BEYOND BELIEF

BEYOND BELIEF

MY SECRET LIFE INSIDE
SCIENTOLOGY
AND
MY HARROWING
ESCAPE

JENNA MISCAVIGE HILL
with LISA PULITZER

WM

WILLIAM MORROW
An Imprint of HarperCollins*Publishers*

HarperCollins books may be purchased for educational, business, or sales promotional use. For information please write: Special Markets Department, HarperCollins Publishers, 10 East 53rd Street, New York, NY 10022.

Designed by Jamie Lynn Kerner

Library of Congress Cataloging-in-Publication Data has been applied for.

ISBN 978-0-06-224847-3 (hardcover)
ISBN 978-0-06-226343-8 (international edition)

13 14 15 16 17 DIX/RRD 10 9 8 7 6 5 4 3 2 1

I would like to dedicate this book to my many good friends who are still in the Church. I love and miss you all and I truly hope you someday have the courage to stand up for yourselves and get the chance to leave and really live your life. You all deserve so much better.

Contents

Author's Note

TALKING ABOUT SCIENTOLOGY IS HARD—NOT JUST BECAUSE OF the memories that it stirs up or because Scientology itself is a complex and layered religion—but because in the past, Scientology's practices have made it difficult for anyone to criticize or talk about life in the Church.

The story in the pages that follow is true to the best of my recollection. The dialogue has been re-created to the best of my recollection. I have changed the names of some individuals in order to preserve their anonymity, and the goal in all cases was to keep certain names confidential without damaging the integrity of the story. Towards this end, the following names are pseudonyms:

Joe Conte

Karen Fassler

Maria Parker

Cathy Mauro

Melissa Bell

Eva

Naomi

Caitlin

Teddy Blackman

Sondra Phillips

Sophia Townsend

Olivia

Julia

Mayra

Laura Rodriquez

Kara Hansen

Melinda Bleeker

Steven

Linda

Charlie

Molly

Sylvia Pearl

Tessa

Mr. Wilson

BEYOND BELIEF

PROLOGUE

RAYS OF MORNING SUN POKED THROUGH THE CLOUDS AS I STOOD toward the back of the line of children waiting to meet two important adults in the Church of Scientology. I didn't know exactly how long I'd been there, but it seemed like forever. At seven years old, minutes seemed like hours when I was waiting for something. There were at least ten kids ahead of me, so my two friends and I were singing songs and playing handclap games to pass the time. Although I was certainly giggling along with them, I was mostly distracted and anxious. The two visitors were recruiters from the Church's international headquarters in Hemet, California, and they were standing at folding tables that had been set up along the road to the School House.

I'd been too far back in line to hear the exact explanation of why the two had come to "the Ranch," the Scientology boarding school where I lived with about eighty other kids whose parents were executives of the Church. Whatever their reason, I figured it was important, or they wouldn't have made the twenty-mile trip from the base to speak with us in person. Dressed in naval-style uniforms complete with lanyards and campaign bars, they looked impressive, even powerful. I knew they were members of the Sea Organization, Scientology's most elite body comprised of its most dedicated members. My parents had joined the very same group years earlier, just before my second birthday.

Several songs later, my turn to approach the tables was upon me. The faces of the two recruiters were stern and intimidating. Eager for adult attention, I tried to please them by being cute and smiley. When they did not seem impressed, I changed my tactic and tried instead to seem smart and inquisitive.

One of the two handed me a sheet of paper bearing the Sea Org coat of arms and the word "REVENIMUS" printed at the top, with places for dates and signatures at the bottom.

"What does '*revenimus*' mean?" I asked, most curious about that.

"It is a Latin word meaning 'we come back,' " the recruiter responded. She further explained that it was the official motto of the Sea Organization, seemingly pleased for the opportunity to enlighten an eventual candidate.

"Come back to *where*?" I asked.

"We come back lifetime after lifetime," she explained. "You are signing a billion-year contract."

"Oh, right," I said, realizing how silly and ignorant my question must have sounded.

As Scientologists, we believed that when our current body died, the spirit inside it would begin a new life in a new body. Our founder, L. Ron Hubbard, said that, as spirits, we had lived millions of years already, and we would continue to do so with or without bodies. I had believed this as far back as I could remember.

On this day, I was all too willing and ready to commit myself to the cause that was so dear to my parents. Being in the Sea Org had meant so much to them that when I was six, they had placed me at the Ranch so they could dedicate all their time to the Church's mission. They only saw me for a few hours on weekends. Nobody's parents were at the Ranch to share the moment we pledged our loyalty to the Sea Org. Signing this document, though, meant I would be one step closer to joining them in the Sea Org, and hopefully to seeing them more frequently.

"Where should I write my name?" I asked eagerly.

The woman pointed out the spot, but directed that I read the document first. The unavoidable final line was:

"THEREFORE, I CONTRACT MYSELF TO THE SEA ORGANIZATION FOR THE NEXT BILLION YEARS (As per Flag Order 323)."

Before I signed, images from the *Little Mermaid* flashed in my mind, particularly when Ariel signed the Sea Witch's magic contract. I knew that contracts meant I had to keep honest to my pledge, so I made mental notes of the things I was agreeing to: following the rules and mores, forwarding the purpose, and serving a *billion* years.

I can do this, I said to myself. And with that, I tried to write my name in my best possible cursive with the proper connectivity of letters, exactly the way I had been learning in school. I wanted my signature on this important document to be perfect, but the recruiters were rushing me, still having to enlist the rest of the children behind me. As a result, my signature didn't turn out as nicely as I had hoped.

Still, I had goose bumps as I walked away. Nothing about the billion-year contract was strange to me. I knew that my parents were with me in spirit, wherever they were. My contract was the same commitment they themselves had signed for the first time when they were teenagers. Besides, at my young age, I had little understanding of larger numbers. To me, a billion years was no different than a hundred years—both an unfathomably long time. If I wanted to be with my parents and friends for the next billion years, the obvious thing to do was to sign my name.

One by one, my friends wrote their own names down on their contracts—each pledging his or her service to a cause that none of us could possibly fully understand. As I stood there in the road between the playground and the pink and white oleander trees, I didn't know the true significance of what I had just done or the full extent of the expectations that would now be placed on me. Just like that, I had gone from singing "Down by the bank with the hanky pank" to full-on committing my soul to a billion years of servitude to the Church of Scientology. Whatever my future held for me, one thing was now certain: my life was no longer my own.

CHAPTER ONE

IN THE NAME OF THE CHURCH

ONE OF MY EARLIEST MEMORIES OF SCIENTOLOGY WAS A CONVER-sation that happened when I was about four years old. At the time, my family was living in Los Angeles in an apartment that had been provided to us by the Church, and one Sunday morning, I was lying in bed with my mom and dad wondering what it would be like to be out of my body.

"How do I go out of my body?" I asked.

My parents exchanged a smile, much like the one my husband and I share when our son asks one of those difficult questions that can't really be answered within his frame of knowledge.

"Can we all go out of our bodies together and fly around in the sky?" I asked.

"Maybe," my father responded. He was always eager to indulge me.

"Let's do it now," I demanded impatiently. "Just tell me what to do."

"Okay, just close your eyes," he instructed. "Are they closed? Now, think of a cat."

"Do we all think of it at once?" I asked, wanting to make sure I was doing it right.

"Yes," was Dad's reply. "Okay, one, two, three . . ."

With my eyes closed, I waited, but nothing happened. I could hear my parents laughing, but I didn't understand what was funny, and why they weren't helping me. Were they not allowed to help me out of my body? Could they only help at certain times? Could I only get out of my body when I was older? Was something wrong with me?

I knew I was a Thetan. I had always known I was a Thetan and had never believed anything else. *Thetan* was the term Scientologists used for an immortal spirit that animated the human body, while the body itself was essentially a piece of meat, a vessel that housed the Thetan. A Thetan lived lifetime after lifetime, and when the body it currently inhabited died, it picked its next one and started over again.

The idea of having past lives fascinated me. I would often ask grown-ups to tell me stories about their past lives. I couldn't remember any of mine, but I was always assured that they would come to me eventually. My father's secretary, Rosemary, would tell me things that had happened in a past life of hers, when she had been a Native American girl. They all sounded so amazing and romantic to me. I couldn't wait until I could remember one of mine. I hoped I hadn't been a bad guy or a solitary old man. Surely, I must have been a princess at least once.

Back then, as young as I was, that was what Scientology seemed to be about: past lives, leaving your body behind, being a Thetan. Beyond that, there wasn't much that I knew about it, but for a child who really couldn't understand the layers of complex belief, there was an excitement to it all. I was a part of something bigger, something that stretched into the past and the future; something that seemed impossible and yet somehow was completely believable.

And so, I sat there, eyes closed, waiting to fly around the sky with my parents at my side, waiting to leave my body behind.

I DIDN'T KNOW THEN THAT ONLY SCIENTOLOGISTS BELIEVED IN Thetans. Everyone I knew was in the Church, and as a third-generation Scientologist, my life was Scientology. My grandmother on my mother's side had started reading books by L. Ron Hubbard, the science-fiction writer and founder of Scientology, in the mid-1950s. On my father's side, my grandfather had come into the Church in the 1970s when an acquaintance told him about it. They'd each gotten hooked right away.

In Scientology, there was no god, no praying, no heaven, no hell—none of the things that people generally associate with religion. It was a philosophy and a self-help program that promised greater self-awareness and the possibility of achieving one's full potential. This unconventional self-help quality was precisely what drew both of my grandparents to it. Each, in their own way, liked Scientology's focus on controlling one's own destiny and improving one's life through a series of clearly laid out steps; each brought children in, nine on my mom's side and four on my dad's.

Once my parents joined the Church as children, they stayed. By the time I was born in Concord, New Hampshire, on February 1, 1984, they had been Scientologists for more than fifteen years.

From my first breath, I was a Scientologist, but it wasn't until shortly before my second birthday that the Church actually began to shape the course of my life. That was when my parents decided to give up the life they had started in New Hampshire, move our family to California, and dedicate our existence to service in the Church. Prior to that, we had been living in Concord, where my parents had built their dream house, a four-bedroom, two-bathroom wood-and-glass home on a parcel of land. Mom and Dad both had well-paying jobs at a local software company, and my nine-year-old brother Justin was a fourth grader in the local public school. At least on the outside, our family had all the markings of a normal, suburban existence.

All that changed in the fall of 1985, when my father, Ron Miscavige, Jr., went to Scientology's Flag Land Base in Clearwater, Florida. Covering more than a few city blocks, the Flag Land Base was a massive complex that served as the Church's spiritual headquarters, a place where Scientologists from all over the world gathered and stayed for weeks to months.

My father went down for a couple of weeks, and on this particular trip, the clergy of the Church, known as the Sea Organization or the Sea Org, was in the midst of a massive recruitment campaign. The Sea Org recruited and employed only the most dedicated Scientologists, who were willing to devote their lives to spreading Scientology to all mankind. L. Ron Hubbard had created the group in 1967 aboard a ship called the *Apollo*, which he referred to as the *flagship*. L. Ron Hubbard was a Navy man and had a passion for naval traditions. The word was he had taken to the seas to research the spiritual component of Scientology without interruption or interference. There was speculation that he had moved into international waters to avoid accountability to the United States Food and Drug Administration, after some of his medical claims, such as applying his teachings could cure psychosomatic illness and other physical and psychological ailments, had been criticized by members of the medical community, who debunked his miracle cures as fraudulent.

Regardless of the reason he operated at sea, he mandated that the members of this special group wear naval-style uniforms and gave the Sea Org its own navy-like rank and rating system, which set its members apart from other Scientologists. He went so far as to have crew members address him as Commodore and high-ranking officers as "Sir," whether they were male or female. He even selected his own group of personal stewards within the Sea

Org who ran programs, related his orders, and followed up to make sure they were carried out. He called this important group the Commodore's Messenger Organization, CMO.

In 1975, the Sea Org moved onshore to the Flag Land Base in downtown Clearwater, where members lived and ate communally in facilities provided them. Even though the organization was no longer stationed on ships, it still kept the naval terms from its sea days—living quarters were "berthings," staff dressed in naval-style uniforms, and L. Ron Hubbard was still the Commodore.

Ten years later, this was where my father found himself in the midst of the all-out recruitment effort. Dad later told me there were Sea Org recruiters stationed at various locations around the Base looking for young, successful, competent, ethical Scientologists. Anyone who entered the Sea Org would have to sign a billion-year contract that bound their immortal Thetan spirit to lifetime after lifetime of service to the Sea Org. Its members also had to work grueling hours, seven days a week—with minimal time off to spend with their families—often for as little as fifteen to forty-five dollars per week. Qualifications for membership included having never taken LSD or angel dust, having never attempted suicide, and having no anti-Scientology immediate family members.

My father had once been a member and felt he still fit the bill. He was a dedicated Scientologist, he was willing to make the full commitment, and he was the older brother of David Miscavige, one of L. Ron Hubbard's top executives and a rising star in the Church. At only twenty-five, my uncle Dave was chairman of the board of Author Services Inc., which oversaw all of the financial aspects of L. Ron Hubbard's copyrights, texts, and intellectual property from his writing. Like my father, Uncle Dave had been a Scientologist since my grandfather had introduced the family to the church. From the start, Dave was so passionate that, with my grandpa's permission, he dropped out of high school at sixteen to join the Sea Org.

When my father returned home to New Hampshire, he informed my mother that he had decided to accept re-recruitment into the Sea Org. Although my parents had been in the midst of settling down, he again felt the calling and wanted our family to move to the Church's Los Angeles base, where we would begin our new life. Mom would have to reenlist in the Sea Org as well, as Sea Org members could not be married to non-Sea Org members. Without hesitation, my mother agreed.

As impulsive as this was, my parents knew what they were signing up for. Not only had they both in the Sea Org before, they had first met at the Flag Land Base when each was only nineteen. At the time, they had each been married to someone else in the Sea Org. My father had a stepson, Nathan, and my mom had two-year-old twin boys, Justin and Sterling. My parents became romantically involved, got in huge trouble for it, as it was a violation of Church policy, and had to work hard to make amends for their behavior. Eventually, they got permission to marry, and Mom's ex-husband remarried, too. Sterling lived with his dad and his dad's new wife, and Justin lived with my parents, but both twins were able to spend time in both households, an arrangement that made everybody happy.

My parents made a handsome couple. My father was five foot eight, slender but strong. He had sandy hair, a mustache, blue eyes, a warm smile, and was an all-around friendly guy. My mom, Elizabeth Blythe, known as "Bitty" to everybody, was beautiful, five foot six, and quite slim. She had hazel green eyes and brown hair that came down to her waist. Her ivory skin had just a few freckles. Unlike my father, she was a smoker, and had been since she was a teenager. Around strangers, she was shier and more reserved than my dad, but when she was with her friends, she was confident, blunt, and funny, with a very dry sense of humor. Mom was opinionated, and sometimes judgmental, but also an amazingly capable, woman.

Even with the huge time commitment that the Sea Org required, my parents had actually been happy there until the late 1970s, when they started getting frustrated with the management at the Flag Land Base. In 1979, after being in the Sea Org for five years, they both quit. While that was a breach of their billion-year contracts, at that time leaving was not catastrophic. They were allowed to remain public Scientologists, loyal to the church, but without the full-time commitment of service to the Sea Org.

For years after they had left, my parents' lives were normal. They lived in Philadelphia with my dad's parents for a bit before moving up to New Hampshire, where they lived a typical middle-class life—two working parents with job security, two children at home (they'd retained full custody of Justin after they'd left the Sea Org), a nanny for the daytime, and a house built to order. Much of our extended family, including my father's sisters, Lori and Denise, and my grandmother on my dad's side, was also living in New Hampshire, and we were on a path to settling down surrounded by family. It seemed like rejoining the ranks of the most die-hard devotees of Scientology could not have been further from my parents' minds.

And yet, with one rash decision, they did just that, returning to the Sea Org and putting all of our lives on a drastically different path. What my parents knew at the time, and what I would only learn later, was that being in the Sea Org meant that they would spend a lot of time away from me. But that didn't change their decision. The Church was their priority, and their minds were made up.

Later, my parents would tell me that their decision was made spontaneously, without much thought, and in hindsight it was the worst decision of their lives. While I can't say whether they considered the impact that their choice would have on me, most likely I was just one of the many sacrifices they were willing to make in the name of the Church. They had quit once, so perhaps they figured that they could leave again if it didn't work out. Another part of their thinking may have been that they really believed it would be awesome to raise a child in Scientology, because I would experience Scientology from the beginning of my life.

There was likely a restlessness in them, a feeling that something was missing. They preferred being out in the world on an important mission and serving some higher purpose than being in New Hampshire, working nine-to-five jobs, and raising children. They were motivated by the Church's mission and they wanted to be involved in something bigger. One thing is clear to me: That decision was when normal stopped having a place in our lives. There had been an opportunity for our lives, for our family, to look very different; my parents considered that future, then walked away from it.

CHAPTER TWO

LRH DROPS HIS BODY

LIVING IN CALIFORNIA WAS GOING TO BE A MISCAVIGE FAMILY reunion of sorts as my dad's father, Grandpa Ron, and my dad's brother, Uncle Dave, already lived there. The year before, my grandpa had also succumbed to the recruitment effort, when he decided to leave Philadelphia and join the Sea Org. Meanwhile, Uncle Dave, who'd been a rising star in the Church for years, was quickly becoming one of the most powerful figures in all Scientology, and what none of us knew then was that, before long, he would be leading it.

On December 11, 1985, after a long cross-country drive, we arrived at our new home, the Pacific Area Command (PAC) base in Los Angeles. The first Church of Scientology had been established in the city in 1954, and L.A. still had one of the largest populations of Scientologists anywhere. The PAC base was comprised of many buildings within walking distance of each other, most of them along Fountain Avenue, Franklin Avenue, and Hollywood Boulevard. The "Blue Building" at 4833 Fountain Avenue was the heart of the PAC Base. Once Cedars of Lebanon Hospital, it was the most recognizable Church building in the city. High on its roof was an eight-pointed cross, a religious symbol of the Church, and the word "Scientology" in huge letters. At night, they were lit up and visible for blocks. The seven-story building now housed the Church's administrative offices, some staff housing, and the galley and mess hall. Uncle Dave and his wife, my Aunt Shelly, had an apartment in the Blue Building, although their main residence was two and a half hours away at the Church's international headquarters in Hemet, California.

Our first apartment was in the Fountain Building on Fountain Avenue, a block from Sunset Boulevard. It was in a somewhat dodgy area of Hollywood with some crime and known gang activity. The apartment consisted of two dingy and dark rooms, each about fifteen by fifteen feet, and one bathroom. The smell of mold hung in the air. In an attempt to make the place nicer, my parents had the original chipped linoleum floors covered with carpet. They also went to a nearby discount store and bought a bunk bed for Justin and me as well as some other furniture, placing the bunk bed in one room and their bed in the other. I still preferred to sleep with my parents in their bed.

Those hours asleep with my parents were just about the only time I had to be with them. The typical Sea Org member was required to be on duty for at least fourteen hours a day, from about nine in the morning to eleven-thirty at night, seven days a week, with a break for an hour of "family time" in the evening, when parents were allowed to see their children before heading back to work. On occasion, they would get a day off for liberty, or libs, but libs was not a guarantee—at most it was one day off every other week. It was a reward for good performance.

As arduous as the days were, my parents didn't complain. My dad's office was conveniently located across the street from our apartment. He had been assigned a management post in a branch that dealt with computerizing Scientology, known as INCOMM. In Scientology, almost every division, building, office, department, or base was identified by an acronym. Even the job positions/posts and the courses we took used them. L. Ron Hubbard himself went by the acronym of his initials, LRH.

My mother was put in charge of the Ship Project, a massive venture involving the purchase of a new ship to be used as a floating base. It would be called the *Freewinds* and would operate much like the original flagship *Apollo* had during the early days of the Sea Org.

Because my parents were working long days and nights, Justin and I were watched by other caretakers. When we first got to L.A., I spent my days at a nursery in the Fountain Building, where I stayed until my parents came to pick me up for dinner, which was served in the mess hall. Afterwards, Mom, Dad, Justin, and I would go back to the apartment for family time. I was taken back to the nursery when Mom and Dad went back to work. There were plenty of cots and cribs where the children could sleep until pick-up time, which was typically 11 p.m. or later.

During the day, when I was at the nursery, Justin went to the Apollo Training Academy (ATA), another building on Fountain Avenue. The ATA was for older children of Sea Org members. They were considered to be cadets, basically Sea Org members in training. I didn't know what they did there all day, but Justin hated it enough that he begged my parents to let him go back to New Hampshire where his friends were.

Justin's and my daily routine soon became normal. I was too young to understand that seeing your parents only one hour a day was highly unusual. I didn't know what parents were supposed to do, I only knew that mine were seldom around.

WE HAD ONLY BEEN IN LOS ANGELES FOR SIX WEEKS WHEN ON January 24, 1986, L. Ron Hubbard died at the age of seventy-two. He had been living in seclusion in a remote area of the desert in California for the previous six years, tended to by a married couple, Pat and Anne Broeker, his two closest confidantes. He hadn't been to the base or made public appearances in years, but everyone said he was actively working on new, ground-breaking research, so his isolation had been understandable.

To Scientologists, LRH had always been respected as a researcher and philosopher whose stories about his discoveries for the Church were riddled with colorful tales from his own travels and life experiences. By the time of his death, he had become almost godlike, a charismatic figure who'd developed the path to salvation for all Scientologists. Everyone viewed him as a personal friend, whether they knew him well or not at all. To us, he saw the good in all mankind.

L. Ron Hubbard had been a prolific writer of short pulp fiction tales for fifteen years before he published his first serious work, *Dianetics: The Modern Science of Mental Health*, in 1950. *Dianetics* was a self-help program, and the philosophy behind it was that people had to get rid of moments of pain, which were obstacles to personal growth. These moments were what held us back, impaired our health, and undermined our quality of life. However, by addressing and overcoming them, we could conquer just about anything that made us suffer.

When it was released, *Dianetics* quickly sold millions of copies, with readers becoming rabid fans of the program overnight, saying this new guide to mental health was filled with amazing ways to heal and improve your life. Of course, *Dianetics* also had its skeptics and outright critics who questioned the alleged science used by LRH. For his part, LRH dismissed his naysayers as feeling threatened by his new perspective.

Despite the naysayers, *Dianetics* became such a sensation that LRH opened Dianetics centers in cities across America, so that people could engage in one-on-one study with a trained coach whom LRH referred to as an *auditor*. In these sessions with the auditor, the student, or "pre-Clear," was guided back to his painful moments. They could be anything physical or emotional from childbirth to a car accident or any kind of actual moment of pain, as well as the sights, smells, emotions, and words heard or associated with that painful moment. L. Ron Hubbard believed there were chains of painful moments, and with an auditor's help, they would disappear one by one. The goal of Dianetics was to address each and every one until finally the mind was "cleared of the entire chain." Dianetics was a continual process of locating such chains, of which there could be thousands, and following them all the way back to the earliest incident. Only then would they disappear, bringing the pre-Clear closer to a state of "Clear." When you were Clear, the goal of Dianetics, you no longer had psychosomatic illnesses, neuroses, or psychoses. You also experienced a giant lift in IQ and had perfect recall of your past. You were free of what LRH called your Reactive Mind.

By 1952, L. Ron Hubbard had moved past thinking of Dianetics as simply a self-help regimen. In his research, he had discovered that pre-Clears were demonstrating chains of painful moments that preceded their current lifetime. In fact, they could go back many lifetimes, indicating the possibility of past lives, which naturally opened the door to the realm of the spirit. This led LRH to another discovery: that man existed in three parts—the body, the mind, and the spirit. He called the spirit the *Thetan*. It was immortal, and it was also the most important of the three parts. Without it, there would be no body or mind. A Thetan wasn't a thing, but rather the creator of things and the animator of the body. The mind was the computer, the body was the vessel for the Thetan, and the Thetan was the life force. Thus, Scientology was born.

The Thetan quickly became a vital part of Scientology. By offering followers a spiritual component, LRH took the first step toward making Scientology a religion, a designation that came with a variety of benefits. Suddenly, the claims of dubious science that had surrounded *Dianetics* were irrelevant; if Dianetics was part of religious practice, it didn't need to be proven scientifically. There were also financial incentives and tax exemptions that made becoming a religion attractive. However, perhaps the most important part of Scientology becoming a religion was that, unlike Dianetics, in which people could simply become Clear, get fixed, and never return to another auditing session, Scientology, with its infinite spiritual component and its journeys into past lives, was designed to keep people coming back indefinitely.

LRH developed a curriculum that specified the order in which Scientology was to be taught. This step-by-step program was called the Bridge to Total Freedom and was divided into two parts: *auditing*, which was a type of one-on-one counseling; and *training*, a program by which to learn how to audit others. Under this road map for Scientologists in their journey to spiritual freedom, everyone had to start at the bottom and move up one level at a time. You could go up one side of the Bridge or both. There were also many courses that weren't actually on the Bridge available to Scientologists, as well. But as for the ascent itself, a person had to attain a certain level of awareness before he or she could advance to the next level and ultimately cross the Bridge to Total Freedom.

The levels on the Bridge up to a State of Clear were based on LRH's Dianetics' research. However, with the discovery of the Thetan, he had to decode the spiritual levels beyond a state of Clear. These became the highest levels on the Bridge, known as the Operating Thetan, or OT Levels. There were eight levels, the final one being OT VIII, enticingly called "Truth Revealed."

LRH warned that no one could bypass any level to get to this ultimate mystery and said proper preparation was imperative. Doing levels out of order, he claimed, could result in serious injury or even death. For this reason, people who had already achieved this knowledge were forbidden to share it with those below them on the Bridge. Additionally, the OT courses could only be delivered by specially-trained Sea Org members. A number of Sea Org bases around the world could deliver OT Levels up to Level V. The Flag Base in Clearwater delivered Levels VI and VII. The *Freewinds*, the ship my mother was preparing for service, was going to be the only place in the world that would deliver OT VIII, the highest level yet decoded.

Even though LRH spent his last years in self-imposed exile, he let it be known through communications from the Broekers that he was hard at work on advanced, never-before-revealed levels beyond OT VIII.

The day after LRH's death, both my uncle Dave and Pat Broeker addressed a capacity crowd of Scientologists at the Hollywood Palladium, the 40,000-square-foot art-deco style concert hall on Sunset Boulevard. Uncle Dave told everybody that LRH had "moved on to a new level of research." There were a few gasps of disbelief, occasional muted applause, but mostly the auditorium was in total silence. Dave went on to explain that it had been L. Ron Hubbard's decision to "discard" his body because "it had ceased to be useful and had become an impediment to the work he now must do beyond its confines."

"The being we knew as L. Ron Hubbard still exists," he told his followers, helping to diffuse the shock.

The fact that LRH had orchestrated his own journey, combined with the fact that he hadn't been seen in years, made his departure bearable.

Since both my uncle and Pat Broeker were onstage that day, it wasn't immediately clear who LRH's successor would be. Reportedly, there was a power struggle between the two men over who would assume leadership of the Church. There were opposing stories of exactly what transpired, but accusations emerged that my uncle used some questionable tactics to oust Pat from the leadership position. Regardless of how it happened, in the end my uncle prevailed, eventually becoming the head of the Church, with his official title being Chairman of the Board, Religious Technology Center. From this point forward, everyone in the Church referred to him as COB, but to me, he was just Uncle Dave.

My father, Ronnie Miscavige Jr., was actually three years older than Uncle Dave. He was the oldest, followed by Uncle Dave and his twin sister, Denise, and Lori, the baby of the family. When they were kids, my dad and Dave shared a room and got along well, even teaming up to play pranks on their sisters. Dad was very athletic, and although he played football in school, his real passion was gymnastics. He even landed a place on the Junior Olympics team in his region. Dave also enjoyed sports, but because he had asthma, he was sometimes held back from competing and doing other physical activities. Denise was kind, free-spirited, and loved to dance, but she was often in trouble with my grandparents, because they didn't approve of some of the boys she dated. Little Lori loved to dance along with her big sister.

Their father, my grandfather, was Ron Miscavige Sr. He had been born and raised in Mount Carmel, a small coal-mining town in southwest Pennsylvania, where he grew up Polish Catholic. He worked as a salesman, selling things from cookware to insurance. He wasn't particularly tall, but he was loud, gruff, gregarious, and a little intimidating. He joined the Marines when he was just eighteen, and in 1957, the year after he was discharged, he married my grandmother, Loretta Gidaro, a beautiful young woman with thick brown hair, olive skin, and the brightest blue eyes. Grandma Loretta was a coal miner's daughter of German and Italian descent, who was humorous, kind, and always looking out for the welfare of her family. The two settled in Cherry Hill, New Jersey, outside Philadelphia, where she worked as a nurse until taking time off when her children were born: Dad in 1957, David and Denise in 1960, and Lori in 1962.

Being in sales, Grandpa was very much a people person. He would frequently invite characters home to have dinner with the family, where they would tell their entertaining stories over a nice meal. It was through a fellow salesman that he first heard about the Church of Scientology. He wasn't drawn to Scientology because he had a particular personal issue, but rather because he was always hungry for answers about spirituality and our minds. At the time he was thirty-four, but he had always been interested in philosophy of one kind or another. When he was just a kid, he'd read *The Prophet* by Kahlil Gibran, and became fascinated by the questions about human life and spirituality that it raised. Early on, he'd been curious about social anthropology, how humans came to be here, and why we did the things we did.

This interest in the origins of man led him to visit a local Scientology mission in Cherry Hill and buy one of L. Ron Hubbard's books. As Grandpa would later say himself, after that trip to the mission, he needed no convincing—he was sold. After buying a few more books, he went to the mission and began the auditing process. He said that in the next few months the benefits of Scientology helped him become the top salesperson in his company, and he claimed he was even featured in *Newsweek* for his success. His boss was so impressed that he sent the whole company of twenty or so employees down to the Cherry Hill Mission, because, if this was what Ron was doing, they had better check it out, too.

For her part, Grandma Loretta didn't object to his interest in Scientology; in fact, she liked it and started taking services at the mission as well. Pretty soon, Grandpa was bringing all four of his children for auditing, beginning when my father was twelve. In addition, Grandpa had heard that Scientology had produced promising results in treating ailments such as asthma, so he thought Dave could really benefit. According to Grandpa, Dave's improvement was impressive, further convincing him that Scientology had the answers he had been looking for. It had helped him succeed at work, made him feel better about important decisions, and now it appeared to be improving his son's health.

Ultimately, Grandpa liked that Scientology was more of a self-help philosophy than a religion. He liked that, instead of discussing heaven, hell, and sin, it promised breakthroughs in relationships and marriages, careers, communication, and physical and emotional well-being. He also liked that there was a utopian quality to Scientology. It held a point of view that man is essentially good and in charge of his own spiritual salvation, but that salvation depended on a cooperation with the universe. L. Ron Hubbard felt it was possible to clear the world of human misery, end wars, and promote harmony. It was idealistic but somehow rational at the same time, a combination that appealed to Grandpa. The fact that it was unlike any religion or belief he'd ever known didn't bother him in the least.

Two years after he discovered the Church, he took a leap. He decided to sell his three cars and use the money to move the entire family to Saint Hill Manor in Sussex, England, where the Church's main headquarters had been located for more than a decade.

In 1959, L. Ron Hubbard and his family had moved to Sussex and bought a fifty-acre estate with a mini-castle from the Maharajah of Jaipur, which became the headquarters of the Church of Scientology. Saint Hill soon became a gathering place for Scientologists from around the world. LRH was often there, always continuing and discussing his research, which gave people the feeling they were at the forefront of something new and important.

Despite Grandpa Ron's desire to be close to the center of the Scientologists' world in Saint Hill, my fourteen-year-old father was skeptical. Understandably, he wasn't that interested in moving from Pennsylvania to England and leaving his friends in the middle of high school. More important, he would have to give up his gymnastics and his dream of getting to the Olympics. However, my grandpa was doing what he felt was best for the family, and reluctantly, my dad went along with it.

Those couple of years in England succeeded in fully committing my father to Scientology. After being surrounded almost exclusively by Scientologists, he became increasingly devoted to the cause, so much so that, at seventeen years old, he enlisted in the Sea Org and moved to the Flag Land Base in Clearwater.

Uncle Dave joined him there in 1976, after quitting high school on his sixteenth birthday to devote himself to the religion. In Clearwater, Uncle Dave began to work closely with L. Ron Hubbard and was rewarded for his efforts with important posts. Eventually, he was based at the international headquarters in Hemet, California, where he quickly rose through the ranks to the point that, during L. Ron Hubbard's self-imposed exile, Uncle Dave had become a powerful figure in Scientology. Now, with L. Ron Hubbard's death, he was more than just the face of the Church—he was the head of it all.

CHAPTER THREE

THE GREATER GOOD

ABOUT A YEAR AND A HALF AFTER MY UNCLE TOOK OVER THE Church, the Fountain Building where we lived was severely damaged in an earthquake and subsequently condemned. My family moved nearby to the Edgemont Building on Edgemont Street, where the apartments were much nicer. Each had two bedrooms, a small dining area, a kitchen, and a small living room, but even though they were bigger, each apartment was occupied by two families or two couples, so they were crowded.

We shared our apartment with Mike and Cathy Rinder, old friends of my parents who were also dedicated Sea Org members. Mom and Dad occupied one bedroom, and Cathy and Mike had the other. Justin and I shared the living room on bunk beds and couches with Mike and Cathy's daughter, Taryn, and their son Benjamin James, B. J. for short. Taryn was around ten, a little younger than Justin. B. J. was a few months older than I but, by then, we were both two.

My mom had met Cathy when they were both teenagers and stationed on the *Apollo*, where they became good friends. While it was a bit odd to suddenly have another family around, I enjoyed Cathy's great sense of humor and the fact that she drew silly cartoons in which everyone looked like a pig. Mike was a bit different. An Australian, he was quiet and, like my parents, rarely in the apartment.

We had no reason to complain that the apartment was crowded. It was fun having so many people around, especially so many kids. Because the earthquake had taken out the Fountain Building, B. J. and I had to go to a large day care/kindergarten center for children of Sea Org members located on Bronson Avenue, next to what is now known as the Celebrity Centre. It was far enough that we had to take a church-provided bus. About eighty to one hundred kids went there, from infants up to age six. We were divided into different classes, not so much by age, but by our parents' status in the Church.

Most afternoons, I rode the bus home with Justin or Taryn, who was also in the ATA. They boarded when we stopped at the academy to pick up the students there. On some days my brother would take me off when we stopped at the ATA and we'd walk back to the apartment together, stopping for Push Pops from George's General Store across the street from the ATA. While Justin was a little young to be watching me, the Edgemont was a Scientology building, and perhaps my parents took comfort in knowing that there were other Scientologists in close proximity and that their offices were right on the block. Additionally, there was a roving nanny on duty in the building who would stop by the various apartments and check on the children and was available in case any emergency arose.

Over the months, B. J. and I were becoming really good friends, despite the fact that he was into bugs and robots, and I was into Barbies and baby animals. He wasn't a big talker, but I was fascinated by him. He was always teaching me some new fact about bugs or doing a new magic trick. We did pretty much everything together, and it didn't take long for B. J., as well as Taryn, to become like family.

Shortly after we all moved in together, we started to see less and less of Mom. Because she was getting the *Freewinds* going, she was often on location in Curaçao, British West Indies, where the ship was to be based. If she wasn't in Curaçao, she was at the International Base in Hemet. She would visit when she could, and bring me presents from her travels. Although I loved the gifts, especially the small painted musical jewelry box with a tiny spinning ballerina, they didn't make her absence any easier. Family time was when I missed her the most. Usually it was just Dad and Cathy who came to the apartment for the hour. Dad would bathe me, read me stories, and we would play.

That was how the routine went for about a year. The four of us—Justin, Taryn, B. J., and I—formed a makeshift family of our own. Although they weren't yet teenagers, Justin and Taryn were babysitters to B. J. and me. Together, we hung out, had snacks, and played around. They generally looked after us until our parents came home for dinner or had a day off. All that changed, though, one day in early 1988 when Cathy came home at family time.

That particular evening, I saw her speaking privately with B. J., who looked upset. From where I sat on the couch, I could hear Cathy tell him this would be their last daily family time together. From now on, she and Mike were only going to be able to see him once a week, on Sunday mornings, since the rest of the week they were going to be somewhere very secret doing important things for the Church.

Even though we were just four years old, B. J. and I were both used to the Scientology explanation that our parents gave us about why they had to work so much. They would explain how they had to help lots of people and sacrifice personal time for the Scientology cause. We nodded our heads that we understood, pretending that the explanations would make us miss them less.

Now, though, looking at B. J.'s face, I knew there was no way he could pretend to not be devastated. He didn't talk a lot, and as his mother carefully laid out what was going to happen, he just listened and stared at the floor. Afterward, I tried to comfort him by putting my arm around him and telling him how sad I was for him, but all I could think was how unlucky he was to lose this cherished hour with his parents. That's when Cathy told me that my parents would no longer be coming home at family time, either.

"I don't believe you," I told her defiantly, but when I paused to think about it, I realized I had only been seeing my parents less and less during the week for the past few months. While my mom was often traveling, my dad, bit by bit, had been coming less and less frequently in the evenings on weeknights. From what Cathy was telling me, this separation was now official.

As it turned out, my parents had already relocated, and I hadn't even realized it. A series of new policies had been enacted by the Church that severely restricted the amount of time Sea Org families could be together. For instance, Sea Org couples were no longer allowed to become new parents. If a Sea Org woman did become pregnant, the couple had to leave the Sea Org and go to a non–Sea Org mission, which was a demotion. There, they would still be on staff and work at a Scientology church, but they wouldn't be allowed back in the Sea Org until the child was six years old, and even then, they would have to reapply. For Sea Org members who already had children, there were changes as well. On the positive side, their kids would be accommodated with improved facilities for care and schooling, but on the negative side, the nightly family hour was essentially canceled, and children over the age of six would be raised communally at locations close to Sea Org bases.

While Uncle Dave hadn't written these policies, it was impossible for him not to know about them. They weren't the kind of changes that could have happened without his approval. It was hard to say why they did happen. Uncle Dave never had kids himself, which probably played a role; I've always believed not having children was a conscious decision on his part, as he had married Aunt Shelly before this rule was put into effect. Perhaps, through other Sea Org members, he saw how much work kids were and the facilities and personnel they needed. Most likely, though, it was because kids were a distraction that caused the parents to become less productive and more emotionally invested in something other than the Church.

I never doubted that my parents loved me. I accepted that the time they had for me was extremely limited. Even now, looking back on their dedication to the Church, I have no doubt that its teachings played an enormous role in their putting their Sea Org responsibilities before their family at all times. In many ways, they sacrificed family for what the Church considered to be for the "greater good." In Scientology, we said, "The greatest good for the greatest number of dynamics," meaning that when making decisions, Scientologists had to use a basic Scientology principle called *The Dynamics of Existence* to determine exactly who and what any decision would benefit. There were eight dynamics of supposedly equal importance:

1. Self
2. Family, children, and sex
3. Group
4. Mankind
5. Plants and animals
6. MEST Universe, MEST being Matter, Energy, Space, and Time; the physical universe

7. The Spirit
8. God or Supreme Being

When my parents reenlisted in the Sea Org, they knew their service would mean focusing on dynamics three, four, six, seven, and eight. They believed their work would serve each of those areas. Had they chosen their family, they would only have satisfied the first and second dynamics. As a result, because the Sea Org satisfied five dynamics and their family satisfied only two, it meant joining the Sea Org was the right decision. It offered the greatest good for the greatest number of dynamics.

In truth, this dynamic system meant that families and children were usually unable to compete with the Church's larger mission. In most religions, families and children were a central part of the religion's quest; in Scientology, they were subjugated by it. Similarly, the long hours and low wages of Sea Org employees were for the greater good of Scientology, and as long as the greatest number of dynamics was served, then it was right, even if children and families became collateral fallout.

Being four years old, I wasn't sure how to deal with the idea that Mom and Dad were no longer living with us. They had already moved to the International Management Headquarters, also referred to as "Int," the "Int Base," or the "Gold Base." The only thing I knew about it was that Uncle Dave and Aunt Shelly lived and worked there. Located in Hemet, California, about two and a half hours east of L.A., the Int Base was shrouded in mystery to the point that its actual location was kept secret even from family members of those who worked there. Only people who received special clearances were allowed to go there.

The Church said the security and secrecy were to protect the Int Base from any outside enemies who might try to hurt Scientology. They said that these "suppressive persons" hated that we helped others, so they had to keep it confidential. In actuality, I think it added a sense of superiority to those who were important enough to know its location. Also, with the intrigue, there was an air of importance to the subject matter of Scientology.

Mom and Dad told me they had their own quarters in an apartment complex near the Base for the time they lived there during the week. On Saturday nights, my parents would drive back to L.A. to visit. They'd only stay until Sunday morning, because they had to leave around eleven for their drive back to Hemet. Every week, I would be upset to see them go, although I tried hard not to show it. Justin never cried, so I tried to behave like him.

My mother used her executive clout to arrange for a regular guardian for me. Her name was Pat, and she was a member of the Sea Org. A lot of kids with parents at Int stayed in the after-school nursery overnight, but because I had Pat, I was allowed to sleep at the apartment. During the day, Pat worked at the Manor Hotel on Franklin Avenue, which was part of Scientology's Celebrity Centre.

With Mom, Dad, and Cathy and Mike Rinder no longer home on a daily basis, our schedule changed a bit. B. J. and I still took the bus to and from the nursery every day, but we didn't go straight to our apartment in the afternoon. Instead, our teachers would take us to another apartment two doors down from ours that served as an after-school nursery. Eventually, my brother or Taryn would pick us up when they got home from the ATA to take us to our apartment. The roving nanny was still on duty, so there was an adult available to us, if we needed anything. Pat would arrive there sometime after seven and spend the night with the four of us. By default, she became B. J.'s nanny, as well as mine.

As much as I missed Mom and Dad, the time away from them wasn't always bad. Some days, Taryn would invite her friend

Heather, whose parents were also at Int, to our apartment. I loved pretending I was a princess, so the two girls would dress me up in costumes and fancy dresses, fix my hair, give me a wand and a crown, and make me beautiful.

Justin also liked to invite friends over. Mike, the son of our father's secretary Rosemary, and Teddy, a friend whose mother worked with Mom on the Ship Project, were two of his favorite guests. They would practice their karate on B. J. and me. We would pillow fight them back. Teddy and Justin liked to go skateboarding, and they'd bring B. J. and me along to watch.

My father made it down to Los Angeles most Saturday nights. Usually, he would try to make the weekend visits as special as possible by bringing me little gifts or doing something fun with me on Sunday mornings. Sometimes, we would relax at home, but at other times we would go out for breakfast, hang out at Griffith Park near the Santa Monica Mountains, or look around the mall. Because of her work, my mom was able to come less often.

One Saturday night, though, she called ahead and told me that she and Dad had a surprise for me. I tried to wait up, but I had fallen asleep by the time they came in. The next morning, I ran into their room. "Where's my surprise?" I asked excitedly. Mom reached under the bed and pulled out a kitten, a silver tabby, absolutely adorable, but scared to death. I named her Sarah Kitty. At first, B. J. and I were scared of her because she was vicious, but eventually we made peace with her.

B. J. and I were at the apartment one afternoon when Sarah Kitty suddenly came sprinting out of the dollhouse to investigate a newcomer, a boy around Justin's age whom I had seen around the Base before. He had barely stepped into the living room when Sarah Kitty dashed up to him and climbed him as if he were a tree. He was screaming, partly in fear and partly in pain at having been scratched, so B. J. and I ran to grab her. Once we had her and our laughter under control, we stood staring at the boy, wondering who he was.

Justin was home and made the introductions. "This is Sterling," he said to me. "He's your brother." I knew that Justin had a friend named Sterling, but I didn't know that he was actually his twin. He and his family had been living in L.A. for several years and were also members of the Sea Org.

It took me a while to get used to the concept of having another brother. Although Sterling and Justin looked nothing alike, they both loved sports and got along fairly well. He even started picking me up from the nursery some nights and stayed until Pat arrived.

Dad, Mom, or both left L.A. every Sunday morning at 11:00 a.m. When they left, Justin and I liked to be outside to wave them off. I'll never forget the Sunday when my parents were backing their car out of the garage and B. J. and I were riding the garage gate. My leg got caught in between the bars as it was sliding to the right to let the car out. Justin tried to pull me off, but I misunderstood his intention and thought he was teasing me as usual. The gate had no safety stop and my leg got stuck between the gate and the wall, and I was trapped. In unbearable pain, I started to scream my head off.

My dad jumped out of the car and literally bent the metal bars with his bare hands to free my leg. I was crying uncontrollably as he carried me to the elevator and back upstairs. My parents called a local Scientology doctor, who instructed them to ask me to try to walk. When I couldn't do it because of the pain, she told them that unfortunately my leg was probably fractured, and that I should get an X-ray in the morning.

Mom and Dad stayed with me for as long as they could, but they had so many urgent phone calls from Int that they were unable to stay past dinner. Someone in charge insisted that they come back to the Base, even though he knew I was seriously injured. Orders had to be obeyed, and my parents reluctantly went. The ramifications for insubordination were significant and depended on the wrath and power of the person you disobeyed. My parents didn't want to displease their senior and suffer the consequences. After all, it was for the greater good.

After my parents left, Pat remained with me and took me to the doctor's office for an X-ray the next morning. My knee was indeed fractured. The only thing the doctor could do for me was to wrap it in an ACE Bandage.

I was back at the nursery two days later. My leg hurt so much that my limp caused me to lag behind during our daily strolls along Franklin Avenue. Rather than slow the group down, the teacher would become irritated at me and tell me to hurry up. She seemed to think I was putting on an act. B. J. defended me, telling her that my knee was fractured.

"Well if you fall behind, you are going to get left behind," she scolded. She told me that I needed to "make it go right!" This was a common Scientology saying, which referred to the Church's belief in mind over matter. All I had to do was not let the pain dominate my thoughts, and it wouldn't feel as bad. A few months passed before my knee finally stopped hurting.

Right before my fifth birthday, Justin told me he was leaving L.A. and going to live at a place called the Ranch. I didn't know what the Ranch was or where it was, but I didn't want him to leave me. I already saw so little of Mom and Dad. He said it was close to where they were living and he would come and visit me once in a while, like they did. To make things worse, Taryn was going, too. I didn't know how to feel, but I didn't like it.

Now, with no one to pick us up, B. J. and I had to stay at the afterschool nursery, where we waited for Pat, who would usually come to get us around 8 p.m., except on Thursdays when she had to work late—often past midnight. All the kids at the after-school nursery ate dinner sitting on the kitchen floor, took an evening shower, played a little, then went to bed on one of the cots lined against the wall of the living room. This was where I first learned about touch assists. We were taught to perform them on each other before bedtime each night. We would be paired with another child and instructed to use one finger to touch him or her on the arm. The touch assists were procedures created by LRH to put the Thetans into better communication with our bodies, so as to improve the healing process.

"Feel my finger?" I would say to my partner, who was supposed to say, "Yes."

I'd say, "Good," and repeat the exercise on the other arm. We would all do this on each other's fingers, toes, arms, legs, and face. I didn't totally understand the concept. I just knew the touch assists helped put me to sleep.

While many of the kids stayed there overnight, B. J. and I got a pickup, when Pat took us home and put us in our own beds, or my parents' bed, where she would sleep with me. She was amazingly nice, and I loved her very much. On Sundays, she would pick us up at the apartment and take us back to the nursery after my parents left for Int.

Every few months, Pat or Rosemary would take me to an international Scientology gathering, which was usually held in the Shrine Auditorium, a huge entertainment hall and expo center on West 32nd Street. Hundreds of Scientologists and Sea Org members, some from the Los Angeles area and some from the Int Base, would be in attendance. Pat would always dress me up and curled my hair for the occasions. Together, we'd sit in the audience and listen to the speeches. I didn't know what the presenters were talking about, but my father would often be one of the featured speakers. Seeing him at the podium, I would get so excited that I would scream out, "Hi, Daddy! I'm over here," and wave madly.

If my Uncle Dave spoke, I was equally animated and would yell, "Uncle Dave! It's me! It's Jenna!"

When I would see them in the greenroom afterward, they would tell me that they had winked at me or waved with their pinkies when nobody was looking. I had no idea how important these events were, but they always went on for several hours, they were filled with standing ovations and loud, long cheers, and the reception had great food.

B. J. and I had been living in Los Angeles on our own for a little over a year when Pat told us that we were going to be moving to the Ranch, where Justin and Taryn were living. We were both thrilled, even though we didn't know why we were leaving L.A. It turned out that someone had been shot right in front of the Edgemont Building, so my parents insisted that I be taken to the Ranch immediately, and naturally, B. J. would be coming, too.

The next morning, we packed up our stuff and waited for Rosemary, Dad's secretary, to pick us up. When she arrived, B. J. and I climbed into the backseat anticipating that Pat would get in, too. But she didn't.

"Why are you standing there?" I asked. When she broke the news she wasn't coming with us, I was shocked. We both started crying. We had been together for two years, and I was devastated. Although I knew that at the Ranch I might be able to see more of my parents, I was still really emotional. I had spent more time with her than with my own parents. I told her how much I loved her, and I promised to visit often. After one long last hug, I got into the car, and Rosemary pulled away from the curb.

CHAPTER FOUR

THE RANCH

It was a long drive to the Ranch. At first, B. J. and I were excited and chattering, but after a while, boredom set in. I fell asleep briefly, and I woke with a jerk of my head smacking against the window, the result of the car hitting a bump on the winding dirt road we'd apparently turned onto. It was March of 1999, springtime, and everywhere I looked was lush and green. At one point, we crossed a bridge that spanned a very large running creek and came to an oasis of tall oak trees. Each turn in the road seemed to present a new vista.

Difficult as it would be not to have Pat with me, the excitement that I would be only twenty miles away from my parents made me forget about Pat for the time being. From time to time, I had wondered what the Ranch would be like, but I really had no idea. Whenever I'd tried to get clues from my brother during his trips home, he always teased me and I wound up with no information in the end. While I didn't know for sure whether being closer meant I'd be able to see my parents more often, I certainly hoped it would. Despite the uncertainties, just the thought of being closer to them made me think that life at the Ranch would be worthwhile.

The fact that Rosemary was going to stay for a couple of days to help us settle in was also comforting, although she was no Pat. As we drove up to an old wooden gate, Rosemary victoriously declared that we had arrived, setting off a cheer from B. J. and me. She pushed a button on the call box attached to the gate.

"Hello, I have Jenna Miscavige and Benjamin Rinder," she announced, when asked her business. At that, the gate opened and we proceeded up the dirt road around a hill, passing a few outbuildings along the way. Soon, Rosemary parked in front of a low-slung, rundown-looking building, where older kids in uniform—light blue shirts and dark blue shorts—were milling around. When I stepped out, the first person I saw was Justin, with a big smile on his face. He gave me an embarrassed, awkward brother-to-little-sister hug, happy to see me, but still being cool in front of his friends.

Taryn was waiting there, too. B. J. had barely gotten out of the car when she swooped him up into a suffocating hug. B. J., always the quiet type, accepted the hug with no fuss. "Come here, little sis!" Taryn said to me, as she forced me into the same overwhelming embrace.

A few older kids, my brother included, grabbed our stuff out of the trunk and led us toward the buildings called the Motels. We followed them into an open courtyard with large birch trees in the center. Around the courtyard were thirteen doorways, each with its own small walkway.

B. J. and I were assigned to Room 12. Apparently the room had been chosen for us, because its refurbishment was the closest to being completed. It was pretty big, about twenty feet square, with two small windows on the back wall. Although the floor was carpeted, it was completely empty.

As I stood looking at the room wondering how this could be a bedroom, someone behind me yelled, "Coming through!" Two older boys, carrying a twin bed frame, followed by two older girls carrying a mattress made their way through the doorway. This was repeated until three twin beds were set up while we were standing there.

Room 12 was connected to Room 11 by a shared sink room and bathroom. Room 11 didn't even have carpet, just a concrete floor with a single mattress on it. Someone who had been asleep on the mattress suddenly sat up, and I saw that it was my brother's friend, Teddy, who I had always had a little-girl crush on. Teddy explained that he was sick and running a fever, and that Room 11 was the isolation room. Sick kids stayed there to keep away from healthy kids until they were better, so he told us we should stay out. The room didn't look very comfortable to me, especially if you were sick, but I figured that they must know what they are doing; after all, this was the Int Ranch.

B. J. and I went back to our room and made our beds. We let Sarah Kitty out of her crate, but she was not happy. She started snarling and hissing, her hair standing on end, scratching at anyone who came near her as she was hiding under the bed.

After we finished making our beds, Justin and Mike gave us a tour of the property. The Ranch was sprawling, covering about five hundred acres of land at the back of the Soboba Indian Reservation in the San Jacinto Hills in Riverside County. They told us they had heard the property had once been a convent, but didn't know for sure. The main dwelling cluster included the Motels and six or seven other buildings, some small, and one big one spread across five of the acres. There was a small swimming pool in a state of disrepair, with a few dead rodents floating in it. They said they couldn't use the pool until it got fixed, and they said the same about many of the other buildings as well. The rest of the property was mixture of green trees, dusty desert, and mountains.

The boys showed us the Big House, a very old and soon-to-be gutted two-story house that sat at the top of a hill. On the second floor, it had a few holes in the walls and floors. Even in that condition, the upstairs was being used for dormitories for the young girls. Once the renovations of the Motels were complete, everyone who lived in the Big House was going to move there.

The downstairs of the Big House was the mess hall. For each meal, the food was driven in from the galley at the Int Base, about twenty miles away. The meals were always set up buffet-style, although each kid was assigned to a certain table. Each week, a different child from each table took his or her turn as the steward, responsible for setting the silverware and plates and serving the food and drinks. As it turned out, the food was actually quite good. The meals were hearty and varied, and each day, we got freshly baked bread. Most nights, we even got dessert.

Next, Justin and Mike showed us the School House, which was slated to be renovated soon but currently was being used as storage, so there wasn't any actual school there. They also took us to see the Cottage, the project that they were currently working on, which consisted of a small building, now completely gutted, that was going to be adult berthing for the Ranch faculty when it was finished.

The Ranch may not have been fancy, and there were certainly a few holes in the walls, but none of this put me off. It needed work, but it seemed like an adventure that I would get to participate in. The landscape was unfamiliar, but the kids seemed so proud of the place. Looking back on it now, they were probably eager to show off to us younger kids, but their attitude was infectious, making me feel like I was somewhere special.

It was also a relief not be confined to a tiny apartment as well.

Back in L.A., we were never allowed outside unsupervised, but the huge, expansive land at the Ranch made me feel like I could breathe easier and not have to hold someone's hand every time I went outside. For the first time I could remember, I felt like I had space to run around and imagine things. And, if that weren't enough, being reunited with Justin and Taryn made feel me like I was getting to do all this with family.

As we walked around the property, B. J. and I learned that that there were five dogs living at the Ranch who would be keeping us company most of the time. They weren't guard dogs, but they were protective, friendly watchdogs, who would follow the kids around everywhere and keep an eye on us. Each had its own distinct personality. Brewster, a German shepherd, was the alpha dog. Tasha, the female German shepherd, was extremely loyal. Ruby was a very old, lazy, grumpy Labrador with a bark that sounded like a toad. There was also Jeta, a middle-aged female Lab. Bo, the fifth dog, looked like a wolf, with his hair always coming out in clumps.

Our first few days at the Ranch were spent exploring with the dogs at our side. B. J. and I hardly noticed the sweltering heat as we walked through the desert in search of different cacti. In the morning, cows would roam the fields around the Ranch; for some reason, we were supposed to chase them away, which we would do with the dogs. The farther we walked, the more we could see just how big the Ranch was—the property itself was immense—as though we would never be able to explore the whole thing. I had always worn incredibly frilly dresses that my grandma, Aunt Denise, my godparents, and Uncle Dave had sent me for my birthday and Christmas. Suddenly, at the Ranch, those dresses were out of place, as they seemed to soak up dirt the moment I stepped out the door.

• • •

After I'd had a bit of time to take everything in, I was still unsure what to make of all this. I loved it there. Whether it was the dogs or simply the way that we lived, it was dramatically different from life in Los Angeles. For the first few months, there were only a few adults to watch the approximately fifteen kids at the Ranch. For the most part, the older kids were the ones who took care of B.J. and me and told us what to do. At the time this seemed much better to me as they were young, seemed cool, and were nice to us, although they often made fun of my dresses.

Not long after we arrived, we met Joe Conte, or Mr. C, for short. He was introduced as the head adult at the Ranch. There was also a rotating security guard and a woman by the name of Karen Fassler, or Mr. F, as we called her. In Scientology, both sexes, male and female adults, went by Mister or Sir. Mr. F was pretty, fairly nice, and in charge of logistics, uniforms, food runs, and other business. Mr. C was friendly and easygoing, tall and thin, with a mustache and a bald head. He was rugged with an outdoorsy look about him; he struck all the kids as smart and very cool. My favorite books at the time were the young readers versions of *Chronicles of Narnia* and, in my mind, Mr. C was Professor Digory Kirke.

The kids themselves were essentially responsible for all of the various renovations going on at the Ranch. Projects involving electricity and plumbing were usually done by a specialist, who was an adult at the Int Base or a hired contractor, with kids helping. Everything on site faced city and county inspections, so the work had to be up to code. B. J. and I were still much smaller than the other kids, so our first projects were picking up trash, handing screws to my brother while he put up drywall, or varnishing our new dressers.

One of my favorite things after a hard day's work was the "wild ride." Mr. C would put upwards of ten kids into the back of his blue Nissan truck before driving it off road like a madman, over crazy bumps at high speed. When I first got to the Ranch, I was told that I was too small, but I finally convinced Mr. C to let me have a go, and the big kids held on to me for dear life as we tore around the property.

Every Saturday morning, a team of adults from the Int base would come and stay all day long to help and oversee what we were doing—sometimes even Dad would come and I'd get to work with him. We referred to Saturdays as "Saturday Renos," short for Saturday renovations. All the kids were involved in one way or another, but as I was so young, not much was expected of me. I was usually just fetching drinks, remembering measurements, or holding screws for the adults, who were always perfectly friendly. Except for the few adults who came for the Saturday Renos and the occasional contractor, the older kids were the labor pool for fixing up the Ranch—just as they were during the week. Their involvement didn't strike me as odd, though, because, even though my brother and his friends were still kids, to me they seemed essentially like grown-ups.

Between the kids work during the week and the Saturday Renos, the Motels and the School House were fixed up in that order. At the Motels, each room got a paint job, carpeting, curtains that were hand sewn, and a box AC/heater unit. Three or four bunk beds were set up in each room, accommodating seven or eight children. Every pair of rooms shared a bathroom with one toilet, one shower, and two sinks. We each had our own dressers, the same ones we had varnished and stained as our early projects. All the beds were provided with matching blankets and bedsheets. The mess hall was moved from the Big House into a very large room in the Motels. A laundry room was also added, equipped with a few washers and dryers. At some point, the swimming pool was cleaned, patched, and returned to a usable state, as well.

Next, the School House was renovated. The walls were painted with murals of the *Apollo* and the *Freewinds*. I even helped on the mural project, although I mostly messed it up with a few stray strokes at the bottom. Seeing the finished picture of the *Freewinds* was a thrill, though, because I knew it had been my mother's project for so long. Besides the murals of the ships, the School House also had portraits of L. Ron Hubbard, supplemented with several of his quotations on the walls. The floors were tiled with linoleum, and the classrooms were furnished with long foldout tables and plastic chairs rather than individual desks.

Soon after the School House renovations were completed, a woman named Maria arrived to the Ranch. We were required to call her "Mr. Parker." Mr. Parker was the adult responsible for education and activities. After with her arrival, more kids began to come. The School House had only two large rooms, one usually reserved for teenagers, while the other room was for younger kids, generally between four and twelve years old.

Right away, we started splitting our time between renovations we were helping with and classes. B. J. and I were far ahead of the other children, likely because the other children with us were much younger. All subjects were taught in the one room designated for our age group. Our main focus was reading and writing. There were no grades or report cards, and the teacher didn't lead the class in instruction.

We all had to go to our berthings a little before nine o'clock in the evening. Lights out was around nine. Some nights a woman by the name of Mr. Jane Thompson, a new adult at the Ranch, came to our room with a guitar and sing "Take Me Home, Country Roads," by John Denver, to help us go to sleep. There was always something comforting to her voice that never failed to remind me of when I was very little and my mom, on the nights she was home, would sing to me and stroke my hair to help put me to sleep.

• • •

My favorite thing about the Ranch was Saturday nights. As had been the arrangement in L.A., every Saturday night was when we'd visit with our parents. Only now, instead of them coming to us, Rosemary would pick Taryn, B. J., Justin, and me up at the Ranch and take us to our parents' apartment at the Int Base. The apartment was in a complex not far from the base, and it was a two-bedroom unit with a balcony on the second floor. Like the arrangement in L.A., Mom and Dad had one bedroom and the Rinders shared the other. For our Saturday overnights, Justin claimed the couch in the living room, so I'd sleep on the bedroom floor.

It didn't take long for us to settle into a new Saturday night routine, in which we'd stop first at the video store to rent a movie or two to keep us occupied while we waited for our parents. Although my parents had a television that got network broadcasts, it was not allowed at Int; at one point, Mom and Dad caught wind of a campaign to confiscate the televisions, and they'd been forced to hide theirs. However, once a week we were allowed to watch rented movies, and lots of kids would join us. In Justin's age group, that could be Sterling, Taryn, and often Mike, Rosemary's son. Another additon was Kiri, a girl that B. J. and I had played with sometimes when we lived in L.A., who arrived at the Ranch a few months after I did. Kiri was my best friend.

Together, we'd all stay up as late as we could. Mom and Dad usually got home around midnight, but sometimes it was even later. Most Sunday mornings, they would make breakfast for Justin and me, but depending on how much money they had, they might take us out to eat at Marie Callender's, or to Walmart for shampoo, socks, or maybe shoes. As fun as it was to be out with them, it was difficult because the visits were always too short. My parents always had to be back at work by one on Sunday afternoons, which meant they had to drop us off at the Ranch an hour or so before that.

Even with us being brought to our parents, we still didn't see that much of them, and often it was just Dad because a lot of the time, Mom was away on one special project or another. Once the *Freewinds* was launched, she was often in Los Angeles running renovations at the Celebrity Centre International, which was often undergoing improvements. Located in the old Manor Hotel on Franklin Avenue in downtown Hollywood, the seven-story building had been modeled on a French Normandy chateau and, in the 1920s, had been one of the area's most glamorous hotels. It was purchased by L. Ron Hubbard in 1969 and opened to the Scientology public in 1972; over the years it had been in various stages of repair. Despite the name, the Celebrity Centre catered to all Scientologists; however, celebrities often used the facilities there because L. Ron Hubbard thought famous people of arts and letters were great assets to the church. Because he had become a writer of international fame, he appreciated the arts and also recognized that celebrities were instrumental in disseminating the benefits of Scientology.

When Mom finished at the Celebrity Centre, she moved on to Clearwater, Florida, where she ran renovations at the Flag Land Base. She was eventually given an apartment in the berthing complex there. Just as Uncle Dave had apartments in Flag, PAC, and Int, other important execs had more than one berthing. It wasn't unusual at all for married couples to be stationed at different bases, as the greater good might be served this way. Since Mom was almost always at Flag, I'd speak to her on the phone at some point while I was at my parents' apartment.

Though my mom was rarely around, Dad tried his best to be involved in my life. Eventually, he started coming on Fridays during his lunch break to visit my brother and me. He could only stay a short time, usually, at most, twenty minutes, but I always appreciated it when he came. We would usually just talk by his car or chat in my room. Sometimes, he'd bring me a little present.

I especially liked when he brought me near beer, a nonalcoholic beer. Other times he would bring me my latest book shipment. He had signed me up for a Book of the Month Club where I would get a few books a month, which I *loved*. I always loved reading.

Very few parents came to see their kids at this time, but I wasn't prone to wondering where the other kids' parents were. Seeing Dad was such a rare thing—every minute that we were together felt precious.

CHAPTER FIVE

A CADET'S LIFE

WITHIN SIX MONTHS OF MY ARRIVAL AT THE RANCH, EVERYTHING became more regimented, as new kids began coming at a steadier pace. Mostly, they were kids closer to my age, although some of them were younger. In time, there were more than eighty kids there. With the major work completed on the Ranch, the adults from Int stopped coming for Saturday Renos. We were all given new uniforms—khaki pants or shorts, and red T-shirts with the "The Ranch" on the front in white letters. We also got sweaters and down vests for the winters and sweatpants for phys ed. Because boys and girls could no longer room together, I left B. J. in Room 12 and moved to Room 4 with six other girls. Previously, our Saturday pickup had been at around four or five in the afternoon. Now our parents, or in our case Rosemary, could pick us up only on Saturday at nine or ten at night.

This added regimentation was not a good thing; almost overnight the tone of the Ranch changed. Earlier, when there had only been a few of us younger kids and a lot of older kids, we had a fair amount of freedom, but suddenly they began to schedule us down to the minute. In a matter of weeks, I went from enjoying life there to loathing it.

Several additional adults arrived as well, including two new teachers: Melissa Bell, Mr. Bell to us, who was an intimidating chain smoker, and Mr. Cathy Mauro who was kind enough, with short brown hair and glasses.

Traditional education was not viewed as crucial to success in Scientology. Neither my mother nor my father had finished high school, and they were both respected senior executives in the church. Even Uncle Dave had dropped out at age sixteen, and he was the head of all of Scientology. Given my family's history with school, I was under the impression that dropping out was kind of cool; my mom always sounded proud when she told me about her schooling and how she had decided that the Sea Org was more important than finishing high school.

The kids were separated into three different groups: Children, Precadets, and Cadets. Children were generally the youngest kids, six years old or younger. Precadets were mostly seven to nine, and Cadets nine to sixteen. The grouping wasn't determined exclusively by age, but also by how far along you were in your academic and Scientology studies. There were some eight-year-old Cadets and some twelve-year-old Precadets. When I first came to the Ranch, I was a Precadet, but as I neared my seventh birthday, I graduated to Cadet.

One of the first things I did as a Cadet was sign the billion-year contract pledging my commitment to the Sea Org. It was the same contract that was signed by the adult members of the Sea Org, because Cadets were considered Sea Org members in training, and thus were supposed to pledge with equally binding loyalty.

At first, I didn't know much about the contract. I'd heard bits and pieces when I was younger, but it wasn't until that day that they explained what the contract was all about. Signing it was part of our curriculum, part of becoming a Sea Org member and moving through our training as future Sea Org members. Even though it was for a billion years, I felt no hesitation—they asked me to do it and it was my job to follow their lead. Besides, at seven, any large number feels pretty unfathomable, whether it's a thousand or a billion, and the irrational magnitude of that time frame simply didn't register with me. Sure, we were making a long commitment, but it was the same long commitment that our parents had made.

On signing day, all the kids stood in a single-file line at tables where the contracts were laid out. One by one, we each signed. I really didn't have anything else I wanted to do in life except to be a Sea Org member, so it would have been silly to pause and consider my options, as I wouldn't have even known what they might have been. All I wanted was to be with my parents and work with them every day. I knew that if I graduated from the Cadet school and became a full-fledged Sea Org member and was ethical and compliant, I would have a post at the Int Base, and I'd see my parents more than once a week. That alone was enough to make me eagerly sign the document in the blank space.

WITH THE NEWLY IMPLEMENTED REGIMENTATION ON THE Ranch, the Cadet Org became a lot like a military boot camp, with grueling drills, endless musters, exhaustive inspections, and arduous physical labor that no child should have to do. From the moment we woke up to the time we went to bed, there was little downtime; the only real break we'd get was seeing our parents Saturday nights and Sunday mornings. Between drills, chores, duties, posts, and studies, we were scheduled to the minute. The fact that my uncle was the head of Scientology didn't protect me or offer me any special treatment.

In truth, it was around this time that my serious indoctrination into Scientology began. Until then, my parents had been the ones in the Sea Org, and my life had been dictated by their schedules and service to the church. Now I began to have my own schedules and responsibilities. However, the changes were more than strictly organizational; they were about learning the Sea Org point of view. Much of this indoctrination was aided by the extreme separation that existed between us and the outside world. Except for a few rare occasions, we were completely isolated from non-Scientologists and had no interaction with anyone of a different faith. The trips we took off Ranch were most often to the equally isolated Int Base, which of course was stocked with Scientology's most ardent defenders, including all of our parents.

Even if we'd been allowed to travel into the outside world, it wouldn't have mattered much. Few of us possessed curiosity about life beyond our borders, because we had been led to believe the outside world was filled with ignorant people whom we called *Wogs*, short for "Well and Orderly Gentlemen." From what we were taught, WOGS were completely unenlightened; after we'd been trained in auditing and Scientology, it would be our job to "clear" them. Wogs were to be avoided because they were unaware of what was really going on, and their unawareness was reflected in their shallow priorities. Wogs liked to ask a lot of questions. We were led to believe that they would find our lifestyle alarming, so we had to be careful that, when speaking to them, we spoke in terms they could understand.

Questioning attitudes and nonconforming behavior was kept in check through threats, punishments, and humiliations in front of the group. Any time you were late, flunked an inspection, or behaved in a way that was not considered ethical, you would get a chit, sometimes several chits a day, depending on how many people had decided to write one. A chit was a kind of written demerit; one went to you, and a copy went into your ethics folder.

Every child had an ethics folder, which was kept locked in the Cottage to prevent any file tampering. A Master-at-Arms was responsible for keeping our ethics files in order, doing inspections, and making sure we toed the line. In order to graduate from the Ranch, we had to have great Ethics and Production records to receive clearance for the Int Base.

Virtually all of the chits issued had nothing to do with an adult observing bad behavior, but rather another kid in the group reporting it. The rule was that we had to speak up if we saw or knew of anyone who was "out-ethics," or unethical, or else we would be considered an accessory to their crime and would receive the same penalty. Self-policing inside the group made it difficult for anyone to trust anyone else. LRH believed that a group's success depended on all its members enforcing a code of mores, and making each other accountable.

Chits and humiliations were an essential part of keeping Cadets of all ages in line and cooperative. It was amazing how quickly even young kids would find themselves captive to this system, making even the most unruly eight-year-old eager to please. While teens were more resistant than the younger kids, if given the proper set of embarrassments and punishments in front of the group, they too would fall in line quickly.

On the occasion that a chit was written on me, an anxiety always built in my chest. The chit was usually for something unfair or an exaggeration of the truth because someone was angry at me, but no matter how misguided the reason behind the chit might have been, getting one was always enough to make me think twice about doing or saying something that was in any way contrary.

The sense of order these punishments created was incredibly important to life on the Ranch, because, whether you were seven or seventeen, nearly everything you did was about the group.

• • •

Each morning, we woke at six-thirty to the sound of an alarm clock. As soon as one of us was up, we would go to the courtyard and yell, "Wake up time!" We had until seven to get ready and complete our various cleaning stations in our dorms, such as laundry, sweeping, and trash collection. My assignment was cleaning the bathroom. We also had to prepare our uniforms for daily inspection, which meant shining our shoes, tucking in our shirts, and trying to hide holes in them by wearing a sweater.

Seven o'clock was muster time, when all our various units would line up. The Cadet group had a structure slightly different from the Children and the Precadets. One of us was named the Commanding Officer, or CO, Cadet. The rest of us were divided up into seven different Divisions, each led by a Division Head. Each Division had three departments. Different divisions had different duties they were to carry out. I was assigned to Division 5.

At the morning muster, each Div Head would account for each member of his or her division. The Commanding Officer would direct us to stand at attention, then a formal military-style report was done by the Master-at-Arms, also a kid. Each division head had to call out his group's accountability with a salute.

"Div One, all present and accounted for!" would begin the roll call, and so it continued for each unit. Throughout the day but especially at morning muster, lateness was unacceptable and every instance was reported. In addition to it being embarrassing, the penalties for lateness were stiff, varying from having a bucket of ice water dumped on your head in front of everyone at the muster to having a chit written on you.

Our division accountability reports were finished in about two minutes, and we were then given a "Left face!" command. We all turned left so our Div Head could walk down the line and do a uniform inspection. Hygiene was also crucial, so our breath and armpits were smell-tested and our hair routinely checked for lice.

Next, we were given a "Right face!" command, so we would return to facing front. We would be asked to raise our hand if for some reason we had flunked our inspection. As with lateness, an inspection flunk would cause a chit to be written for our ethics folder.

After personal inspections, we would receive the results of our berthing inspections. If your berthing flunked inspection one time, you would be given a chit. The penalties, which increased with each consecutive flunk, ranged from being required to white-glove the room (cleaning the room so well that a person inspecting the room could run their white-gloved hands across all surfaces without getting them dirty) before going to sleep, to being ordered to Pigs Berthing, which meant spending the night on an old mattress in the shell of the Big House, which was filled with bats. I was never assigned to Pigs Berthing, but my friend told me about it in horrifying detail, like how many bats flew near her head and the shrieking sounds they made that kept her up all night. My room, which was now Room 9, would actually wake up fifteen minutes early each day to allow for extra cleaning time to make sure that we never wound up in Pigs Berthing.

When all inspections were finished, we went to Chinese school. Chinese school was parroting; we had to repeat everything we heard exactly as we heard it. L. Ron Hubbard had originally called it Chinese school because he had observed a Chinese classroom and was very impressed with how the students engaged with the instructor.

During LRH's version of Chinese school, quotations from him were written in large letters on butcher paper, so that we could all read them when they were held up at the front of the muster. Someone would yell out a part of the quote, then say, "What is it?" We would then be required to repeat it in unison, loudly and clearly and eventually by memory without glancing at the butcher paper. One in particular was the lesson on "backflashing," which was the Scientology word for talking back. "Backflashes, by definition, are an unnecessary response to an order . . ." We would chant this drill/policy together until everyone said it flawlessly.

The monotony was overwhelming, but it had the impact they wanted. Often, it was hard enough to think about what these slogans meant in order to recite things correctly, let alone question what you were saying. The LRH quotes were also changed frequently, which enabled us to memorize many of them. The whole process was designed to teach us policy by heart. Looking back, however, it was more about teaching us not to question, not to think for ourselves, and to accept without skepticism. We were young enough to sponge up everything we learned, and naive enough not to understand the trouble with trusting everything you're taught.

Sometimes, there were older kids who were willing to take the risk and challenge authority by doing their own thing. Like many Cadets, I struggled to understand why they couldn't just follow the rules. They were asking for trouble, and they were always hauled off and dealt with. Every time it happened, I'd watch them be reprimanded.

At the completion of Chinese school, the morning muster was over, and the next part of the morning—fulfilling our posts— began, lasting until breakfast. No matter what age you were, you had an assigned post, which sometimes changed and was commensurate with your responsibility level. When I first became a Cadet as a six-year-old, I was given the post of groundsman, responsible for the upkeep and maintenance of an assigned area of the grounds. This post entailed physical labor, but not every post was physical; some involved helping the group in other ways. After several months, I was given the Medical Liaison Officer post, MLO for short, even though I was only seven. This post required me to visit each child at the Ranch and make what was called the "Sick List." This meant I had to walk up to everyone and ask him or her, "Do you have any sickness?" Sickness could mean anything from a common cold to poison oak, from dry skin to athlete's foot.

I would write down all the information. Then, I would try to treat them. An adult at the Ranch had given me basic information, such as athlete's foot cream was for athlete's foot, and lanolin was for dry skin.

In addition to daily care, doling out vitamins was a large part of my responsibility. It was my job to make individual vitamin packets for all the kids. Because I knew how to read very well at that point, I learned the definitions of various vitamins and their purposes. It might sound complicated, but in fact it was a lot easier than some of the other materials we were required to read for Scientology. I knew what all the vitamins were and that certain ones, like vitamin A, could be overdosed. I also knew there was some sort of vitamin balance, but I was never sure how to achieve it, so I just did the moderate thing and gave people one of each. The packets I prepared were usually a combination of vitamins A and D, B, C and E, and garlic. On the trace minerals, I just followed the instructions on the bottle. People with colds would get zinc, alfalfa, goldenseal, extra garlic, and echinacea. Before breakfast, I would dump extra vitamin C powder into the orange juice and squirt liquid trace minerals into everyone's cup.

I was also required to make a special concoction called Cal-Mag for everyone to drink before bed. The Cal-Mag's formula, first concocted by LRH, consisted of calcium, magnesium, apple-cider vinegar, and boiling water, which would then be cooled down. It was intended to be a clear drink; however, I didn't know the difference between a tablespoon and a teaspoon, and I would incorrectly add a tablespoon of magnesium instead of a teaspoon, making this already horrible-tasting drink murky and smelling almost exactly like dirty feet. During mealtimes, it was my responsibility to take the meal to anybody who was in isolation.

If someone had a cut, I would clean it with hydrogen peroxide and patch it with a Band-Aid. If it was a hot day, I made sure salt, potassium, and cell salts were available for the kids. If anyone complained of a headache, other ache or fever, I would usually give him an assist. Assists were the special procedures created by LRH that I had been introduced to at the nursery in L.A. They were supposed to help people have better communication with their bodies. In addition to the touch assist that we had done at the nursery, there was also the nerve assist, which was like a very light massage. There were lots of similar assists written by LRH and designed to help people with all sorts of ailments, from colds, fevers, and toothaches to even psychological things, such as bad dreams. In my post as Medical Liasion, I would do as many as I could.

The assists were based on Scientological principles that the Thetan controlled the mind and the body. There were some procedures, like asking a kid to explain his bad dream over and over again, that were supposed to help him get rid of its hold on him. There was also the belief that people got colds because of a loss, so I would ask, "Tell me something you haven't lost lately?" as a part of the cold assist, reminding them of things they still had. There was a giant handbook that had everything from a toothache assist to a temperature assist.

If it seemed as though someone was more seriously ill, I would tell an adult, and an adult would usually visit isolation to see how things were going. I never went to the doctor the entire time I was at the Ranch. The only time I witnessed a doctor's visit, I was accompanying a friend who needed stitches, and wound up fainting at the sight of blood. At least once, they did have a nurse come out, and everyone was given the MMR—the measles, mumps, and rubella vaccine.

One rule that was firm, however, was that no matter how sick a kid was, we never used drugs to relieve pain or reduce fever. Drugs were considered bad and weren't even available. Antibiotics were fine, but you would have to go to the real doctor to get them, which was pretty rare. There were times when I was extremely sick with a high temperature (102 or 103 degrees) to the point of nearly passing out, even vomiting, and I was simply told to drink fluids and get rest. As a kid, I was not responsible enough to take care of myself and follow these orders; once I even tried exercising to get better because my brother told me this was the best way. I have no idea if my parents were informed when I was sick, but I never heard from them when I was, unless I had a chance to tell them about it on a Sunday. Most of the time, though, I was able to stay pretty healthy. As I became a more experienced MLO, everything became fairly routine. Looking back on this time, it's difficult even for me to understand how a seven-year-old child could be entrusted to do a job like this. I hate to think what might have happened if a child had been extremely sick and I hadn't realized the seriousness of it enough to say something to an adult. However, I didn't feel unqualified or unprepared, because this was the only way I knew to do things. They supposedly told me how to care for kids, and I learned how to follow their instructions as best I could.

Post time, when I was on duty as the MLO, was the most enjoyable part of my day, because I liked taking care of the other kids and making them feel better. The adults taught me that there was a practical, clear solution for all medical problems. In many ways, they treated illness as if it were the same as hunger or a lack of toilet paper—it was simply an obstacle on our journey to become Sea Org members. The solution was to rely on the people who made the food, supplied toilet paper, or, in my case, helped my fellow Ranch kids become healthier.

Breakfast was at eight-thirty. We ate at assigned tables; each table had a Mess President and a Treasurer, who collected one dollar here and there so that we could have extra condiments, such as honey or jelly. They were on sale at the canteen, and we could purchase them ourselves or pool our money and purchase them as a group. Because there was a no-sugar policy at the Ranch, these were rare commodities that went fast. The meal was over at nine, and the dining room/dishwashing process began. We all had cleaning stations. Some kids did dishes, others did sweeping and mopping, some cleaned the tables, but everyone had a chore.

The second muster, which began at nine-fifteen, signaled the beginning of decks, or the labor-intensive projects. They lasted almost four hours, until twelve-forty-five, Monday through Friday, and all day Saturday. This added up to twenty-five hours of deck time per week, but if you included the time we spent at our morning posts, and the time we spent white-gloving the entire Ranch on Saturdays, that brought the total hours we were working to more than thirty-five hours a week: a full-time job, and we were only kids and young teenagers.

Unlike our posts, which were specific jobs that rarely changed, the decks had us working in small groups; the projects themselves changed constantly. Depending on how many projects there were to be done on any given day, we were all divided into units—and worked with our units. It didn't matter how old you were, everyone worked on these labor projects.

Each unit was assigned a kid who was in charge, and he or she had a sheet of paper that laid out exactly what the project consisted of, how long it should take, and the tools that were needed. The projects themselves varied from the fun ones, such as doing the laundry or cleaning the swimming pool—often considered one-person jobs—to weeding for fire protection, rock hauling, planting trees and other plants, and digging irrigation trenches.

Often there was landscaping involved. We would spend long hours on dig-and-plant projects, using a shovel to dig five-foot holes for each of the hundreds of new trees in the tree nursery, sometimes in pouring rain and hail. We worked in teams to haul hundreds of trees all over the property, plant them, and make sure they were properly fertilized. On hundreds of days, we planted the hills with an ice plant called red apple. We'd weed and irrigate a hill, lay burlap on it, and then one kid would dig holes with a pickax while another would place the plants into the holes.

Rock hauling to build stone walls was another arduous deck project. We would pick up rocks from a creek that ran nearby and put them into a pile, where another group of children would load them into a wheelbarrow and carry them to the site of the newest rock wall. Once the rocks were in place, yet another set of kids would lug around cement bags, and the older, more skilled kids would use the cement to secure the rocks in the wall.

Because the buildings on the Ranch were older constructions, part of the renovation job of the Big House involved loading piles of roofing by hand or shoveling them into wheelbarrows and taking them from the Big House demolition/construction site to a huge hole, about a quarter of a mile away, where it was to be buried. The insulation itself was brittle, about an eighth of an inch thick, and would crack like cement if you hit it on a rock. It was a reddish, pinkish, brownish color. On at least one occasion, we were told that some inspectors were coming to the Ranch, and there was a big rush to hide the giant pile of roofing, which seemed a little odd, but we did it nonetheless.

When we weren't planting, constructing rock walls, or moving debris, we frequently pulled weeds to keep the Ranch safer in case of brushfires. The parched desert land around the Ranch was peppered with scrub that could easily catch fire during the dry summer months, and so, for fire protection, we were required to pull out weeds by their roots along several miles of the road. No matter how hot it was—temperatures were often well over 100 degrees—the older girls couldn't wear tank tops or sports bras because they were too suggestive, which was confusing, because the boys were allowed to take their shirts off. We were always told to wear gloves, but none were ever provided, at least to me, so I, like many kids, had a thick layer of brown, chapped skin between my forefinger and my thumb from holding the rake.

To cope with the heat, there was usually cold water, as well as the salt and potassium tablets, which were supposed to keep us hydrated. Kids would take four or five of each because none of us really knew how they were supposed to be taken. At least I didn't know. So we just took them because we heard they helped prevent overheating. We were also allowed five-minute breaks, although they were few and far between.

We were told that the labor was simply an exchange for being able to live on the Ranch. It was our chance to earn our way, rather than getting things for free. This was important because, as Scientology taught us, our supervisors were actually helping to prevent us from becoming criminals, since only criminals got things for free. Furthermore, this hard labor was training us how to have pride in production, to face tough situations head-on, and to confront MEST, an acronym that Scientology used for Matter, Energy, Space, and Time. MEST was the term that referred to physical objects as opposed to anything in the spiritual realm that had to do with nonphysical things, such as Thetans, thoughts, and intentions. Because we were doing physical labor, we were dealing with MEST, which would someday make us better Scientologists.

Frequently during decks, the adults would wander from project to project to see how they were coming along. Sometimes, they would help out a little, but the projects really were primarily carried out and overseen by the children. In fact, the adults would push us to work harder, faster, and more thoroughly. We were controlling and handling the MEST in our way. Confronting it through physical labor was seen as therapeutic and helped to clear our heads, even though the projects and assignments were often incredibly labor intensive.

Very rarely during my time at the Ranch did anyone ever step forward to say they thought the work was too much or too extreme, probably because the adults did not see it that way. After all, they were the ones who wrote the project orders and determined whether or not we had satisfactorily completed our decks project. If not, we were sometimes required to finish it through our lunchtime. No project was considered finished until an adult or another specially appointed kid inspected it and signed off.

In the end, we either complied with our decks assignments or we were sent to an adult. If we were repeat offenders, we could end up in the HMU, the Heavy MEST Work Unit, where we did heavy manual labor. This unit was for people who repeatedly broke rules or backflashed. The harder work, such as deep trench digging, was reserved for this group. They were also required to eat and study separately and we weren't supposed to talk to them.

Despite the fact that our Scientology supervisors didn't seem to think it was strange that kids were doing this kind of work, every now and then we'd come into contact with outside contractors who did. Usually, they were hired to do the more technical projects on the Ranch, like laying the cement for a sidewalk. These outsiders didn't come around often, but when they did, I always had a little bit of hope that they would advocate for us or that our work shifts would be cut back a few hours or even days. Most of the time, our supervisors just tried to keep us as separate from these Wogs as possible, but once, while the contractors were there, they actually complained when they saw a couple of young kids hauling a railroad tie, because they thought they were too young for that kind labor. What they didn't know was that, since railroad ties were a featured element all over the property for edging pathways or creating planters, we hauled railroad ties all the time, usually two kids per tie. After the complaint by the outsiders, we were not allowed to work anywhere near hired contractors.

Not surprisingly, the older and stronger we got, the easier the physical labor became. Some children, such as my brother, didn't seem to have trouble keeping up with the deck work. Justin would usually make fun of me or call me a slacker when I would walk instead of run or complain that I was tired. I was a seven-year-old girl, and he was a fifteen-year-old boy, so it was just different.

I didn't like the work at all. My legs always hurt, my hands were extremely chapped, and I was usually either overheated or freezing cold, because we worked no matter the temperature. We often wound up wearing shorts in the winter because the funds weren't there for new uniforms and, as kids, we grew quickly. The rule was that everyone had to run while on decks, so if I was caught walking, I would hear "Jenna, run!" or "Jenna, get to work!" Adults and kids alike would yell this out. There was nothing polite about it. If we backflashed, moved slow, or refused to do a project, which almost never happened, we were told to stop "nattering" (the word LRH used for complaining or talking badly about something) and we would get a chit written on us.

The work itself was never-ending. We would finish a project one day, and then have a whole new one the next. It was incessant and repetitious, like being told every day to push a boulder up a hill and knowing full well that tomorrow another boulder would be there. We were making the Ranch into a beautiful place, but for whom? I'd certainly lost all appreciation for its beauty, and I longed for the days when the Ranch had been more run-down and I had downtime to enjoy it.

To this day I don't know whether the real motivation behind these projects was the virtually free labor, a way to keep us out of trouble, or to make us better Scientologists. Most likely it was a combination of all three. In the end we were a group of children who devoted hours of every day to doing the kind of physical labor that no child should have to do.

We got calluses and blisters. We had cuts and bruises. Our hands lost feeling when we plunged them into the frigid water of the creek bed for rocks. When we pulled weeds from the scorched summer earth, our hands burned from the friction and stung from the nettle. The conditions we worked under would have been tough for a grown man, and yet any complaints, backflashing, any kind of questioning was instantly met with disciplinary action.

However hardened the adults who demanded the labor were, the bottom line was that the beliefs in Scientology itself enabled it. In the eyes of Scientology, we weren't kids; we were Thetans, just the same as adults and capable of the same responsibilities. The only difference was that our bodies were younger. *We* were not necessarily younger, just our bodies were. So, the fact that we were children was irrelevant. I knew this was the thinking, so when I felt like it was just too hard or too much, I figured there was something wrong with me and that I would need to toughen up, however wrong that conclusion was.

My insecurity was only reinforced by the adults and the older kids around me, who would call me a slacker and tell me to toughen up.

When I look back and consider why I didn't rebel, the reality was that doing so would have just made life harder. If I didn't follow the rules, I would have been separated from the group, not allowed to talk to my friends, forced to make up for my behavior, not allowed to have libs, or attend special ceremonies and events. The only place to go from not following rules was back to following rules. Insubordination would only make it harder for me to graduate and leave the Ranch.

CHAPTER SIX

BEING A CADET, PART II

IF OUR MORNINGS AS CADETS WERE ABOUT WORK AND LABOR, then our afternoons were about schooling.

When decks ended, we had lunch and cleanup, followed by schooling, which began around one-forty-five. Our academic education encompassed the usual subjects: math, geography, reading, spelling, and history, but we were expected to learn the subjects on our own, using textbooks and checksheets that were assigned to us, not from a formal lesson given by a teacher. In fact we didn't even use the word "teacher" because it had been replaced by "course supervisor." Similarly, the name "classroom" had been replaced with the name "course room," based on an L. Ron Hubbard policy letter aptly titled, "What Is a Course?"

During our course period, we were now required to get a daily meter check, to be administered by a supervisor. The supervisor would use an LRH invention technically called an electropsychometer, but everybody called it the E-Meter. The person being assessed held two soup cans. Then, a tiny electrical current was passed through the cans into his body as he was asked questions. The E-Meter had a needle, and after each question, the needle would fluctuate; those movements were then interpreted by the person operating the machine. By carefully watching the motions of the needle, the operator supposedly could figure out whether someone was telling the truth. The idea was that the E-Meter could locate moments in your subconscious that you might not be aware of, but that needed to be discussed. These moments would then have to be addressed with Scientology auditing. In other words, the E-Meter was viewed as a tool that helped the auditing process.

The daily meter checks were used to see if we had come across any words in our studies that we didn't fully understand. In Scientology, there was the belief that if you encountered a word in the text that you didn't understand and you continued to study past that word, it would cause you to fail in your studies and in life. LRH said that trying to study past a misunderstood word was the prime factor in stupidity and was at the root of all wrongdoing and misbehavior that might lead to criminality. As LRH wrote, "Reading on past a word that one does not understand gives one a distinctly blank feeling, a washed-out feeling, a not there feeling, and a sort of nervous hysteria can follow that." This, he said, could produce a "blow," which could make you give up on your studies or leave the classroom.

Clearing a word consisted of finding the correct definition in the dictionary, then using it in sentences until you were comfortable with it. The process would be repeated with each of the remaining alternate definitions of the word, including any synonyms and idioms. God forbid that, during the process of learning these various definitions and origins of the word, you came across another word inside the definition you didn't understand. This would cause word chains, which meant there were even more words to clear, and you could be piled high in dictionaries for several hours just so you didn't fail your meter check. You also had to know etymologies.

If you flunked your meter check, you were required to start at the beginning of your course and write down and clear every word you didn't know the meaning of. Then, you were required to restart your course from the first misunderstood word you found.

I really disliked meter checks; they made me extremely nervous. They were done in front of the entire course room, and everyone heard if you flunked. The course supervisor would ask:

"In your recent studies, have you encountered any word or symbol that you didn't fully understand?"

Then, she would expectantly look down at the E-Meter to see whether you had passed or flunked. If you flunked, she'd let the whole class hear it.

Aside from the meter checks, the course supervisor offered little to no guidance. Any time you didn't understand something in your text, she would ask you what word you didn't understand, instead of helping you to figure it out. The thinking was that if people couldn't understand what they were reading and were asking for explanations, this meant that they'd read a misunderstood word. A supervisor explaining it was doing them a huge disservice, because passing by misunderstood words led to failure. Not surprisingly, I started to hate school. Before becoming a Cadet, I had always been a pretty smart kid with a love for reading, but it didn't take long for these tedious and robotic instruction methods to discourage me. Whatever educational value there may have been in learning the definitions of different words was undermined by the stunted and impractical process of the learning itself. Even though I'd been able to read and write at a very young age, all the focus on individual words caused me to lose interest in both.

The E-Meter checks were particularly nerve-racking for me, and I went to great lengths to avoid them. No one could be meter checked if he was in the middle of clearing a word, so I developed a system to get around meter checks by always having a dictionary open, pretending I was looking up a word and using it in sentences. While my system saved me the embarrassment of flunking meter tests, it didn't help me get through my studies. It was a complete distraction; I became so tied up in understanding the meaning of words that I actually wasn't able to understand the bigger text that I was supposed to be reading. I would sometimes ask my friends to explain certain concepts to me, but we were not allowed to talk to other students. If we did, we would often be yelled at in front of everyone across the course room, possibly even sent to the Ethics Officer.

Academic studies went from one-forty-five until six, with one fifteen-minute break. We were allowed to grab a snack, either something we bought at the canteen, or an orange or apple, which was free. We could also play in the playground that we had built. After break, there was another roll call before classes resumed. Some days, we had a forty-five-minute physical education class, which was probably the least structured thing we did. Once a week, a fitness trainer would come to the Ranch and give us a physical fitness test. Since we were all in good shape from the deck work, though, passing was not a problem. On the days that the fitness trainer wasn't there, we did whatever came to mind. Some people played soccer or volleyball, but there were no set teams, no coaches, and, usually, the sixteen-year-old boys were playing sports. It was impossible for a young girl to play on the same team without getting trampled, which I learned from experience. So like many others my age, I just gave up and would go to a room where we would all do so-called gymnastics or aerobics.

DINNER AND CLEANUP WERE BETWEEN SIX AND SIX FORTY-FIVE, after which point our Scientology studies would begin. While our academic studies focused on subjects meant to supplement our Scientology studies, these evening sessions were tied to the actual introductory courses of Scientology. Of course, by that point in the day, exhaustion often set in. By the time we began these studies, we'd already been going for more than twelve hours.

Like our academic studies, these course periods were crowded with forty or so people per room. Students were on different levels, so some kids would be working on drills, while others were listening to audiotapes of LRH lectures, making models in clay, or reading LRH books and policies. We worked at our own pace, using a checksheet to show what we'd accomplished.

The courses that we took covered many different aspects of Scientology, from learning about the Thetan, mind, body relationship to understanding the importance of misunderstood words. We also took what was called the Children's Communications Course. It had been adapted from an adult course designed to teach older Scientologists how to audit, although a lot of it had been lost in the adaptation. The communications courses had various Training Routines or TRs, which were supposed to perfect communication. They were done in succession, from TR-0 through TR-4. The goal of the TRs was to help us isolate and practice various communication skills. Some were long practical drills to help us confront adversity and distraction.

For all the TRs, we were paired with a person assigned to be our drill mate, called our twin. In TR-0, we were instructed to sit in chairs facing each other pretty much knee to knee. One of us was the coach and the other was the student. We had to look at each other until we were comfortable, not moving, not blinking excessively, not smiling, not looking away, just staring. The stated aim was to learn how to face another person without anxiety but, in actuality, it felt more like a mindless staring contest. In time, the stare would morph into a hypnotic trance, as the person across from me always blurred into a gauzy haze of lines and colors.

Next was TR-0 Bullbait, by far the hardest one to pass. We again sat facing each other, only this time, instead of silent stares, we had to endure our coach making fun of us, saying joking or insulting things. No matter what was said, we were supposed to stay stone-faced. The other kids in the course room could hear the bull-baiting, so of course they'd laugh, too, making it almost impossible to stay focused. The objective of TR-Bullbait was to learn how not to react, but it was never clear to me why it was so important not to laugh at things that were funny. At times, it was hard to maintain composure, let alone not break out into loud laughter.

Oddly enough, *Alice's Adventures in Wonderland* was an integral part of TR-1 and TR-2. In TR-1, called "Dear Alice," we read passages from Lewis Carroll's *Alice's Adventures in Wonderland* out loud in order to practice making ourselves heard without over- or under-projecting. It was our twin's job to flunk us, literally announcing the word "flunk" at every mistake. TR-2 was the extension of "Dear Alice." In this exercise, one person would read random quotes from *Alice in Wonderland,* and the other would acknowledge that he had, indeed, heard him by saying "thank-you," or "good" every time. This acknowledgement was important, because that was how Auditors were supposed to let pre-Clears know that they have been heard during an auditing session.

At the time, the exercises didn't feel strange. In retrospect, these TRs were bizarre. TR-3 was an exercise focused on the technique of getting a typical question answered. The student would ask questions, "Do birds fly?" or "Do fish swim?" and the coach was supposed to try to distract the student by deliberately saying unrelated things like "Well, dogs fly," or "I'm cold," thereby forcing the student to repeat the question. The whole exercise was a cycle looping over and over again—until the coach decided to give the correct response.

TR-4, Handling Originations, had us practice keeping our twin on topic. For example, we would still ask, "Do birds fly?" But our twin was not supposed to answer the question, instead saying something off topic, such as "I need a tissue." We would then say, "Okay, here you go," and hand over a tissue. We'd immediately return to our original question, "I will repeat the question. Do birds fly?" and so forth.

All the TRs were grounded in repetition and were supposedly meant to teach us about how to control communication. I truly believed the goal was to improve our communication skills, but the monotonous, repetitive nature of them in many ways had the opposite effect. I began to feel the need to look right at someone when I talked to them or to make sure I acknowledged everything he said. In reality, the TRs made me feel like it was wrong to react or express my emotions. In our everyday life, if we started to get upset by something someone said or did, we were told "Get your TRs in." I was supposed to be in control of my emotions at all times, and the courses helped me to do that, even if that meant burying those emotions inside me.

Although the TRs seemed to encourage uniformity in our interactions, it was apparent that the adults at the Ranch believed taking these courses at such a young age would make us better Sea Org members in the future. We were people who grew up with the technology of Scientology, so our parents and other adults were excited and even a little envious that we were being exposed to this stuff so young. It was almost like a privilege they never had.

At nine, our Scientology study period would end. We then had to fill out Student Point Slips, which were essentially point-based progress reports for each day. For example, reading one page of an LRH policy was worth ten points and each definition we cleared in the dictionary was three points. We would then total our points and mark our number on a daily graph to see whether we were up or down from the previous day. If we were down, we would be first in line the following day for our daily meter check.

Once our graphs were completed, the supervisor would ask if anybody wanted to share a win. A win was something you had learned and could now apply. If someone shared a win, everyone clapped. Typically, three or four wins were offered every night. I assumed the purpose of sharing our wins was to show our course-mates that there was a lot to be gained by applying Scientology techniques, and you could have a win, too, if you listened to the Church's teachings. Conversely, not having wins meant maybe you were doing something wrong or that something was wrong with you.

We always ended each course period the same way, with three cheers to L. Ron Hubbard. The cheer began when we would all turn and face his picture on the wall. Even though LRH had dropped his body, everyone still thought of him as our hero, a man who had cared enough about the human race to help us through his wisdom and technology. It didn't matter what room we were in; there was a portrait of LRH in every one, includ-ing every dormitory. This felt weird, as if he was watching me wherever I went.

The supervisor would then shout, "Hip! Hip!" We'd reply "Hooray!" and then we would clap for a couple of minutes.

After our salute, we would return to our rooms and get ready for bed. I lived in a dorm room with seven girls. We would all take showers at night because there was never enough time in the morning. While waiting for the shower, the sixteen of us who shared it would hang out, chat, and brush our teeth. It was one of the few occasions during the day when we could just talk to our friends, although it was just thirty minutes.

Lights went out at nine-thirty sharp, and the Master-at-Arms would be around to ensure everyone was in bed. The next day, we'd wake up and do it all over again.

OUR WEEKDAY SCHEDULE WAS THE SAME, WITH THE EXCEPTION of Thursday afternoons. In Scientology, the week begins and ends on Thursday afternoon at two, and as part of starting a new week,

Thursday afternoons were spent on the tedious job of putting together all of our numerical data for the week, so that our supervisors, who were usually kids themselves, could evaluate our progress. We all assembled in the School House at precisely two o'clock for two hours of what we called "Thursday Basics." This was when we tallied up our daily statistics from the Student Point Slips, made charts to graph them, and reviewed them ourselves to see if we were improving or declining.

Thursday Basics was also when we compiled our weekly statistics for our posts. Every day, we were inspected to make sure we marked our activities on our daily post graphs to reflect what we were accomplishing. In my case as Medical Liaison Officer, that meant that every day I was being evaluated based on how many healthy Cadets I saw.

On Thursdays, I'd tabulate the results from these daily graphs. When I emerged from what felt like a mountain of data and weekly numbers, my graph would indicate whether I was moving in a good direction (up) or a bad direction (down). Based on the direction and slope of the graph's line, I had a corresponding condition formula, which was supposed to help me determine how I would improve my post statistics; depending on what the formula said, I would have to take different steps the following week in order to improve or maintain my statistics.

Condition formulas didn't just govern our progress at our posts; they were also integral to evaluating whether we were improving as people. According to LRH, there were twelve conditions or states of well-being that were ranked, and Scientologists were always supposed to be trying to improve their condition, since improving one's condition would result in increased happiness, prosperity, and survival. Everyone started in a condition of nonexistence and through the steps laid out in a corresponding conditions formula, a person could improve his condition and therefore his state of well-being.

The conditions from best to worst were:

Power
Power change
Affluence
Normal operation
Emergency
Danger
Nonexistence
Liability
Doubt
Enemy
Treason
Confusion

Any condition below nonexistence was considered a lower condition and would be treated with varying degrees of punishment. "Lower Conditions" meant you were on the outs with the group, had done something that violated the mores of the group, and needed to be corrected. There was often humiliation involved in being in lower conditions. You might have only beans and rice to eat or be excluded from org awards or have privileges revoked or reduced. Lower Conditions could also be a form of punishment, so, as part of the atonement for doing something wrong, you'd get lowered in conditions, and then have to work your way up again. Everything from severe backflashing to insubordination or even losing your keys could earn you lower conditions.

As medical liaison, I had to graph my weekly progress on a chart. If I showed improvement in my post, my condition would improve as a result. If tons of kids came in sick, my graph might show a downward trend, which would require me to reverse it by applying the formula for the Condition of Danger. You could also be in different conditions in different aspects of your life. For example, you could be in "doubt" in your finances and "affluence" in your health.

As a seven-year-old girl, tallying and graphing all these numbers seemed ridiculous and unimportant to me. I was not a perfectionist, and the attention to detail was always stifling. Thinking back on it now, it's hard to believe that we were expected to do this: not only was the analysis of these numbers wearisome; it was also incredibly time-consuming. It forced us to focus just on numbers and the formulas with little thought about what it all meant. We had to look at the results, draw conclusions, and follow the prescribed next steps. All this work with numbers, statistics, and trends was a fundamental warm-up for our adult lives as Scientologists. The more we grew accustomed to having our life be quantifiable every week, the less likely we were to have a problem with it in the future.

Another part of Thursdays was our weekly E-Meter checks, which were different from our E-Meter checks during academic study. During these checks, we'd wait in line together, and then each of us would sit down and hold the cans. Unlike our daily study meters, no questions were asked. The adult meter-checker would simply observe the meter's needle, and, depending on the needle's pattern, the reading would either be clean or dirty, pass or flunk. A pass was indicated by a "clean needle" or "floating needle," when the needle rhythmically swept back and forth. While I would often try to think happy thoughts so that I would pass the check, I wouldn't know the results until later in the evening when they were announced in front of the group.

If we flunked, we would be required to do an O/W write-up. O/W was short for "Overts and Withholds," which essentially means sins and secrets. Overts were sins or transgressions, while withholds were secrets, anything we were trying to hide. Essentially, we were writing down confessions. The format was precise: First, we would write down the nature of the transgression; then, we would write down the Time, Place, Form, and Event. We would keep writing until we had told everything and felt better, at which point we would receive another meter check. This second time, we would be asked, "In this O/W write up, has anything been missed?" If we failed again, we had to go back and write more until our needle floated.

During Thursday Basics, we also had to write Weekly Reports for our parents. These were prepared forms with blank spaces for name, date, a spot to show which courses we had completed, whether our stats were up or down, if we had any wins, and anything else we wanted to say. Writing anything negative wasn't a real option. Adults read the weekly reports before they were sent to Int, so complaints would be discovered and treated as nattering. This was true for not only our Weekly Reports but our letters, whether they were to our friends, family, or parents. Whenever I received a letter from my parents or anyone, it had already been opened and stapled closed. This happened to other children at the Ranch as well. I didn't know what the purpose of monitoring our correspondence was. Perhaps it allowed the adults to make sure we weren't enturbulating our parents, who were very busy with their work. "Enturbulating" was a Scientology word for disrupting or upsetting. So, in addition to not being allowed to complain at the Ranch out loud, we couldn't complain about it in letters, either.

Friday evening had a different routine. After dinner, we would have graduation, where kids would be given certificates for the courses they had completed. Graduation would begin with all of us gathering in either the mess hall or the lounge for a Scientology media presentation. Sometimes this was a Scientology music video, but more often it was the Sea Org recruitment slide show. Inevitably, the show would have images of people in uniforms, some of them our parents, along with awesome background music and catchy slogans such as, "Many are called; few are chosen."

Almost every week, there was a showing of LRH's "Mission into Time." It featured L. Ron Hubbard recalling his past lives going back hundreds of years and chronicling his journey to connect with those past lives. From only his own recall of these past lives, he named locations around the world where, in these previous lives, he had buried various unknown items. The slide show then told the story of the first Sea Org members, who had taken on the mission of traveling to these locations in search of the items. They went by boat around the world, and sure enough, they found them all. Watching the slide show gave me goose bumps every time.

After the slide show, kids who had finished courses would receive certificates and be applauded. Then there would be awards such as "Student of the Week," "Cadet of the Week," and "Division of the Week." Graduation ended with clapping to the picture of LRH and three cheers to him as well.

The best part came after graduation, when we got our five-dollar allowance. We had to sign for it, because we had to have our deductions taken for Social Security and Medicare, so it was more like $4.50. There were also deductions taken for collections toward adult and executive birthday presents for anyone celebrating that week. If overall Cadet Org stats were up, we would sometimes have org awards, which meant we could all watch a movie and have popcorn before bed, or maybe even take a field trip. And, when it was all over, we'd head back to our rooms to prepare for bed.

Saturday was a no-school day, but we still had to do deck work, which on Saturdays was intense white-glove cleaning of our berthings and the buildings. My assignment was the School House. In spite of the intense cleaning, I liked Saturdays because we were going to be seeing our parents, and Saturday night dinner was now the only time we got dessert—usually chocolate-chip cookies. By the time white-gloving and inspection were done, it was about ten in the evening. It was tiring, but leaving for the relative luxury of my parents' apartment was worth working for.

CHAPTER SEVEN

RUNAWAY

WITH ALL THE WORK BEING DONE, THE RANCH SLOWLY BECAME a more and more beautiful place. The roads were paved, and the houses were uniformly painted a barn-red color with white trim. There were gardens, tree nurseries with pomegranates and apples, beautiful stone walls bordering the property, lush ice plants covering the hills, and freshly mowed sports fields. Eventually, it was hardly recognizable as the arid dusty earth that it had been when I arrived. At first glance, it was easy to see how someone might have thought this was an appealing place for children to grow up, almost like a sort of permanent summer camp. For me, though, it was hard to appreciate the improvements after all my effort.

I no longer enjoyed being at the Ranch or being a Cadet. The deck work routine felt unbearable, the course work overwhelming. While the physical labor took its toll, what really stressed me was that we were expected to have the minds of adults. With all of the procedures, information, and responsibilities that filled our heads on a daily basis, there was little or no room for the imagination and whims. It's difficult to understand how, as kids, we possessed the mental capacity to keep track of multiple sets of daily and weekly statistics, identify trends in that data, and then strategize how to improve the statistics by applying complex formulas and writing daily battle plans to achieve our goals. Whether it was being required to sign out for tools or the fact that every dining room table had its own hierarchy of mess president, treasurer, and steward, every process was rigid and bureaucratic. Cleaning had to be done in a specified manner, which LRH had laid out in "The Cleaning Course." It had policies on exactly how windows and brass must be cleaned, as well as the exact sequence for cleaning a room. Every day, our beds were inspected to make sure we had proper hospital corners, which we all learned to do in a "how to make a bed" course. Even riding a bike required us to pass a course first.

In addition to this tedium and minutiae, we had at least three areas that we were responsible for cleaning on a daily basis. In the event of fire, intruder, or earthquake, we all had an assigned duty, which ranged from damage control to evacuators, and we were drilled and timed thoroughly every week on these duties.

Simply getting time off required an incredible level of accountability. If I ever wanted time off—if, for example, my mom was visiting Int—then I had to request it in a formatted proposal that required me to find replacements for each of my various responsibilities. We would only be granted permission if the requests were every other week, if our statistics were up, and if we were not in Lower Conditions. If all those things were in order, then my proposal would have to be approved by no fewer than four people.

The list of duties and procedures went on endlessly, and the result of all this process, paperwork, and regulation was that there were no children at the Ranch—only little adults. At special events, we were dressed up in cute outfits and paraded in front of our parents and Int crew to make it seem as though Scientology was creating a normal and joyful childhood, when in fact we were all being robbed of it. Any sense of normalcy that existed did so because we practically were each other's parents, taking care of each other when we were sick, consoling each other when we couldn't sleep, disciplining each other when we acted out, feeding each other meals when we were hungry, and helping each other with schoolwork when we were confused. Yes, we were responsible for our post work, deck work, academic work, Scientology course work, and cleaning—but, more than anything else, we were responsible for each other.

I spent most of my days just trying to keep my head above water, and nights were even worse. I was deathly afraid of the night. Often, after lights out, we'd hear coyotes howling outside, and although the doors were closed, I knew that the wilderness wasn't far away. My huge imagination didn't serve me well in the dark. Sometimes I'd wake up in the middle of the night so scared that I would crawl into bed with one of my friends for comfort. The better nights were when I would dream about having days off with my parents, but even then, I'd have the disappointment of waking up to realize that I was still at the Ranch.

Reassuring as it was to be closer to my parents, I still missed them terribly. While living with Justin gave me some support, he could also be a big brother in all the hardest ways. For my first several months on the Ranch, having him around had been crucial to how I adjusted to life there. By the time I became a Cadet, though, he was caught up with his friends and his own struggles on the Ranch, and he wasn't always able to, or interested in, making me feel better. He wasn't my parent, after all. Sometimes when I was upset, he would try to help, but other times he only succeeded in making me angrier.

I didn't blame the Church or my parents for what was going on at the Ranch. Instead, I blamed the adults who I thought were treating me poorly. If I could just tell other people what was going on, I was certain that things would change. It was hard to know just how much my parents had been told about what it was like for me at the Ranch. Because of comments they'd made from time to time, I knew they had seen photos of me working, so, on some level, they were aware I was doing physical labor. My father had occasionally participated in the Saturday Renos with other adults and witnessed firsthand what the kids did. Even so, I assumed that neither of my parents knew the full scope of how difficult the conditions were for me, and I figured that once they had heard, they would immediately correct the situation. I mean, if they knew how bad it really was, how could they possibly allow me to stay there?

Still, something prevented me from telling them. As much as I wanted to tell them the truth, I was hesitant, not because I was afraid of getting in trouble, but because I was terrified that the problem wasn't with the Ranch, but with me. All around me, other kids were completing their decks and clearing their words, and the fact that I, along with a few others, was struggling made me feel like there was something wrong with me. I had no one around me to reassure me, or to tell me that kids weren't meant to do work like this. My fear was that if I went straight to my parents and told them what was happening I would only disappoint them. I didn't want to let them down, so I did the only thing that made sense to me: I kept quiet and decided to run away.

BY THE TIME I'D BEEN AT THE RANCH FOR A YEAR, I WAS DONE. Luckily I wasn't alone in my unhappiness. My friend Rebecca didn't like it, either. She had arrived a short while after me. Her mother worked in the Religious Technology Center at an administrative job and lived at Int. About a year older than I, with straight dark hair and light eyes, Rebecca had a true love of animals, which made her perfectly suited for her post of taking care of all the various animals on the Ranch. She tended to the goats, the ducks, the hens, and the horses that lived in a corral on the property. Even though she had a post that she was well suited for, everything else about our routine—the decks, the course work—was intolerable to her as well.

One day in early May, Rebecca and I crafted a plan to escape. For at least a week, we strategized about what we needed and where we'd go. One thing we did know was that we couldn't go to the base. If I made it the twenty miles to the Int Base, my parents most likely would have to turn me in, so I had to find a new place to settle down. The rough plan I had was to live in an underground cave/mansion that I was going to dig myself, and I was going to eat croissants, which I planned on stealing from an imaginary bakery, which were undoubtedly everywhere in the Wog world.

On Thursday night, May 1991, the time had come for Rebecca and me to make our move. I packed my clothes and the kangaroo sweater that had once belonged to my mother. Earlier that day, I had stolen some vegetables from one of the gardens we maintained and some eggs from the chicken coop. These eggs were hatched specifically for Uncle Dave. Chickens were brought to the Ranch and kept in a special coop with a caged outdoor area. The kids gave the hens feed and cleaned their cages. When the hens laid the eggs, we gathered them to be taken to Uncle Dave at the Int Base for his consumption only.

It was actually not my first time stealing Uncle Dave's eggs. I had snatched some a few months back because I wanted to hatch the chickens in my drawer at the Ranch. I'd gotten into trouble when somebody caught me. Mr. Parker and Mr. Bell were furious when they found out. They made it clear that when my uncle found out, I was going to be in serious trouble. I was told to write him a letter to confess that I was the one who had taken his eggs, but to my surprise, and I think the surprise of Mr. Parker and Mr. Bell, he was very nice about it. He wrote me back and explained that my drawer was probably not warm enough for the eggs, and that I would need an incubator if I wanted to succeed in hatching them. Now I'd stolen eggs again. I knew I was taking a big risk, but I didn't have many other options. We were going to need food.

Rebecca hated Mr. Parker in particular. The woman could be intimidating, but she didn't seem to be as difficult with me as she was with other kids. Rebecca insisted that we write her a letter before we left, a sort of in-your-face note. We told her that we had had enough, and that we were going out into the Wog world and weren't coming back. Rebecca added that we hated her and that she was really mean. We also told her to say goodbye to our parents, because we were on our own now.

My heart was pumping when we put the note on Mr. Parker's desk in the Cottage. I could see the fear in Rebecca's face as well. Despite all the confidence of our note, we were both so anxious about getting caught mid-escape that we hadn't thought much about what we would do once we had gotten out of the Ranch. Suddenly, I wasn't so sure, but it was too late to stop. We ran to the bike parking lot and got on our bikes. Mine was a pink Huffy with a basket in the front, which my dad had bought for me. We had a backpack with our food, and I put it into my basket. We rode the quarter of a mile or so down the road to the front gate. We knew we had to be as quiet as possible going under the gate, because otherwise they would hear us through the intercom box.

I hadn't thought of how hard getting my bike under the gate with a basket full of groceries was going to be. Of course, everything fell out. Rebecca scrambled to help me reload, and soon we were back up on our bikes, pedaling down a steep hill and going a little too fast for my comfort. When we started over the bridge that traversed the creek, we were both wobbling so much that we looked at each other in total fear. Rebecca encouraged me, telling me we could do it. When we finally got to the other side, we were so relieved.

The sun, which had been fading when we had slipped under the front gate, disappeared as we walked our bikes over the cattle grate. I had always heard that you could break your leg on it, so we were particularly careful. The cattle grate was where the Ranch property ended and the Indian reservation began.

After we had pedaled another mile or so down the road, we saw a vehicle with its headlights on approaching in the distance. We quickly put our bikes to the side of the road and ditched them before running behind a small hill to wait. We figured the car would just pass by, but instead, to our horror, we heard the sounds of shoes hitting the dirt, followed by slamming doors.

There was a crunch of footsteps on the brush. We looked at each other totally frozen, unable to move. I was sure it was an Indian coming to get us. There were always rumors floating around the Ranch that the Indians sometimes shot at people who drove by if they didn't recognize them. We had also heard of people getting killed outside the nearby Indian casino, which was at the beginning of their property. We hadn't quite gotten that far, but it could have been one of the gamblers on his way home.

However, the vehicle didn't contain strangers. I looked over and saw Joe Conte, with Taryn and her friends Jessica and Heather riding in the back. Our escape was officially a bust.

"You're such an idiot," Taryn sniped. She grabbed my stuff and pulled us back to the truck. Heather and Jessica grabbed our bikes. "Now we're gonna miss the beginning of the event because of you two twerps," she scolded me.

I had forgotten that the night we picked for our escape was the anniversary of Dianetics, May 9. In celebration, the Church organized an annual international event that was telecast via satellite at all the Scientology bases, including the Ranch. Taryn, Jessica, and Heather had been rushing back to record it for everyone at the Ranch. Having to track us down made them miss the beginning, which was the best part, since it usually featured performances by dancers or singers. Now, not only would Rebecca and I be in trouble for trying to run away, but we would have to be accountable to everyone who had missed the opening performance.

Rebecca had tears running down her face, and I was feeling sick to my stomach as we rode back to the Ranch in the bed of the truck. We were freezing cold and surrounded by all the bigger girls, as the sharp turns of the winding road threw us from side to side. Someone opened our backpack and pulled out the carrots I had taken from the garden as well as the eggs stolen from the coop. All at once, they broke out laughing in unison and started shouting belittling questions, which they had no intention of letting us answer.

"Were you going to survive on carrots and raw eggs?" one of them asked.

"Where were you planning on going?" another one asked.

"Into the Wog world, away from all of you meanies!" I shouted. I didn't understand why nobody was taking us seriously—I had fully intended to be in the Wog world by now. They simply looked at each other and doubled over in hysterics all over again.

When we finally stopped in front of the School House, Justin and Sterling were there, laughing at us and making jabs about how ridiculous we were. I would have been infuriated by the teasing, had I not been so terrified about what was in store for us from Mr. Parker.

She was inside the School House and I quickly learned that the staff had known we were escaping before we had even reached the front gate. Mr. Parker was angry and quite disappointed. She yelled at us for a bit and said we were both assigned Lower Conditions and would be starting with our amends first thing in the morning. The punishment was actually mild compared to what I expected, but I hated Lower Conditions. We were assigned Liability, which meant we had to make amends. With Liability, each group member had to sign a piece of paper that he or she had accepted you back into the group. If the majority didn't agree, you would have to do more amends until there was a consensus.

"If you even attempt to run away again, your penalties will be doubled," she threatened.

Rebecca's punishment was harsher than mine. In addition to the lower conditions, she was demoted from the rank of Cadet to Child for several weeks. I knew that it was unfair that she had gotten a worse penalty than me, but I wasn't about to question it. Taryn didn't let it go, though, calling me a spoiled brat for getting off easier than Rebecca.

Rebecca and I went to bed too ashamed to talk to each other or anyone else. When I woke up in the morning, I was so anxious that I couldn't stop projectile vomiting. With breakfast, it only became worse.

My friend Eva was worried, but Taryn wasn't the least bit concerned. "Well, look what you pulled in," she said, matter-of-factly. "Pulled in" was a Scientology concept whereby if you did something bad, you would "pull in" or have something bad happen to you. "Pulling in" was kind of like karma, the difference being that pulling in was guaranteed if you did something wrong. The idea was that you, the Thetan, caused something bad to happen to you in order to punish yourself for the wrong you had committed.

Mr. Parker echoed Taryn's sentiment on that as well, telling me, "Don't think because you are sick, you can get out of doing amends." All I wanted was to be able to keep some food down. I had never had anything like this happen to me before.

Rebecca and I were assigned to work with Mr. Cathy Mauro, separated from the group. The assignment could definitely have been worse, but we were to weed the rock gardens at the Cottage. We preferred being with Mr. Mauro rather than Mr. Parker.

Rebecca and I were not allowed to attend the screening of the international Scientology event. All the kids were informed that it was because of us that the beginning of the performance had not been taped, and the kids who were in attendance told us that we were severely booed after that announcement.

For most of the next week, Mr. Parker kept her distance from me, but that Friday when my dad came, she told me I needed to tell him what I had done. I said I would, but of course, I really didn't want to—I was too afraid he'd be ashamed of me. When Dad arrived, we walked to the playground, which was normally only used during break time, to meet Mr. Parker. "Hi, sir," she greeted him.

My father was a senior executive of the Church, so that was how he was addressed. To me, it was always weird to hear other adults call my parents "sir," because it seemed like they were the boss of everyone.

"Did Jenna tell you what happened this week?" Mr. Parker asked Dad.

My father was clearly baffled. "What is she talking about, honey?" he said to me.

I couldn't keep myself from bursting into tears. "I was gonna tell you how mean everyone here is to me," I burst out. This was not what I had agreed to tell him, but I couldn't bear to tell him I had done something wrong.

Mr. Parker's face tensed—she was clearly irritated by that. She quickly told him exactly what had happened, as I continued sobbing. My dad thanked her and told her that he would take care of it, then dismissed her. As broken up as I was, I couldn't help but notice how strange it was to see her dismissed. I was so used to her being the one in control and dismissing other people. The sudden shift of power was intriguing.

At that, my dad hugged me and asked me why I had tried to run away. I looked at him, thinking about everything I'd been through at the Ranch. I thought about telling him how hard it all was for me, but I just couldn't. I was too afraid that I would disappoint him. Yet there was something else that prevented me from telling the truth: Maybe he already knew how bad things were there, but he believed that what we were being asked to do was in line with Scientology's goal of saving the planet.

Finding that out would be almost too much to bear, so instead I told him I had been sad and wanted to see what it was like in the Wog world. He was smiling, as though he thought my plot had been a cute and a funny idea, which was frustrating. I had been completely serious in my attempt to get out of there. He didn't pry deeper into my reasons and I didn't offer them, and after he left that day, it didn't come up again.

After his departure, Mr. Parker gave me a dirty look, but that was it. I wasn't even really in trouble anymore. I wasn't sure if it had been because I had done enough on the amends, or because my dad had said something to someone in charge. Either way, I did what any good Scientologist was supposed to do: I didn't question it.

Chapter Eight

"DEAR JENNA . . ."

Time passed slowly on the Ranch. Gradually, though, due to the work done by our deck projects, it was barely recognizable from the place it had been when I first arrived. The Big House was now home to the mess hall, the canteen, the offices of the adults, small offices for each of the Cadet division heads, and the Communications Center, where we would receive letters, copies of reports that had been written about us, and commendations.

Along with the physical progress on the Ranch, I made progress in my studies, graduating from one course to another. After my failed attempt at running away, I became more complaisant, but that didn't make the work any easier. However, because I recognized that I had no real choice, I focused on completing my courses and keeping my ethics file as clean as possible, so that one day I could graduate and leave the Ranch behind for good.

I was seeing less and less of my mom. Most of our communication was either via weekly phone calls or, more often, through letters. Her letters in particular were usually newsy and sentimental, and I saved every letter from her in a box in my bottom drawer. Whenever I was lonely, I'd pull them out and read them over again. Seeing her letters, no matter how brief they were, always made me feel like maybe there was somewhere outside of this Ranch where I belonged and someone loved me.

> *Dearest Jenna-bean,*
>
> *Well it's Saturday morning and I'm sitting on my back porch. I thought of you about 100 times so I decided to write you. You are hard to get hold [sic] of on the phones. I miss you so much. I realize I'm not the typical mother who is always around—In fact I've been gone most of 2 years. But do not for a minute think that I love you any less. You mean every-thing to me! You are the brightest spark in my whole life. You are growing up to be better and smarter than I ever hoped for. To me you are so smart and perceptive that it amazes me. Your Dad and I are very proud of you.*
>
> *Things are going good here. It is getting pretty humid but that is Florida.*
>
> *I sent some pictures of me to Dad—they suck. But you can look at them to at least see what I look like.*
>
> *I will call you tomorrow.*
>
> *I love you!*
>
> *All my love, Mommy*

Words like these always offered comfort. While it was true that she was not a "typical mother," she also hadn't had a typical mother herself. My mom had been only twelve when she was brought into Scientology by her mother, Janna Blythe. A chain smoker, Janna was more intellectual than maternal, with an extremely dry sense of humor. She had jobs teaching English, and when she wasn't teaching, she made money underwriting insurance documents. Because Janna always worked, my mom and her many siblings were cared for by babysitters until they were old enough to care for each other.

Janna had an English degree from the University of Illinois and was an avid reader. To be rebellious, she read science fiction books, which at the time were considered trashy literature. L. Ron Hubbard's science fiction impressed her so much that she looked for other books by him, and took to Dianetics in 1957, the same year my mom was born. After reading *Dianetics*, Grandma Janna started using the new-age healing techniques outlined in the book on all nine of her children—Griffee, Jennifer, John, Mickey, my mother, Teresa, Mary, James, and Sarah. The family was very poor, and by using Dianetics, she seemed to save a lot of trips to the doctor. Janna loved the rational approach that it offered, as well as the fact that it seemingly put people more in control of their lives and helped them to deal with the past, regardless of how old or young they were.

For years, her casual use of Dianetics was just that. Then one day in 1969 she saw a copy of the book displayed in the window of a Scientology mission and went inside. From then on, she was hooked. She began taking classes at the mission and two years later she, along with my Grandpa Bill, decided to move the Blythe family to Los Angeles. There, the entire family joined the Sea Org and took up residence on the Sea Org ship called the *Excalibur*.

It didn't take my grandparents long to see that the level of commitment that the Sea Org demanded was substantial. After only a few months, they decided it was not for them. My grandfather, in particular, didn't like the accommodations provided for his children, including the fact that everyone had to sleep on mattresses on the floor. As Bill and Janna prepared to leave, they were surprised when my mom told them that she had no desire to leave with them. She loved that in Scientology, children were treated like mini-adults, with lots of responsibilities but also respect. More than that, though, she was part of a worldwide movement that was gaining momentum; Dianetics and Scientology were so new to the spiritual landscape that they was barely older than she was, and she was growing up alongside them.

My grandpa Bill tried hard but with no success to make my mother come with them. He refused to sign away legal guardianship of her. Many years later, my mom told me how, when authorities investigated the office after reports alleging the mistreatment of children, she was hidden away. Authorities also investigated reports of young kids on the base not attending school, so my mom was sent overseas to Portugal to join her brother on the *Apollo,* at port in Lisbon, because she wouldn't have to go to school there.

Being apart from her parents had not been hard for my mom. Maybe being separated from me was easier for her because of the separation that she had experienced. As a teenager, she'd craved the distance, and on some level, perhaps she felt I'd feel the same way, even though I was younger.

As cherished as my mother's letters to me were, they could not make up for her absence. They lifted my spirits, but they also served to remind me that she wouldn't be back to see me for months:

Dear Jenna,

Thank you very much for your letter. I just got it today and I was very happy to receive it.

The paper you are writing on looks like special printing paper that people use to learn how to print better. And I can tell from your handwriting that you are definitely learning to print better which is good. I will definitely call you sometime this week. . . .

I'm glad Sarah Kitty is doing well. I sometimes worry that she doesn't have anyone to play with since I'm not there but I'm sure that you and J-birdy play with her on the weekends so that is good. Does she still like her grass that you guys grew for her? Does she need any more of it?

I was really surprised when you wrote in your letter that Sterling is only 1 inch shorter than Justin. That means Sterling must have grown a whole bunch which is really good.

What kind of haircuts did they cut? Did Justin get the same kind of haircut that he had last time where the sideburns are really really short and the top part is long?

I was looking at a magazine the other day and I saw a haircut . . . a hairstyle actually that will look very nice on you. You need to grow your hair out so it reaches your shoulders including your bangs in front and at that point we can get it styled at a beauty shop and it will look very beautiful. . . .

You asked me if I live in an apartment and yes I do. It's called the Hacienda Gardens and I live in a room in an apartment at the Hacienda . . . The apartment is very pretty and is renovated. . . .

The office I work in is also very nice. . . . So the one thing good about being in Florida is that I do have a nice place to sleep and a nice place to work. But I would give all that away just if I could be with you. Maybe when you go to New Hampshire you can stop back here on your way and see me for a couple of days? That would be really nice. I don't think you've ever been to Florida but Justin was born in Florida and he could come too and see all the places he used to go when he was little.

I hate to tell you but I will probably be here for a bit longer, maybe even months. But I will set up a line so I can talk to you several times a week at the Ranch—in other words I will call you there. I can also set up that sometimes during these few months that I will be out here that I will be able to come up and see you (fly on an airplane) at the Ranch every once in a while. This way we'll be able to see each other and it won't be bad.

I miss you very very much and I love you even more.

*I do look at your photos and I do read your letters as they
mean more to me than anything. However I know that you
understand that I have to do some very important work here
and therefore it is important that I stay here and do it. . . .
Lots of love, Mommy*

All this long-distance communication meant that the times
when I did get to see her were incredibly special. On the rare occasions she was back at Int for a special event, I would have to file
the necessary paperwork to get permission to leave the Ranch to
see her. Frustrating as this process was, I always managed to get
approval somehow.

Usually the times I saw her were during days off for special
Scientology/Sea Org occasions, like Sea Org Day, which took
place in August. When that happened, I would get to see her for
a whole day.

Sea Org Day was quite a spectacle. People would spend weeks
getting ready for it. Sometimes our decks would be working in the
galley at the Int Base, preparing the special meals. We would work
with the galley staff, slicing cold cuts and baking bread. We'd
also help bus the tables and clean the dining rooms. I would help
Tammy, the executive steward, set the tables; she taught me how
to do fancy folds with the cloth napkins. She also let me draw on
and decorate the vote sheets, which were ballots distributed at the
end of each meal. Diners were supposed to vote for service and
food, the service vote being the statistic for Tammy, and the food
vote being the statistic for the galley staff. Uncle Dave and Aunt
Shelly knew I was the artist for the vote sheets, so they liked to put
in a vote for my artwork. The highest vote possible was a seven,
but their votes were always really high numbers, like two million.

Aunt Shelly had really taken a liking to me, and I liked her,
too. When we would talk during the meals or out by the pool
during the festivities, she would always ask me how I was doing.

She taught me about nutrition, something she was very much into, which helped me at my post as MLO. She was a no-nonsense type of person, but was also caring and loving and had a good sense of humor.

When I was working in the galley with Tammy, I got to watch the rehearsals of the Sea Org's Honor Guard. The members dressed in full white uniforms, similar to those of the U.S. Navy. The uniforms included a hat, gloves, a lanyard, campaign bars, and rank. They marched in time to music coming from the sound system, twirled batons, and did choreographed steps. Some of them carried flags with the Sea Org or Scientology symbols on them. Others stood in two rows and crossed their swords, forming an archway for the senior executives to pass under. It was really cool to watch. Professional and inspiring, the performance never failed to excite me about becoming a member of the Sea Org.

The day following the Sea Org Day ceremony was a day off, filled with fun activities. The base had a full-sized clipper ship built into the ground. The ship, the *Star of California,* had a pool, palapas (tiki huts), changing rooms, and a smoothie bar. This pool was actually for my uncle Dave's use, but on Sea Org Day, he opened it to everyone for swimming competitions and other activities.

It was a great time. Besides the races in the pool, there were soccer matches, basketball games, free swim in the lake, and a picnic with hamburgers and hot dogs. The base had plenty of fields and courts for all the sports, but Sea Org Day was the only time they were used.

In the evening, everyone would return to his berthing to get dressed up. Then we'd come back into the base for a long, delicious dinner. I would always sit with Dad at his table; if Mom was there, she'd join us. At my parents' urging, I'd chat with Uncle Dave and Aunt Shelly at their table for twenty minutes or so while they asked me questions about my studies and told me jokes. I was happy that Aunt Shelly took such an interest in me. With my mother gone so much of the time, it felt reassuring to have an older female relative who gave me sincere attention.

CHRISTMAS WAS ANOTHER TIME I LOOKED FORWARD TO, BECAUSE we would get two or three days off and my mother would be able to leave Clearwater to be with us. My family did not celebrate Christmas as a religious holiday. It would start with the kids going to the Int Base for the Sea Org's traditional Beer & Cheese Party. The kids, of course, weren't allowed to drink beer. In fact, the adults in Sea Org never drank, except at this party. Beer was alcohol, which affected the mind, which would then have to be dealt with in the future by using Scientology. In addition, you could not attend Scientology studies for at least twenty-four hours after alcohol consumption, so it was definitely not condoned.

Even at the Beer & Cheese Party, most of the adults would drink non-alcoholic beer. Uncle Dave liked to point out the people who were drinking real alcohol and getting drunk. One time, he signaled to someone who looked a little red in the face and brought him to the table, where Mom, Dad, and a few other execs were sitting.

"Russ!" he said in his normal booming voice.

"Yes, sir?" I could see the color leaving Russ's face.

"What are you drinking?"

"Irish Cream, sir," Russ answered, looking a little sheepish.

"Ah-hah," my uncle replied, before instructing Russ to keep walking, as though he had no idea why Russ had stopped at our table in the first place. "Well, I really missed his 'withhold'!" Uncle Dave then exclaimed, and the adults agreed in unison. I could tell it was a demonstration of power.

"How many people do you think are actually completely shit-faced right now?" Uncle Dave asked. Then he remembered that I was at the table. "Oh, sorry, Jenny," he said, turning to me with a huge smile. He usually called me "Jenny" instead of Jenna; it was more familiar and what my brother called me as well. "I shouldn't say that bad word," he said apologetically.

"Do I owe you a quarter for cussing?" he asked. I told him he didn't. We swore like sailors at the Ranch. Most Sea Org members did. But I wondered about this bad word.

"What is shit-faced?" I asked, and everybody laughed, except for Aunt Shelly, who took me aside and explained that alcohol was bad and that sometimes it could make you drunk.

The day after the Beer & Cheese Party, the crew at the Int Base would have the day off. Almost everybody used the day to take their family to Big Bear ski resort, which was in California, about an hour and a half from the base. Most people took buses hired for the trip, but we would drive up separately because my dad had a car. Not many crew members had cars. My dad had his BMW and Uncle Dave had a Mazda RX7. I had no idea why people were really impressed with that, but they were. My dad loved his red BMW to the point that, at times, I thought he loved it more than he did me. Once, I even asked him if that was true, and he seemed quite offended by the question and assured me that was not the case.

At Big Bear, our family would often spend the night at a place much nicer than where the rest of the staff was staying. Once when I was nine, we stayed at a huge house in Arrowhead with a ton of rooms, a loft, and an indoor Jacuzzi. The kids got to sleep in the loft. Lots of my Scientology relatives on my dad's side were there: Uncle Dave and Aunt Shelly; my dad's father, Grandpa Ron, and his wife, Becky; my parents; and a man I called Uncle Bill. He was not really my uncle, but he and my dad had been good friends since I had been little, so I called him Uncle Bill. The house belonged to a Scientologist named Paul Haggis, who was a Hollywood screenwriter and director; Uncle Bill was a friend of his, so he had gotten permission for all of us to use his house.

Christmas was unlike just about any other time in the Church. We all sat by the fire to open our presents. I got slippers, jammies, and an album from my mom and dad. My grandmother in New Hampshire sent me a bead and loom kit. It was awesome, because I didn't really have any toys at the Ranch besides the stuffed animals on my bed. Uncle Dave and Aunt Shelly got me a porcelain Tiffany's box, blue with a white porcelain bow. I wasn't sure of its function, but it was very pretty.

At the end of the second day at Big Bear, we returned to the base for a big Christmas dinner and show. We sang Christmas carols, did a play, or made other entertainment, having rehearsed our numbers at the Ranch for weeks before Christmas. Even though all of the older kids acted as though they were painfully embarrassed, I loved performing, and it made me adore Christmas all the more. After the show, the crew would have a dance party. Sometimes, Aunt Shelly and Uncle Dave would sit on the side to watch people.

Aunt Shelly would frequently talk to me, whether she was touting the benefits of carrot juice or telling me that popcorn and peanuts were the worst things you could eat. She would ask about my schooling and tell me that I needed to clear my misunderstood words, because that would help me finish my courses sooner. She was interested in my school progress. More than most people were.

Sometimes, during the Christmas dance, we'd go into Uncle Dave's billiards room, which had a pool table and all sorts of other games. There was a leather couch, comfy chairs, and a phone that looked like a mallard duck, which I always wanted to play with. The bar in the room was usually teeming with stewards attending to all of the execs' needs. The execs were always talking, but I had no idea about what. I was just happy to be with my parents and everyone else.

Everyone at the base treated me well. When I wandered through the dance hall, people I knew grabbed my arm to say hi and give me a hug. Everywhere I looked, people were friendly and inviting—so different from the Ranch. I couldn't wait to finish the Ranch and work at Int, where everybody liked me. My friend Jamie had warned me that people were only kissing my butt because I was David Miscavige's niece, but I was sure he was wrong. I knew them all and believed they were my friends.

When the dance ended, the family would go to our parents' apartment. Mom and Dad would tell me that it was really important to write thank-you notes to the people who had sent me gifts, but I knew they were referring specifically to my uncle Dave. Judging from how everyone treated them, I knew Uncle Dave and Aunt Shelly were important. There were always stewards around, bringing them food and attending to their needs. The stewards attended to my parents' needs, too. Even Mom and Dad always seemed to be more on their toes and agreeable to Uncle Dave.

The next day, all the kids would return to the Ranch and resume our normal schedule. Returning after Christmas was hard for lots of reasons, but especially because I knew that I likely wouldn't see my parents together for a while.

One thing that got me through this tough time of year was the thought of my birthday, February 1. Unless it fell on a Sunday, my parents would not be there, but still I would celebrate it at the Ranch with my friends. It didn't consist of anything more than a birthday cake, which we would have at dinner, and everyone would sing "Happy Birthday." My dad and my mom, if she was in town, would usually get me another cake on Sunday morning. They'd get me presents, too.

I missed my mother most on days like my birthday. Just before my tenth birthday, I got a wonderful surprise. My mother called the Ranch with news that I would be spending it with her in Clearwater, Florida. Getting phone calls at the Ranch was a big deal, because there was only one phone that was open to use, and tracking people down to let them know they had a call could be difficult. Then, by the time you'd finally get on the phone, it was often hard to talk because another person—usually an adult—would want to use it. So, whether I was receiving or making a call, it meant that every time I talked to my mother, which was once a week at most, I had to keep it short, unless I spoke to her on Sunday mornings in my dad's apartment.

Thankfully, this time Mom's news was short and wonderful. I couldn't wait. Clearwater was where my brothers had been born, and I would be able to meet my mom's friends and see the things she always wrote to me about.

It almost seemed too good to be true. Getting to visit her was the best present I could have hoped for. I was going to get to see her not just for one or two days, but for days on end. I was brimming with excitement just at the thought of it.

CHAPTER NINE

CLEARWATER

My flight to Florida would be my first solo foray into the Wog world. The night before, I packed my bag to be ready when Ana, Mom's secretary, came to get me. I hugged Justin, B. J., and Kiri goodbye and climbed into Ana's car for the trip to the airport. There Ana turned me over to the stewardess, who pinned some special wings onto my shirt and got me settled into my seat on the plane.

It was weird and a little overwhelming to be on an airplane by myself, especially surrounded by a bunch of Wogs. One lady asked me where I was going. I told her I was going to Flag.

"Do you mean Fort Lauderdale?" she asked

"No, Clearwater," I told her.

"Oh, you must be going to Tampa!" she said next. I asked her if that was where Clearwater was, and she told me it was close. I spent the rest of the five-hour flight asking people seated near me if we were almost there, and surprisingly, despite my impatience, everybody was quite friendly.

When I stepped off the plane and out the gate at Tampa International Airport, I was instantly struck by how many strangers were standing around, some holding signs with names on them and others clearly waiting for family or friends. I didn't see anybody waiting for me, and the prospect of trying to locate my mother in this crowd of unfamiliar faces was frightening. Luckily, I spotted her before I started to panic. She looked even prettier than I remembered, but as I walked right up to her, she kept looking over my head.

"Mom, it's me!" I said, hugging her.

"Oh, my gosh!" she replied in surprise. "I didn't recognize you!" She was beaming and laughing as she hugged me back. As I took in the aroma of the floral-scented shampoo she always used, a huge wave of relief swept over me: three thousand miles from the Ranch, I was home because I was with my mom.

My mom had brought a guy named Tom to the airport with her. She had always been nervous about driving, and since the airport was outside of her usual driving routine, Tom's role for the day was to drive. Having grown up in the Sea Org, she was used to taking their buses and transportation. Generally, cars were unaffordable to Sea Org members, especially when the cost of insurance and gas was considered. The only people who had cars were those who had bought them before they joined the Sea Org or had some other income source, or the very few who were assigned Org cars as a privilege for their post or duties. My mom had an Org car, a gold Honda sedan.

Mom had mentioned Tom and his wife, Jenny, during our weekly phone calls. She had known them for a long time, and they both worked for her. She had described Tom as an incredibly nice guy, who was also a real kid at heart. I quickly learned what she meant by that assessment. During our tram ride to the main terminal, he wanted us to try standing without holding on to the poles as the tram sped between stops. From that alone, I decided that he was all right by me.

Outside the terminal, the Florida humidity hit me for the first time. I was mystified that anyone could get enough oxygen in the thick air. As soon as we got in the car, Tom turned on the A/C and saved us all.

Mom lived in Hacienda Gardens, a pink Spanish-style apartment complex on North Saturn Avenue, where she had her own apartment and a cat named Poncho. The palm-lined complex had eight buildings, a pool and a canteen. We drove up to the L block, where her apartment was located. Inside, I noticed a security person sitting across the way from her apartment door, as if he were her personal bodyguard. When he saw my mother, he waved.

"Hi, sir," he said enthusiastically.

"Hi, Bruce," my mom replied before entering her apartment.

Inside, a teenage girl greeted us. She was wearing a blue uniform, the kind my mom and dad usually wore at the Int Base: dark blue pants, light blue long-sleeved shirt, a stiff collar, a tie, and a name tag.

"Hi, sirs!" she said to both Mom and Tom. She bent down a little to talk to me. "You must be Jenna! I have heard so much about you!" I smiled shyly back at her. She turned to my mom. "I just put the laundry away, snacks are on the table, and I will be right next door in L2 if you need anything."

My mother took all this attention in stride, but I was duly impressed. I couldn't believe the level of personal service she commanded. She was a senior executive in the Commodore's Messenger Organization International.

The Commodore's Messenger Organization, or CMO, was an important part of management. It was once comprised of L. Ron Hubbard's most trusted personal messengers. To this day, it is a very prestigious unit within the Sea Org and members are discouraged from fraternizing with regular Sea Org members. My mother was one of the highest-ranking execs in the CMO. She was also a member of the Watchdog Committee, the seniormost management body in the Church housed in CMO International. She was clearly an important person with an important position, which made me swell with pride.

"Great, thanks, Sharni," my mom told her. Sharni was a messenger in the CMO in Clearwater, and one of her duties was to take care of my mother's needs as well as those of other senior executives.

After I put down my suitcase, Mom gave me a tour of her apartment. Not only was it much bigger and more luxurious than the apartment she and Dad shared with the Rinders at Int, but she didn't have to share it with anybody. Back at Int, their shared apartment had two bedrooms, but this place had three, all for my mom and the occasional guest; the bathroom had a Jacuzzi tub.

As if the extra space weren't enough, it was also gorgeous, with Spanish tiles everywhere. All the furniture was elegant, even the ornate mirror that hung in the entryway, beneath which was a bowl of delicious candy. The embroidered curtains on all the windows had sheer panels underneath them. The living room even had a television, hidden inside a large wooden armoire. We walked into the dining/kitchen area, where an elaborate snack platter, holding French cheeses and fruit, was waiting for us. There were tall drinks of fresh-squeezed watermelon juice, too, with straws. I opened the fridge to find everything from pâté, which sounded disgusting, to peach juice to English muffins. I was in awe that so much great food was so readily available.

I couldn't contain my excitement. The bedroom she had chosen for me had a queen-sized bed with a large, fluffy comforter in a floral pattern. I jumped on it, enjoying how delicious it smelled, how soft it was, and how I could sink into it, so unlike my linens at the Ranch. My room also had two closets and a big dresser, even though I hardly had any clothes. If I had brought my entire wardrobe, I still wouldn't have been able to fill more than a drawer or two, since I usually wore a uniform. There was even a phone in my room, so that I could call my dad any time I wanted.

I carefully laid out the CDs I had packed on top of the dresser. I brought music with me wherever I went. Mom said she needed to go to the office to get stuff done, but she wanted me to come with her to meet everyone, which I was excited about. Twenty minutes later, we parked next to a tall concrete building on N. Fort Harrison. It was referred to as the WB, the West Coast Building, because it housed the management that was technically an extension of Int Management, which was on the West Coast.

As we walked through the building, Mom was greeted many times with "Hi, sir." We took an old mechanical elevator to her office on the third floor, where messengers were running around.

Mom shared an office with her secretary Alison, Tom, and his wife, Jenny. Tom was the Commanding Officer of CMO Clearwater and Jenny was an executive within the CMO. The offices were very nice, with wood furniture, a tan carpet, and bamboo blinds. Uncle Dave's huge office was at the end of the hall, attached to Aunt Shelly's smaller one. The whole office suite had other rooms for Uncle Dave's staff. He and Aunt Shelly weren't there at the time, but the offices were theirs to use whenever they were in town. There was a kitchenette in the back, where another snack platter sat on the counter. The cupboards of the kitchenette and the fridge were stocked with all sorts of treats. We didn't have access to extra snacks at the Ranch; we were forbidden to take food from the kitchen between meals. A friend of mine had even been assigned lower conditions for stealing food.

Mom said we were going to have lunch with everybody in the conference room. I waited there until lunchtime, sometimes watching a young messenger in her mid-teens making the preparations. She introduced herself as Valeska. "I just ordered you a hamburger, as I wasn't sure what you wanted," she said, smiling.

A few minutes later, an older man wearing a tuxedo entered the conference room and started speaking in a thick French accent. The only thing I could understand was that his name was Steve, but I might have only known that because Valeska had already told me. French-speaking waiters in tuxedos were certainly out of the realm of my experience. I watched in awe as Steve thoughtfully set out the plate with my hamburger, as well as the rest of the food that had been ordered. Valeska told me the meals had been prepared at Hibiscus, the most expensive and the most epicurean of the three restaurants in the Fort Harrison Hotel, which was owned by Scientology. The Fort Harrison was where the public Scientologists stayed when they came to town to take services at the base. It had excellent facilities with three restaurants and more than two hundred guest rooms, outstanding course offerings, and a high concentration of Scientologists. Steve, a Sea Org member, worked at the Hibiscus and our selections had been made to order. I loved the idea that we could all order exactly what we wanted and how we wanted it prepared.

As soon as Valeska was done setting the table, the adults came in. They were talking among themselves, but I was so overjoyed with my hamburger that I hardly paid attention. It had to have been the best food I had ever tasted. Tom seemed to like his meal, too. My mom had fish, which was woven in a puff pastry, with a sprig of parsley garnishing the plate.

In the evening, Mom asked Tom to drive me home. I was disappointed that she couldn't come with us, but at least I felt comfortable around Tom. He was funny and charming, and I was completely at ease with him. When we got back to the apartment, I was delighted to find that someone had unpacked my suitcase for me. Even better, Mom had put some of her special floral shampoo in my bathroom.

As I was settling in, Sharni came in and gently told me some news of how my week would go.

"Jenna, you know your mom is really busy," she began. "She's going to be working long hours, so while she's at work I'm going to be taking care of you."

At first, I was a little down about not seeing my mom as much as I'd hoped. It was still far more than I was accustomed to. I was easily distracted by the novelty of everything around me. Sharni took me down to the pool, and we both swam for a while. I was not used to idle time like this, and I loved it. After drying off, she even took me to the canteen for a Popsicle. While we were enjoying our Popsicles, Sharni pointed out Spencer, a guy she liked. He looked kind of goofy, but the idea of liking boys was entirely unknown to me. At the Ranch, girls were not allowed to have boyfriends. Dating was only for those who were old enough to get married, and we were too young, so what was the point, or so the argument went. Even flirting was something that could get us in trouble and cause us to be assigned to Lower Conditions.

Late in the afternoon, Sharni and I went back upstairs to the apartment. I called my mom at the office and told her I was going to sleep soon, hoping she was on her way home. Not only did I want to be with her, but the truth was I was afraid of sleeping in the room by myself. There might not have been coyotes in Florida, but I was still scared. I was used to having lots of people around at night like in my dorm, which I usually shared with seven girls. Mom was still going to be at the office for a while, but Sharni agreed to stay with me until she got home. Whatever time she did get in, I didn't see her until I got up the next day.

That morning Sharni woke me up. I liked her approach, though. She softly shook my shoulder and whispered, "Rise and shine," so different from the shriek of "Wake up time!" at the Ranch. Plus, I had been allowed to sleep in; it was already eight o'clock.

I went to the kitchen, and I found my mom in her robe watching television. I was a little surprised that she was comfortably watching broadcast television, when it was against Sea Org rules, or at least at Int it was. She was watching some sort of video countdown on VH1. She told me that she loved the program and watched it every morning with breakfast. For me, watching television was the biggest treat of all. While I'd watch movies on weekends, I hadn't watched television since I left L.A.

Sharni had set out a bowl of hot cereal and a plate with two poached eggs and toast on the dining room table. At the Ranch, only the adults were allowed to have toast, because there was only one toaster, so this was an unexpected and welcome treat. When I finished my breakfast, I found Mom in her room getting ready for work. I watched her blow-dry and curl her hair at the vanity table. She was so stylish and pretty, and I admired everything about her, like she was some sort of movie star with a glamorous life in Florida that I had never known about. Her life was her work and her friends, she was waited on and served, she pampered herself, all while working hard for the greater good.

When she was done with her hair, she put on her uniform. She wore the special Egyptian cotton shirts exclusive to executives, while the rest of the crew had to wear cotton-poly blends. Her CMO Int jacket not only had her name embroidered on the front, it also had prominent shoulder boards, showing everyone that she was an officer. Seeing her like this was so inspiring. Her earned rank was Lieutenant, Junior Grade, the third-highest rank in the Sea Org.

I got ready, too, because Mom told me I was going with her to the WB. In the parking lot, staffers in crisply ironed shirts and dark slacks were piling into the Sea Org buses that took them to the base in downtown Clearwater. The Hacienda Gardens was three miles east of downtown; the Sea Org staff took the buses in, since they didn't have cars. Ten blue-and-white buses, all with the word "Flag" written in black script along the side, shuttled people between the buildings that belonged to the church. Everyone in the parking lot was dressed in some type of uniform, white or light blue dress shirts and navy pants, or a tan shirt with brown pants.

Scientology's presence in Clearwater was enormous. The church owned many buildings and was in the process of accumulating more. The Fort Harrison Hotel was one of the most recognizable landmarks in Clearwater, with its magnificent Mediterranean-revival architecture and whitewashed walls. The hotel had a gorgeous marble lobby, eleven floors, three restaurants—the Hibiscus, the Garden, and the Lemon Tree—a swimming pool, a ballroom, a ton of offices, and auditing rooms. This was where the public received auditing.

Down the street from the Fort Harrison was the Coachman Building, where all the training courses were delivered. There was a five-story glass atrium with an arched barrel roof that ran through the entire building, separating it into two halves. Most of the Scientology buildings were within walking distance of each other, and the whole stretch was a stark contrast to what I'd known at the Ranch, both in terms of opulence and upkeep.

The drive to Mom's office took only about ten minutes, but I loved being in the car and seeing the normal world with other cars and freeways, something I rarely saw. Florida, with its palm trees, strip malls, and crowds of people going about their business, was much more exciting than Hemet.

This car ride with Mom was going to be one of the few times I was going to see of her on any given day during my visit. For the rest of my stay, I saw her at lunchtime, some dinners, and late in the evening depending on when she got home, but that was it. It wasn't surprising that she had so much work to do; after all, this is how it had been my entire life. She and Dad had different jobs and different responsibilities, but their dedication to the cause was very much the same. I might have traveled a long way, but that wasn't about to change the nature of her work or her commitment to it.

Looking back, I struggle to reconcile the life my mom was living at Flag to the one I was living at the Ranch. The experiences were so different it feels hard to believe that they both grew out of the same cause, and that, as a parent, she was comfortable living in conditions that were so much better than what I faced. More than just the physical conditions, though, there was a freedom to her life in Clearwater that didn't exist at the Ranch. She didn't have to do manual labor, subject herself to daily meter checks, or get yelled at every day. She didn't have to ask for permission every time she went to the bathroom, something I still do out of habit to this very day.

I am sure she didn't see it that way. This wasn't about neglect or about her being better off than her children. She had committed herself to a cause bigger than herself or her family, and she was following through with it. She truly assumed that I was well taken care of at the Ranch, although she also never went out of her way to understand what life for me there was actually like or, if she did know, she must have been okay with it.

When I saw her way of life at Flag, I wasn't resentful or even jealous. More than anything, I was motivated to figure out how I could leave the Ranch and live like my mother. To me, that trip confirmed that there was a totally different way of life in the Sea Org. When I was back at the Ranch, what I would remember from this trip was the luxury. At the Int base, my father was allowed to have his own comforter or cookies whenever he wanted them—little extras that were prohibited at the Ranch. At my mom's apartment, she had all that and much, much more.

Being in the Sea Org, as I had long suspected, didn't mean simply doing deck work and clearing words forever, there was a better future that awaited me; all I had to do was pay my dues and graduate from the Ranch. Mom's life in Clearwater had given me a glimpse of what my own life could look like, and it didn't involve planting trees or hauling rocks. I believed that through dedication and hard work this life was possible for me, too.

In the end, I had an amazing time during the week I was in Florida. I spent most of my time with Sharni, whom I loved to be around and I also got to see my Grandma Loretta, who gave me a karaoke machine as a gift. Given how much I detested the routine on the Ranch, almost any break would have been welcome, but all the amenities—from the great food, to the downtime by the pool, to my beautiful bedroom at the Hacienda—made it glorious. Best of all was no decks. I fell into the life of leisure without a second thought, and never wanted the week to end.

ARRIVING BACK AT THE RANCH WAS DIFFICULT. THERE WAS NO easing back into things; the first night, I went straight back to sixteen girls to a bathroom. The next day was worse when I woke up to uniforms, dorm inspections, decks, and the rest of the routine. Thankfully, after just a few weeks, news came that I'd be going on another trip: My entire family was going to go to Pennsylvania to celebrate my great-grandparents' sixtieth wedding anniversary. Dad and I flew in from L.A., and Justin was in Florida with Mom, so they came together. Everyone was there: Grandpa Ron and his wife, Becky; Uncle Dave and Aunt Shelly; and Dad's two sisters, Lori and Denise; and their families.

After the party, Mom, Dad, Justin, and I took our first-ever family vacation. The first part of our trip was in Pennsylvania, and our first stop was Knoebels Amusement Resort in central Pennsylvania, where I ate a pierogi for the first time. Though being around so many Wogs always made me a bit wary, on rare occasions we'd taken field trips from the Ranch that had at least exposed me to settings like this. Whether it was Disneyland or the ballet, those extremely sporadic trips were always carefully regimented to make sure that our interaction with the Wog world was limited as much as possible. Because I was with my family, Knoebels was a bit different, and I was able to enjoy the amusement park with more freedom.

Farther east, we enjoyed meatball heroes at a restaurant named after the Philadelphia Phillies' outfielder Lenny Dykstra. From Pennsylvania, we headed across New York and northeast through Vermont to New Hampshire, where we stayed with Aunt Lori and her family, and my dad's mother, Grandma Loretta, at the old house my parents had left behind when they rejoined the Sea Org.

Looking around the house, I found myself imagining what my life would have been like here, if my parents had decided to stay put. The relatives were all public Scientologists, and I would have grown up just like them. This would have been my home. Seeing my cousin Chrissie's room, I thought that it likely would have been my room and my bed, that her closet filled with princess dresses in every color would have been mine. That her life was what might have been.

For all the big differences between my life and theirs, I also came face-to-face with little things, too; in some ways the little things were the most striking. While we were in New Hampshire, we also stayed with Aunt Denise. Her house was amazing. Taylor and Whitney, Denise's oldest daughters, had an unbelievable bedroom with big windows and skylights, and lots of pretty dolls and even a television in their room. It felt like paradise, but seeing all that they had didn't make me envious; I always remembered my place in the Church. I was being raised to be a Sea Org member, and I had a mission to fulfill that was far more important than owning toys. Although it would have been nice to have a few, it was my duty to serve humankind like my parents did, and the thought of having so many toys seemed almost selfish, or at least that is what I told myself.

During our visit, Chrissie and I went berry picking in her backyard just for fun, a concept that felt a bit strange, since any kind of work we did at the Ranch was always a chore. One day, there was a spirited argument between my cousins in the car about who got to sit next to me, and while I was flattered, I was also surprised because we never acted so childishly at the Ranch. My cousins' behavior seemed a bit ridiculous. The Ranch had no tolerance for such behavior, so I'd never encountered it. I didn't know that most kids bickered like this. I didn't know what normal looked like.

CHAPTER TEN

KEY TO LIFE

RETURNING TO THE RANCH AFTER SO MUCH TRAVEL WOULD HAVE been incredibly difficult, but as it turned out, I wasn't going to be back there for long. Mom must have missed me as she was already arranging for me to come back to Flag, this time to do LRH's Key to Life course.

The course focused on the deeper comprehension of the small common words in the English language, as well as English grammar. Only four or five of the older kids at the Ranch had done it, but I was going to be the first to take it in Clearwater. I didn't know anything about the course, because the few kids who had completed it had to keep its content absolutely secret. Mr. Parker seemed doubtful that I could handle it. She thought I was too young, and that it would be too steep a gradient for me. Her lack of confidence didn't worry me, though; more than anything, I was just excited about returning to Clearwater.

When I arrived, I was back at Mom's and in my own room again. Everything looked just as I'd left it: the floral quilt was spread across my big bed without a wrinkle, the bathroom was stocked with my special floral shampoo; and the snack baskets were brimming with goodies, all thanks to Sharni.

For the Key to Life class, Mom had found a twin for me, and for weeks, she had been telling me about her in our phone calls. Her name was Diane and my mother said that the few times that she'd met her, she'd been *so* great and *so* nice. She insisted on calling her "Diana," even though her name was Diane. Hearing my mother beam like this about another girl my age made me a bit jealous.

My unease also came from intimidation. Diane held the prestigious post of Commanding Officer of Cadets at Flag. With a post like that, my concern was that she was probably more ethical than I, but I tried to remember where I was from. Being from the Int Ranch had its own status. The Cadets at my ranch were always touted as being from the best Cadet Org on the planet. My brother had even done special missions for the PAC Cadet Org in Los Angeles to make those Cadets more ethical. Supposedly, the PAC Cadets had been watching television and not doing their decks, so Justin and a few other bigger kids from the Ranch went down there for a few weeks to change things.

The course would take place at the Coachman Building, two blocks from Mom's office, and she had arranged for her secretary Alison to take me there the first day. The Key to Life course room was on the third floor and more refined than those at the Ranch. It had upholstered chairs, tables with wood inlays, and carpets with interesting designs. Like at the Ranch, though, the walls were covered with pictures of LRH, some of his more famous quotes, and some nice Scientology-themed artwork.

Most of the twenty or so students signed up for the course wore civvies, not uniforms. This was because many of them were public Scientologists, who paid for their courses, while others were non–Sea Org staff and had come from Scientology churches all over the world, from Italy, Australia, and Zimbabwe, to name a few. The Key to Life course cost about $4,000, and while Sea Org members didn't have to pay for courses, if we were ever to leave the organization, we would be billed for any services we had taken if we intended to continue in Scientology.

The supervisor for the course was a blond woman in her twenties named Nikki. "You must be Jenna!" she said as she approached. "Welcome!" With that, Alison left, saying she would come get me at lunchtime.

I was looking around for a seat when a girl a year or two older than me with long brown hair and bright blue eyes walked up to me and introduced herself as Diane. From her clear articulation and the look in her eyes, I knew my twin had a correct Scientology stare and voice. She struck me as being smart and a goody two-shoes; when we filled out our check sheets, I noticed she had perfect handwriting.

Nikki handed out a book that used pictures instead of words to illustrate concepts. There were two main characters, Joe and Bill. One character would get frustrated and the other would help him, and vice versa. Their objective was to illustrate twinning. The book had illustrations, but no words.

"Why aren't there any words?" I whispered to Diane.

"Without words, we can't get misunderstood words," she told me. Apparently LRH had designed the course this way to help people conceptualize a meaning without getting stuck on a definition.

When we were finished with that book, Nikki gave us a second one that showed how to do clay representations of Scientology concepts. It had only a few words, and the book defined every one of them for us. For this exercise, Diane and I sat across from each other at a table with a bucket of clay and some molding tools between us. Diane's side of the table had a stack of legal paper and a pen. She was going to be the auditor, and Nikki instructed her to ask me questions and record my answers. Nikki watched as Diane began by writing both of our names on the top of the sheet.

"Are you hungry?" Diane asked.

"No," I replied.

"Good," Diane said as she marked my answer on her worksheet. "Are you tired?" she asked next.

"No," I replied.

"Good." She marked this on her worksheet as well. These were the questions that always started off every auditing session. "Is there any reason not to start this session?" she asked.

"We're doing a session?" I asked, a little surprised.

"Yeah, the one we just read about in the book."

"Oh, okay."

Diane repeated the question. "Is there any reason not to start the session?"

"I don't think so," I said.

"This is the session!" she said in an unusually loud voice and with a particularly intense stare. The loud tone was exactly what she was supposed to do and how every Scientology session commenced. She next wrote the time down on the worksheet.

Nikki told us we would next be using the clay that was between us.

"Make a clay representation of Force/Counter Force," she instructed.

Following the instructions in the second book that Nikki had given us, I did my best to demonstrate this concept by making little men in clay and putting labels on them. When I finished a representation, Diane raised her hand, so that Nikki could make sure it was correct. When she had okayed it, we moved on to the next one, Intention/Counter Intention.

After each representation, Diane asked me if I had had any wins. Usually, my wins were "I feel better," or "My problems don't seem as big anymore," or "I don't have as many problems as I thought I did." I quickly learned that wins had an upside—they were the quickest way out of a session. Once you shared a big win, the session was over. We always had to end a Clay Table Representation on a win.

Alison came to get me at lunchtime as promised, and we drove over to Mom's office. The enthusiasm I got from her co-workers that I had started my Clay Table auditing was very fulfilling, as I wasn't used to people being this energized about anything I was doing. After lunch, I went back to the course room, where I stayed until dinnertime, at which point I went back to the WB and dined with Mom and Tom. Then, Mom had Tom take me home. As usual, she wouldn't get home until one or two in the morning.

Sharni was waiting for me at the apartment when Tom dropped me off. As the course progressed, I spent so much time with her that she quickly became more like an older sister than a babysitter. We would go swimming in the pool at night or, sometimes, we'd watch the current music programming on VH1 or MTV. Since the staff wasn't technically allowed to have televisions, this was a chance for both of us to enjoy it without getting into trouble. If anyone found out, Sharni could get off the hook by saying that she was just obliging me.

Watching me was not Sharni's only Sea Org duty. Along with several other girls, she was responsible for doing the laundry for my mother, Alison, and a few other senior executives. They were also charged with cleaning the apartments and offices of their bosses, making sure their meals were delivered, and providing them with snacks throughout the day. Usually, Sharni was able to get her work done before I got home, but sometimes I would help her if she still had things left to do.

Observing Sharni go about her work felt like I was seeing little pieces of what it meant to be in the Sea Org. I found myself imag-

ining the day when these were my responsibilities. Even helping
Sharni, I felt like I was role-playing a true staffer. Taking good
care of the executives was certainly a prestigious post for Sharni,
and she took it very seriously. On Saturdays, I didn't have class, so
I would hang out with Sharni. Often, we'd visit my grandmother
Loretta, who had recently moved from New Hampshire to Clearwater. I'd never spent a whole lot of time with Grandma Loretta,
but I quickly came to enjoy doing so now. One weekend, Loretta's parents, my great-grandparents Dorothy and Ralph, came
to town. I liked my great-grandma but my great-grandpa Ralph
was crotchety, grumpy, and tended to yell out comments, which
scared me. He was not rude per se, but to a little kid, he could be
intimidating because he was so brash and abrasive. Looking back,
he was probably trying to be nice and to make conversation, but
wasn't aware of how loud he was speaking.

One thing I knew about my great-grandparents was that they
were Catholic. When we sat down to eat, they would pray before
the meal, which freaked me out a little. I wasn't sure what the
procedure for this was, so I just sat in my place awkwardly waiting
for it to be over. Dad had only told me not to say "Jesus Christ!"
or "God damn it!" However, he had never told me anything about
saying grace.

I was wary around them both. They were Wogs, so I never
quite knew what I should or shouldn't say to them. At the Ranch,
we practiced our *shore story*, which was what we were supposed
to tell Wogs if they asked us questions about what we were up
to. The shore story originated when the Sea Org was on ships
and members didn't want their whereabouts known; they would
tell a shore story. Rather than saying we were Cadets training to
be in the Sea Org, our shore story was supposed to be we were
going to a private school called the Castile Canyon Ranch School.
My great-grandparents didn't do too much prodding and probing, though. They were used to their family being involved in the

Church, especially in the Sea Org—after all, David Miscavige was their grandson.

During their visit, my great-grandparents announced that they wanted to take me to Disney World, but I didn't want to be alone with them. I didn't know them that well. When I told Dad about my apprehension during a phone call, he got angry with me and told me I had to go; otherwise it would be bad PR, or out PR, for the family. This may have been the first time I had been ordered to spend time with non-Scientologists. My upbringing had succeeded in making me very apprehensive about Wogs, even Wogs as generous and well-intentioned as my great grandparents were. They weren't about to slander Scientology. However, when my mother saw me crying, she told me that Sharni could come, so my dilemma was solved.

MY CLAY TABLE CONTINUED FOR WEEKS. THE DEEPER INTO THE Clay Table processes we got, the more we were supposed to have a realization called an "end phenomena," basically a win, a floating needle, a very good intention, but I just couldn't get it. Every auditing level in Scientology had a specific end phenomena, or ability gained, that you were supposed to achieve before moving up to the next step. After weeks, though, I hadn't reached the end phenomena, and I was getting really sick of it. I even dreamed what it might be and tried writing the answer down as a win, but as often I guessed, it was never right.

Finally, I was told that I might have gone past it. I wasn't exactly sure how this could have happened, but I was even more confused when they confirmed I had indeed gone by it and that the oversight had been on their part for not realizing it. It was unclear how or when my end phenomena had happened, but as a result, I was now finished with the Clay Table auditing.

As much as I wasn't sure I'd experienced the end phenomena,

I wasn't about to stop them from moving me forward; after all, I wanted to get to the good stuff ahead. Since coming to Flag I'd been encountering more and more people who were further along in their studies, and some of them were quickly becoming inspiring role models for me. I wanted what they had—more knowledge, more proximity to total freedom so if the people in charge of the Key to Life said I'd experienced my end phenomena, well then, I must have. All that was left was to attest to the processing action, which meant going to the examiner and signing off on my Clay Table. Thank God, my needle floated, and that was the end.

I then was assigned to audit another girl on her Clay Table. She was about four years older than I and was so extremely slow at building her representations that it took everything I had to keep from falling asleep. I would sit at her Clay Table for five hours at a time, waiting for her to finish. I wasn't allowed to move to the next step until she finally attested.

The next step was improving our understanding of small, common words. We used a five-inch-thick dictionary written by LRH that contained any common word you could think of, words like "it," "the," "yes," "no," "up," "of," "it," and "out." I had to begin with the first word, read the first definition of that word aloud, then explain to Diane, in my own words, what it meant. I would have to use it in sentences according to that first definition until I fully understood it. Then, Diane would proceed to the next two definitions and so on, until we'd often done more than twenty definitions for each tiny common word. Once we'd moved through all the definitions of a word, we progressed on to that word's etymologies and idioms as well. Tiny words had dozens of idioms that had to be cleared with the same procedure as the definitions. It was mind-numbing at points, and I tried to get through it quickly, but of course, there were meter checks and spot checks in this course room, too.

Our progress was slow, and Diane and I didn't always get

along. She was older, smarter, and quicker than I was. I got bored easily and really struggled to pay attention. How many hours could I spend on the word "of" before going out of my mind? When we got frustrated or upset, we were told to take a walk, so we would go walking all the time. Eventually, though, we got through all the words.

The next step in the Key to Life course had a textbook as thick as the last. *New Grammar* was another nightmare. Because LRH believed that the misunderstood word was at the root of all stupidity and wrongdoing, he wanted to be sure that the meanings of even the smallest and most common words were clarified. He also wanted to stress grammar, since it gave another level of understanding to the English language, which was something we used every day and thus the key to making us truly literate.

It was very hard to understand the material, especially while trying to read it aloud perfectly. While it might have been okay for the older students, it was just too complicated for me. Other than Diane, I was younger than everyone else on the course by about five years, making it even more challenging. I often quietly reread the material later, because every few pages there would be a test to make sure we understood everything. In the end, *New Grammar* took us several months. I don't know how I got through these tests, but I did.

The last step on the course was called the Factors. People talked about this next step as though it imparted some amazing information on how we had all come to this planet. I was curious, because I had been hearing about it for a while now. When we opened *The Factors*, we found pretty pictures of clouds and sunrises, leaves and mountains, lightning, and other natural phenomena. On the last page, there was a quote that read, "Humbly tendered as a gift to man from L. Ron Hubbard."

As cryptic and mysterious as the book was, it felt anticlimactic. I had been hoping for a blow-by-blow of how we had come to be, but instead it said things like, "Before the beginning was a Cause and the entire purpose of the Cause was the creation of effect." It was the kind of winding language with which I was all too familiar. As always, I felt as though I had missed something and, as always, I didn't ask, or else I would just be told to find my misunderstood word.

In spite of all the monotony in the course work, I found myself becoming more and more entranced by the Sea Org life—not by the classes themselves, but by the lives that everyone around me seemed to have.

I'd grown used to the perks that came with having a mother in an executive position. I ate lunch with Mom at the WB, while Diane ate at the Elks Building, the location of the dining services for the non-execs, which, apparently, was gross. Every Saturday morning my Mom got a half day off, once or twice a full day, and we did things I had never done before—we went jet-skiing with Tom, Jenny, and Allison, or to a nature park to swim with the manatees.

My mom had a special hairdresser for her highlights and haircuts, and sometimes I'd go with her, but only to watch. Once, she paid for me to have a manicure at a local spa when she was getting a wax. I didn't even know that highlights, waxes, and manicures were standards when it came to feminine beauty. I had previously never talked about this kind of stuff with my mother. The whole process was incredibly foreign to me—the idea of taking care of yourself like this would have been seen as incredibly selfish on the Ranch, but here at Flag, I didn't question it. It seemed like something my mother deserved, and I looked up to her as a Sea Org role model. She was an outstanding example of just how far you could go.

The longer I stayed at Flag, the more attractive it became and the more I felt my enthusiasm for the Sea Org and Scientology growing. The highlights were the graduations, which took place on Friday nights in the auditorium of the Fort Harrison Hotel. The whole Flag base attended graduations every week, so the hall was always packed. People used this opportunity to share their wins, which were directly related to the courses the graduates had taken or the auditing they had received while at Flag. Each win was really just a personal gain; it could vary from something as small as feeling better to something as big as a miracle. After graduation, there was food being served by roving waiters and, each week, different executives flew in from the Int Base to be guest speakers. Sometimes it would be my father, so we would have the next morning to hang out together. Other times the speaker would be another high-ranking Scientology executive and, occasionally, even my uncle Dave.

In many ways, hearing these speakers amplified all the positive things I'd been feeling about the Sea Org since my first trip to Clearwater. Living like my mom in the Sea Org seemed to be a great dream and I wanted to become just like her. Then I'd see people like my father speaking in front of these massive audiences with the full spectacle of the religion on display, and I'd believe even more strongly that my future was in the Church.

I was especially moved at the annual Scientology events like Auditors Day, the International Association of Scientologists event, and the anniversary of the Maiden Voyage of the *Freewinds*. There would be thousands of Scientologists in attendance, and top executives would take to the podium to share videos of Scientology's work in different parts of the world, even as far as Asia and Russia. The videos often highlighted people from the various countries speaking about what Scientology had done for them. People shared wins about everything from being cured of cancer to walking after being paralyzed, while our audience thousands of miles away sat enraptured, hanging on each word. Afterward, everyone would leap to their feet, cheer, and go wild, and I, too, was energized by the enthusiasm. I didn't understand every word that people shared about their experiences, but the impact that the entire scene had on me was undeniable. A flush of goose bumps would sweep across my body and my ears would strain to take in the pulse of the chants of "hip, hip, hooray" to LRH around me; this was the group in its grandest form, with the power of being a Scientologist on full display.

At these events, Uncle Dave or another top exec would show graphs of how all the international Scientology statistics were on the rise, higher than ever before. The stats would chart things like "well done auditing hours" or "number of books sold to individuals." Uncle Dave or one of his people would always give a motivational speech about how Scientology was making inroads around the world and how some governments were even embracing it.

When Diane and I graduated from Key to Life, it was finally time for me to share a win of my own with the class. I was already insecure and quiet, and coupled with the fact that my win was barely worthy of attention, I wasn't very confident. When Diane presented hers it was long and lovely. I, on the other hand, was a deer in headlights. I had a better understanding of the small common words, and so I felt a more in-depth understanding of what people were saying to me and of the things I read. "I had fun," I mumbled with such awkwardness that I ran out of the room, which only made it more embarrassing. That Friday night, at the graduation ceremony, I was too shy to go onto the stage to get my certificate, which was something everyone usually did.

Unfortunately, finishing my course meant that my time in Clearwater was almost over. My new friends from all over the world invited me to visit them at their homes, an absolutely tantalizing possibility for me. Because my mom had been around the world on her various projects, I knew it might be possible for me, too, someday. I was going to miss my friends; even Diane and

I had grown close, despite the personal competition I had had with her.

More so than ever before, I found myself truly believing in the power of the Church. After months of listening to wins and experiencing Sea Org life vicariously, I'd gradually bought into Scientology in a way that I never had before. For the first time, I wasn't thinking about my frustrations with Thursday Basics and condition formulas or how much I didn't like doing deck work. Now I was just thinking about what I could achieve if I allowed Scientology to help me. I'd always believed in it, but I'd never understood its power or the place that it could have in my life. Suddenly, I felt like I could see my purpose, my future service to the Sea Org, and the reason for my dedication all unfolding right in front of me. Being in the crowd every Friday, I found it hard not to feel that I was a part of something special, something that was going to change all mankind.

CHAPTER ELEVEN

BACK TO THE DRUDGERY

AFTER GRADUATION, I STAYED AN EXTRA FEW WEEKS IN CLEAR-water, then flew back to California with my mother. She had business at Int, and I went back to the Ranch. I'd been away for months, and it gave me a strange sensation to return. It was really hard to go back to the deck work and the drudgery after my taste of freedom at Flag. The experiences stayed with me, and instead of sinking into a depressive rut, I found myself optimistic about what the future held.

My friends at the Ranch were certainly a big part of keeping my spirits high. When I was with my friends, I rarely thought about my family. Naomi, one of my best friends, had a pretty rebellious attitude. She always listened to a punk-music radio station, even though the Church considered a lot of punk bands too explicit, specifically the Sex Pistols. LRH had even mentioned the band by name as being a bad influence on children in one of his advices.

I was also friends with two sisters, Eva and Caitlin. Eva liked putting on makeup and all things girly, and I was really a girly girl at heart, too, even though I tried to be a tomboy, because that was what was cool back then. I liked going to Eva's room with her during meals or during bathroom breaks while on the decks, and going through her bottom drawer and finding cool stuff. Eva, Caitlin, and Naomi seemed more human and less robotic than any of the other kids at the Ranch, which was probably what attracted me to them.

Because our uniforms were laundered at the end of each day, we were allowed to wear regular clothes for evening Scientology studies. Caitlin, Eva, and I liked to swap clothes. We also shared music and exchanged Christmas presents every December.

Hanging out with Caitlin and Eva, it was hard to ignore that we were all getting older, as were the kids around us. Though it was strongly discouraged by our superiors at the Ranch, kids were suddenly talking about things like flirting and liking boys. It all seemed pretty innocent but, before long, I began to see the consequences when it wasn't.

Not long after I got back, I started on the Life Orientation Course, or LOC, which was the course that came after the completion of the Key to Life. This time, Justin was going to be my twin. Because the supervisors at the Ranch were not qualified to deliver the course, we had to take it at the Int Base in the evenings, replacing our Scientology studies, which took place at the Ranch.

In LOC, we learned more about the twelve human conditions and the steps that had to be taken in order to improve our state of well-being as well as other parts of Scientology's Ethics technology. Twinning with Justin was frustrating. We were eight years apart and had a hard time getting along. Just as in Key to Life, we were required to read the text out loud without stumbling or hesitating. If I made a mistake, I had to stop and look up the word I supposedly didn't understand in the dictionary. Justin would stop me if I made the slightest mistake, as he was supposed to, but I would deny it. He had no sympathy, and would get even more annoyed at me for lying. In reality, I had little idea what the whole darned book was talking about, but I couldn't let him know that, either. We were constantly raising our hand to call the supervisor, who was tasked with being our mediator. My brother, peevish and domineering, would make fun of me, and I would be in tears.

Eventually, Justin told the staff at the Ranch that I was in way over my head, and that LOC was too complicated for me. He also told them there was no way I was capable of retaining anything from Key to Life, either. He started spot-checking me in front of Mr. Parker and Mr. Bell, asking me things like, "What is the subjunctive mode?" As much as I had mentally rehearsed these answers for the past three months, Justin was right: I couldn't remember them.

In Scientology, forgetting was considered "blankness," and a symptom of a misunderstood word. Essentially, by forgetting, I was admitting that I had gone past words I hadn't known. This was considered a false attest to a course, which was an offense. Because of his tattling, I was assigned the lower condition of Doubt, which meant I now had to do several weeks of amends before I could rejoin my group.

I also ended up having to redo most of the Key to Life course. I'd go to the Int Base in the mornings to twin with a woman there. I would travel with the morning food run, returning to the Ranch when lunch was delivered. Thankfully, the Key to Life was not as challenging the second time.

Because I missed decks to do the course, I had to make them up in the afternoon, but it wasn't that bad. I got to work with my brother's friend Teddy, who had become a member of the Ranch staff and was now called Mr. Blackman. Our projects were technical things, like fixing the well on the property. I'd ride with him on his motorcycle to the worksite, and sit beside him, handing him his tools. It was much more relaxed than regular deck time, where everybody was under pressure to move fast and produce. Here, I was hardly working at all.

I enjoyed hanging out with Teddy. He'd ask me about Florida, where he had been born. He'd tell me how he just wanted to graduate from the Cadet Org so that he could get a girlfriend. Sometimes, we'd climb up the mountains around the creek to watch the sunset, or hike to a gorgeous waterfall. I had never known that the Ranch property was so pretty, because I had never had time to enjoy it. Teddy became my friend, although as my brother's friend first, he was really like a brother to a pesky little sister.

My friend Eva started commenting about how nice Teddy was to me. She seemed jealous. I thought this was odd, because, as far as I knew, they weren't even friends. Most of the girls at the Ranch had some degree of crush on Teddy. When I was little, I did, too, but he was too old for me and too much like my brother. I actually liked another boy my age named Corwin, who liked me, too, and sometimes came to my dorm at night to talk. We sat across from each other at course time, and other times we hung out during meals. I would watch him skateboard on the ramp at the front of the Big House, innocent but flirtatious. My friends could tell we liked each other, because if there was a minute of free time, we were together.

For a few months, Teddy and I worked decks together until, one day at muster, I saw him being escorted off, clearly in trouble. Prior to this, I had seen Eva, dressed in civvies, being hustled to the Cottage by an adult. Being in civvies on a weekday was never a good sign. Next, I saw Teddy, also wearing civvies, being taken to a different building by Rosemary's son, Mike, who was now also a member of the Ranch staff. I wasn't sure what was happening, but from the looks of it, they had done something together. I heard nothing else until later that day at the deck muster, when the Director of Inspections and Reports from CMO International came to the Ranch. She was in charge of discipline and wielded a lot of power. Everyone at muster was so quiet I could hear my own breath when she stood before us and announced in a very serious tone that Eva and Teddy had been having an "out 2D," "2D" being short for the Second Dynamic. Out 2Ds were any kinds of relationship that went beyond kissing. This was a very serious allegation.

The nature of this offense went back to the eight dynamics, which we were supposed to use when making decisions. Because the second dynamic was dedicated to family, personal relationships, sex, and children, Eva and Teddy being accused of an out 2D meant that they had been charged with something sexually unethical, which violated the mores of the group.

I was scared for them, as they most certainly would be harshly punished. As I stood wondering what would happen to them, the director of inspections had more shocking accusations, announcing that Justin had known about the relationship and hadn't reported it. Failure to report meant he would receive the same penalty that they would. Justin was adamant that he had not known anything, but she clearly did not believe him and had him pulled from the assembly.

The next several days were a witch hunt with all the kids anxious and worried that they might be next. The woman from Int remained at the Ranch, giving meter checks and confronting people on various reports of unethical behavior. She made people write reports about any 2D activity, including flirting, that they had been part of or witnessed. Young as we were, the definition of flirting was often misleading, and if you had a crush on someone or spent time with him, that was enough to raise questions, as it was considered unacceptable.

As a result, I had to respond to a handful of reports that said that Corwin and I had been flirting. Though I knew that all contact between boys and girls was now being taken extremely seriously, I still would have hung out with Corwin had it not been for the disclosure that he had also been flirting with my old friend Rebecca, with whom I'd tried to run away. He came to my door to find out why I was ignoring him, and I was kind of mean. I told him that I just wasn't flirting with him anymore. I could tell that he was a little hurt, but so was I.

Eva and Teddy were in big trouble, although they were allowed to remain on the Ranch and weren't sent to the Rehabilitation Project Force, or RPF, which was standard for this kind of violation. RPF was for people who had messed up badly. They were required to wear all black; they had to run, not walk, while on their decks, wherever they went; they were not allowed to speak to other crew members unless spoken to first. They got half-pay and fifteen-minute meal breaks. If they disobeyed or backflashed, they had to run laps. Their days were divided between heavy manual labor and intense auditing, where they were required to uncover their evil intentions and get rid of them through Scientology processing. Being assigned to RPF was a Sea Org member's worst nightmare. When I first arrived at the Ranch, the RPF program was located there.

Instead of RPF, Teddy had to endure being ostracized. He went from being the coolest guy at the Ranch to the pariah whom nobody spoke to.

"I used to think he was so cool," a friend told me one day, "but now I just think he's a loser."

She wasn't the only one who felt that way. In most people's esteem, he had sunk to the lowest of the low. Later on, I learned from Teddy's mother that he had been assigned to RPF after the out 2D with Eva, but my uncle Dave had saved him from having to do it. I never found out the reason, but I assumed it might have been because Teddy was young and technically a Cadet, not a Sea Org member.

Personally, I couldn't bring myself to feel the same condemnation toward Teddy that other people did. More than anything, I felt bad for him. I didn't look at him and see someone who'd hurt the group or disobeyed Scientology; I saw him as my brother's friend who'd always been nice to me.

As part of his ethics program, he had to read LRH's ethics policies, which were kept in the same building in which the vitamins were stored. I was sure he expected me to be like everyone else and not talk to him, but when nobody was looking, I'd at least tried to say hi. I'd see him there if I was working, and I'd ask him how he was doing. Teddy was grateful for any friends, and a few times, I even saw him break down in tears.

Eva didn't seem to be having as hard a time with being shunned as Teddy. I still talked to her on the sly, although I'd get in trouble when I was caught. One time, I was warned to stop fraternizing with her, or I would receive the same penalties that she had gotten. I continued anyway, as she was my friend.

Meanwhile, I was starting to be grilled about Justin and his relationship with a girl at the Ranch named Tiffany. All I knew was that Tiffany had once confessed to me her undying love for him, and I had never told anyone. During the interrogations, I stupidly said, "I'm not telling you anything about my brother!" which, of course, made the situation more suspicious. I thought my brother would appreciate my loyalty, but instead he was angry with me, and told me I was an idiot.

Eventually, things quieted down and the Director of Inspections and Reports went back to the Int Base, but her work at the Ranch clearly had the desired impact. After being sniffed out and persecuted, we were not just wary about who we were seen with, we were even more careful about who we could trust.

In many ways, though, everything I'd witnessed with Eva and Teddy had the opposite effect on me. Before the visit from the Director of Inspections, I'd sometimes wondered what I would do if I was put in a situation where a friend had done something bad and gotten in trouble with the group. Now, for the first time, I had my answer, and I was surprised at how quickly and naturally my reaction had come to me. No matter what was considered ethical or what Scientology would consider right, friends came first. Ostracizing friends was not something I could bring myself to do.

CHAPTER TWELVE

FLAG AGAIN

I was eleven in the spring of 1995, when Mom told me that I would be returning to Florida to complete my Key to Life redo. She said that, because Flag hadn't gotten me through the course properly the first time, they were the ones who needed to fix it. The whole thing was very embarrassing. I worried that Nikki would be really upset with me for false attesting, but I'd have to deal with that when I got to Clearwater.

When I arrived, I noticed a few things had changed. Sharni no longer worked for Mom; she was working as a cook at the Hibiscus instead. She seemed to really like it, although she said she would miss hanging out with me. Now Valeska was going to be taking care of me. Not only that, she was also going to be my new twin in the Key to Life course.

In addition, Mom had a new male co-worker whom she seemed to spend a lot of time with. His name was Don Jason, and he was the right-hand man to the captain of the Flag Service Organization, a very high rank. He was a nice-looking man, with close-cropped blond hair and pale blue eyes, and his wife, Pilar, was an executive who worked in Mom's office. Don would sometimes join us for meals, and Mom talked about him a lot.

That first day when I arrived at the course room, I was a little nervous about what Nikki would say to me, but I was relieved when she didn't come down hard. The Key to Life course room had all new students this time around. I became friends with a huge boy named Buster and his twin Jason, who I thought was cute. Waiting for roll call, Valeska, Buster, Jason, and I would play twenty questions.

Valeska and I would take the bus home together after class. We'd go swimming, make silly videos, or paint each other's faces. I'd sometimes help Valeska with her work, like laundry and snacks. That was when she'd tell me stories about her childhood. She had been born in Switzerland, and when she was young, her father wanted to join the Sea Org in England, but her mother did not want to. Despite the disagreement, the family decided to drive from Switzerland to England, and during a pit stop, her mother got out of the car, saying she was going to get coffee. She never came back. Upon arriving in England, Valeska's father sent Valeska and her two siblings to the Cadet Org, even though none of them spoke English.

The story was horrifying. I had never heard anything like it in such detail. Back at the Ranch, I'd known some kids who had one parent who caused problems, so they never saw that parent, but I never paid too much attention to those stories. Still, Valeska's story sounded believable. If her mother hadn't wanted to join the Sea Org but the father did, there was no way they could be together. However, the thought that this had happened to someone I felt so close to was upsetting, so much so that when my mother came home that night, I told her about it. She said offhandedly that it couldn't be true. I wasn't sure she had really been listening, but I was wrong. The next night before I went to bed, she said, "Okay, no more sad stories tonight."

Talking about difficult things was not something we did often. Mom and I were in the kitchen at her office one day when, out of the blue, she told me sad news.

"Just so you know, your grandma Janna dropped her body," she said, somewhat dejectedly.

I hadn't even known my grandma was sick, but I also hadn't seen her since I was five. A couple of months earlier, I had tried sending her a Christmas card, but I must have had the wrong address, because it was returned to me.

"Oh, shoot," I said, not knowing how else to respond. In Scientology, there was no specific ritual we practiced when a person died. A lot of people chose to get cremated because that was what LRH had done. Usually, a very sentimental announcement was sent out saying all of the good things the person had done. If he had been a Sea Org member, the announcement usually said that he was being granted a twenty-year leave from his billion-year contract, so that he would have time to find a new body and then return. Typically, there was a memorial service. I had never attended one. A part of me felt bad that Grandma Janna had died, but I tried to remember that she would get another body.

For her part, Mom didn't seem too broken up. "Are you okay?" I asked.

"I'm sad," she replied. "But your grandma and I haven't spent much time together in years, so I'm kind of used to not having her around. I'll get an auditing session on it."

It may sound strange, but Grandma Janna's death had little impact on me. Though she had been the person responsible for getting my mother into the Church, I hadn't spent much time with her, and Mom seemed to be handling her death okay.

Living in Mom's apartment, I quickly settled into a routine that I thrived in. Having Valeska take care of me was also a huge help. More than just a Scientology role model, Valeska was my classmate, and our friendship became incredibly important to me.

My main focus was the Key to Life course—I didn't have any academic studies to think about, only my Scientology course work. In what seemed like no time, I wrapped up Key to Life and moved on to LOC, the course I'd originally taken with Justin as my twin but never completed. This time, LOC didn't bother me because it meant that I got to stay at Flag for even longer.

Because I was living with Mom, I also began to see Uncle Dave more. He had a lot of business at Flag, so he came to Clearwater often. Sometimes, he'd stay for long periods of time. My mom directed me not to come around the office when he was in town and to eat lunch at the Lemon Tree. She told me to go home with Valeska after the course, rather than look for her at the WB.

I was at the office, anyway, one afternoon despite her instructions. I was writing a letter to Justin, back at the Ranch, and I wasn't quite finished when I heard my uncle coming down the hall. I ran across the room to hide, but I was too late. Uncle Dave, Aunt Shelly, and Mom all saw me crouching behind the bookshelf when they opened the office door. Uncle Dave looked confused.

"Why are you hiding from us, Jenny?" he asked.

I stupidly explained it was because Mom had told me not to be in the office when he was there. Uncle Dave looked at my mom, who put on a baffled face.

"I never said that," she said. She had told me only a few days earlier, so I was confused as to why she would deny it now.

"Were you doing something you shouldn't have been?" Aunt Shelly wanted to know.

Before I could answer, Uncle Dave cut in. "You don't have to run away from me," he said reassuringly. He gave me an awkward hug and said they had to run now, but that he would see me tonight. He and his entourage then headed down the hall to the elevator. I wasn't sure what he meant by "seeing me that night," but I went back to course.

As it turned out, I ran into him in the elevator a couple of times that day. "I see you!" he'd joke, with a big smile. That night, Mom, who had seemingly forgotten about the incident earlier that day, told me to put on my pajamas because we were going upstairs to Uncle Dave's.

"Jenny!" he greeted, as we walked in. "Come sit on the couch!" My mom seemed proud that I was getting so much attention from him. "Do you want some popcorn?" he asked.

Before I could even answer, he turned to his steward, Georgiana, and commanded, "George, get her some popcorn."

I sat down on one of the leather couches. The room was filled with top Scientology executives, including Norman Starkey, who was the trustee of LRH's estate. We were all going to watch *Star Wars*, but, first, a couple of people had to fix something with the tape.

Uncle Dave was chatting with someone about plans for everyone to see *Apollo 13* in a few days when it came to the Clearwater movie theater. "Do you want to see that movie, Jenny?" he asked me.

I said I did, but that I really wanted to see *Batman Forever*.

"Aha! Of course!" Uncle Dave responded. "Who do you like in that movie?"

"Jim Carrey, and it has Nicole Kidman, too."

Uncle Dave turned away from me and proceeded to engage in gossip about some of the celebrities in the film with the others in the room.

They all seemed interested, but still he turned back to me. "Jenny, when we adults are having a conversation, do you feel like you can understand it yet?"

"Um, sometimes, not always," I replied.

He beamed at me, and with the video fixed, we all watched the movie.

In the next weeks, we finished all three parts of the *Star Wars* trilogy, once watching one in Mom's apartment. Uncle Dave and Aunt Shelly thought my bedroom was beautiful. Uncle Dave even borrowed my CD collection. I thought it was pretty cool that he liked my music enough to borrow it. He returned it a few days later.

My father would sometimes fly to Flag for big events. One evening, when we were hanging out together in the greenroom, I overheard Uncle Dave discussing a sound system glitch that had happened during that evening's event. A few minutes later, he gruffly summoned the three sound techs, who had flown all the way from Int to produce the show. They looked very sheepish as they entered the room, as if they dreaded what was coming. I knew they were most likely about to get a Severe Reality Adjustment, which meant they were going to be acerbically yelled at.

My dad took me down the hall to keep me away from the action. I told him I knew what was going to happen. My father didn't really know what to say. Clearly, he wasn't aware of how much yelling went on at the Ranch. I had never seen Uncle Dave chewing anyone out, but I imagined it would be pretty severe. A few minutes later, someone from the room came into the hall to tell us we could come back. The three men were no longer there, and Uncle Dave greeted me as though nothing at all had happened.

It was hard for me to reconcile the impressions that people had of Uncle Dave and Aunt Shelly with the way they treated me. To me, they both seemed kind, even loving. I enjoyed being around them, because it made me feel more like I was spending time with family. I could tell that people seemed to fear both Uncle Dave and Aunt Shelly, and that they wielded so much authority that they were probably intimidating to most people. Sensing all this, I was always careful what I said and did when they were around. How they acted toward me was kindly, so I didn't really understand the full extent of why people were so cautious around them.

When Uncle Dave and Aunt Shelly were in town, they usually spent leisure time with Mom and me. We'd play mini-golf or go to a hockey game. I would get ready with Aunt Shelly; she would put on her makeup and I asked what purpose her lip liner served, and she told me that when you were old like she was, the lines of your lips disappeared and lip liner defined them again. She said I was young and pretty and didn't need makeup.

Another time, when I was at their apartment, Tom was there to look into a problem with the phones. She was telling Tom to make sure the phone lines in their condo got fixed. She told him that several times now, she had been on the phone with Kelly Preston or John Travolta, and could hear another phone conversation going on at the same time. Kelly had even noticed the other conversation and asked what it was, thinking it was "out-security," a term for a security breach.

This wasn't the first security breach that I'd heard of. In my LOC course, I'd met an ex–Sea Org member, now a public Scientologist, who told me that he had gotten in serious trouble over a celebrity leak. He said he had been accused of being the one who had let the media know that Tom Cruise was a Scientologist. He told me he had known about Cruise's Church connection, but the only person he had told was a close family member; the story had made headlines shortly after that, and he got the blame.

Although Mom and Tom still worked closely together, Don seemed to be in the picture more. She and Don got along very well. Not only did they both have a dry sense of humor, they seemed like kindred spirits, because they had had similar upbringings and saw things the same way. They were becoming better and better friends. Because Mom thought so favorably of Don,

I wanted to like him, too. He was a nice guy and liked to joke around, but sometimes he was slightly intimidating, but it may have been more because of the way my mother talked about him so reverently, I felt the need to impress him.

As Don and Mom started getting closer, she and I were growing more distant. I used to wait up for her to come home at night, but now she said I shouldn't do that anymore, because I needed to get enough sleep.

There was an edge to her that hadn't been there before—at times that edge could become downright rude. One day, I was standing with a group of people when she handed me a paper bag that contained deodorant. I had never used deodorant, and I didn't understand why she was handing it to me now.

"Why are you giving this to me?" I asked, with a bit of confusion.

"Because you stink," she said, and she started laughing. A few other people in the office laughed, too, but I could tell that they felt a bit bad for me.

The longer I stayed at Flag, the more I could feel her drifting away. Finally, in the fall of 1995, when I was getting toward the end of LOC, Mom told everyone in the office her news: Uncle Dave had offered her a position in RTC, the Religious Technology Center, at the Int Base. The RTC was the highest governing body of the Church, and was responsible for policing ethics violators and upholding the proper application and use of Scientology materials and technology. Not only was this a huge honor, it meant that she would be back home on the West Coast with Dad, Justin, Sterling, and me. She seemed hesitant, saying she really didn't want to be in RTC, as she liked her current job. But she acknowledged that since Uncle Dave had made the offer, she couldn't say no.

Everybody showered her with gifts at her going-away party. The staff at Flag really seemed to love her, and gave her a whole living room set, including an ornate white couch, an antique trunk, a hutch, and a few other items. That week, I planned to add my own celebration for Mom as well. Some Fridays, after the graduation ceremonies, I'd put on some kind of show for Mom and the various Scientology executives that she entertained at her apartment. My performances were kind of ridiculous. One Friday, I did an out-of-fashion fashion show, where I put on mom's clothes and paraded around. Another time, I did a tap-dance show, even though I had no clue as to how to tap dance. And so, in celebration for Mom's move back to Int, I plotted my biggest show ever for the Friday night postgraduation crowd at Mom's.

I made a whole cardboard structure and sewed an outfit for myself out of kitchen rags. I painted Valeska's and my faces and was just about ready to clean things up when Mom came home early. She was furious that the house was filthy and that people were coming over, and she started yelling at me. She said that I was dressed with nothing more than a kitchen rag, that there was trash everywhere, that I had a CMO staff member getting cardboard for me when he should have been on post, and that I was spoiled. She turned on Valeska next. "And you," she barked, "grow up!"

Valeska clearly felt ridiculous with her face painted and a silly hat on her head and almost burst into tears. Mom signaled to her to leave, and she did.

I had never yelled at my mother before, but I couldn't stand to see her treat Valeska like that, or me. I told her that I was not afraid of her like other people were. I even cussed at her several times, telling her we were just trying to put on a show for her benefit, and that we had been about to clean up when she burst in. She screamed back at me not to cuss at her, and I shouted at her not to yell at me.

After some vicious back-and-forth that brought us both to tears, she finally turned to me with a heavy sigh.

"I'm sorry, Jenna," she said. "Give me a hug; I really am sorry."

Emotional and exhausted, I looked at her. We'd never had a fight like this, so we'd never had to make up like this, either. Reluctantly, I gave her a hug.

That night, her friends still came over as planned, and Mom acted as though nothing had happened. A few days later, we boarded a plane bound for the West Coast, Int, and the Ranch.

Chapter Thirteen

THE GOLDEN AGE OF TECHNOLOGY

I RETURNED TO THE RANCH WITH NEW CONFIDENCE. IT WAS hard to say whether it was because I'd finally finished the Key to Life and LOC courses successfully, because of all the excitement about the Sea Org that I'd experienced at Flag, or simply because I was getting older, but the end result was an optimism I'd never felt before.

Part of my enthusiasm came from the fact that, at the end of the LOC course, I'd been tasked with finding my purpose, or my "hat in life," as Scientologists say. I'd begun talking with Mom about this, and asking her lots of questions about the different Sea Org roles she'd had. From those discussions, I'd decided that I wanted to be in the Commodore's Messenger Office, the CMO, which offered a new clarity and focus to everything. Although I still had to graduate from the Ranch before I could join the CMO, for the first time I had a plan for what I wanted to do with my life; now all I had to do was follow the rules.

In truth, following the rules felt a lot easier now—even deck work, which I hadn't done in ages because I'd been at Flag, didn't seem as bad. I was nearly twice the age I had been when I'd first arrived at the Ranch, and I was much more able to do physical work. I even started receiving praise for being a hard worker, something I wasn't used to. My old post as medical liaison had been taken by someone else in my absence, so my new post put me in charge of the Harvest, making sure certain fields were properly harvested, but soon I was promoted to the head of Division 2, an executive position. In this role, my duty was to oversee the Children's group.

One of the changes that had been made since I'd arrived was that there was no longer a pre-Cadet category, only Cadets and Children. Among my responsibilities, I had to make sure the children under my care made it to morning muster on time, had good hygiene, were ethical, and did their deck work. Some of them were well behaved; some of them weren't. I wanted to build good relationships with all of them; I hadn't forgotten what it was like to be their age, living at the Ranch. I nurtured them as best I could. If they came to me and told me they didn't like the post they were assigned, I would try to help them find a post that suited them better. Their posts were simple, things like supplying the dorms with toilet paper, picking up trash, or gathering vegetables, but I tried to work it so that everybody was happy. I took my post seriously and was even recognized as Cadet of the Week.

My academic schooling wasn't going as well, though. I was almost two years behind because of the time I had spent at Flag receiving no academic education. One of the results of my experiences at Flag was that, now, I only wanted to do Scientology studies, since I knew that to be a Sea Org member, those were what really mattered. When I argued with my course supervisor that academics were not that important, she escorted me to a small storage room where the books were kept. She was only eighteen or nineteen, although she was much bigger than I. I started fighting to get out, but she punched me in the face pretty hard. I only got a small bruise, and I didn't complain to anybody at the Ranch.

However, when I did tell my mother, she just asked me what I had done to deserve it. I wondered if she would speak to someone about it, but I was too afraid to ask, because she seemed to think it was my fault.

In the evenings, I was assigned to audit a girl named Trisha on her Clay Table. The two of us would go to the Int Base at night with the food run, and I would audit her after dinner. It wasn't too difficult, because she was a friend and pretty easygoing. Being at Int most nights meant that there were more opportunities for me to run into Uncle Dave. One time after course, he came to pick me up on his motorcycle. We drove to his office, where I chatted with my aunt Shelly, and I played with his dogs. He took pictures of me at his desk answering the phone, pretending that I ran the world.

For all that he was the head of the Church and a powerful figure who inspired fear, moments like these showed a normal side to him. There were times when I could tell he just wanted to be a fun, normal uncle, goofing around with his niece, and in these moments, it was almost possible to see some sort of longing for a family, a humanity that was hidden much of the time. From how he treated me, it seemed apparent that he didn't want me to be afraid of him in the way that most adults were. Sadly, these tender moments were going to become fewer and farther between. As the years went on, I saw that side of him less and less, and perhaps, given how he eventually seemed to change for the worse, it eventually ceased to exist entirely. But I never have forgotten Uncle Dave's gentle, human side.

I stayed in touch via letter with all of my friends at Flag, especially Valeska, Tom, Jenny, even Don and Pilar. My dad would sometimes make comments about the letters I received from Don, saying things like, "Did you get your letter from your best friend Don?" He'd say it in a weird, jealous tone, but I would just ignore it. It wasn't just those comments that struck me as odd. It seemed like my parents were arguing a lot, and that the arguments were getting worse.

Christmas was at Uncle Dave's apartment at the Int Base that year. Mom and Dad got Dave an expensive pen, and Mom got a cute green Ann Taylor suit from him and Aunt Shelly. Aunt Shelly told me I should not get too enmeshed in fashion, as it was a bit of a trap. She also sat me down and talked to me about issues like skin and acne. I was having lots of breakouts and pimples and didn't really know how to take care of my face. Aunt Shelly suggested some natural solutions to help me clear it up. Although it was embarrassing, I was thankful for her guidance.

Soon after Christmas, a policy change went into effect that kids could no longer stay at their parents' berthing on Saturday nights. I was ambivalent about the change. I had always liked going to my parents' berthing; staying at the apartment was so much nicer than staying at the Ranch. If this had occurred just a few years earlier, I would have been devastated. My parents were now living on the Int Base, which meant I didn't really get to see my friends on Saturday night and Sunday mornings anyway, so I wasn't really too bummed about the change. My dad was furious, though. It meant that family time was even more limited, and if parents wanted to see their children, they had to come to the Ranch, making it difficult for most of them because they had to take the bus. They also lost the Sunday morning time to go shopping with their kids for socks, underwear, toiletries, and such. I was still allowed to go to Int on Sunday mornings, but I didn't go as often.

Justin and I didn't see each other much anymore. He'd officially joined the Sea Org, so he was living and working at Int. When I did see him, he didn't have much to say to me. Therefore, I was surprised when Taryn approached me one afternoon, anxious to share good news with me about my brother. Like Justin, she was also working at the Int Base as a Sea Org member.

"Aren't you so excited that Justin decided to stay!" she exclaimed, waiting for me to agree. When I looked baffled, she could tell I had no idea what she was talking about. She brought me aside.

"Justin has wanted to leave the Sea Org for several years," she told me quietly, "but your dad finally convinced him to stay."

As I heard these words, I couldn't make my mind up as to which was more shocking: that my brother had contemplated leaving, or that Taryn was telling me about it. In the Sea Org, you were forbidden to talk about leaving or even hearing that someone else was considering leaving. If you did, it was considered a Suppressive Act, so just by her telling me, she was taking a huge risk. Aside from telling someone that you were thinking of leaving, other High Crimes that might be considered Suppressive Acts were things like talking negatively about Scientology, practicing Scientology outside the umbrella organization, asking for your money back, taking legal action against Scientology, or speaking or writing negatively about Scientology to members of the media. Suppressive Acts could cause you to be declared a Suppressive Person, an SP. If this happened, you were considered evil, and people who were still Scientologists had to disconnect from you in every way, or they would be considered SPs, too.

As I turned over Taryn's words, things started to make more sense. I knew that Justin had been unhappy. He always seemed to be in trouble for one thing or another—even when he wasn't doing anything wrong—so the idea that he'd contemplated leaving wasn't a total shock. However, there was a big difference between contemplating it and almost doing it. Until now, I hadn't realized just how close I'd come to losing a family member. I wouldn't have been able to have any kind of relationship with him. It scared me that I had come so close to losing someone I loved.

In the end, I felt relieved that it hadn't happened, but I also hadn't known enough to worry about it. Everyone seemed to know about his discontent except me. It was the first time I'd heard of someone this close to me doubting their commitment to the Sea Org. It wouldn't be the last.

ON MAY 9, 1996, THE DAY WE WOULD CELEBRATE DIANETICS Day, Uncle Dave was going to unveil the next great steps in the future of Scientology. Scientology, he said, was undergoing a renaissance of sorts, and he had decided that there were imperfections in the way people were being audited. As a result, he wanted to improve the training program for auditors with new, more sophisticated E-Meters and perfected auditing drills, thus enabling Scientologists to ascend the Bridge to Total Freedom more thoroughly and efficiently. These improvements were going to be called the Golden Age of Technology, and from now on, they would help train Scientologists to be perfect auditors.

One of the changes brought on by this Golden Age of Technology was that new E-Meters were going to be created for training auditors. In the past, the checksheets that had been used for training auditors asked the coach to squeeze the cans to simulate E-Meter readings for the student. Now, instead of having a coach squeeze the cans, there was an actual machine on which one could push buttons and the desired reading would show up. With these better E-Meters and the heightened training that these new procedures produced, for the first time the process of teaching auditors would be flawless, so the auditors would be flawless as well.

I was very excited to be among a small group of cadets chosen to help on the Golden Age of Tech's new E-Meter, called the "Mark Super VII Quantum," manufactured by a division of Golden Era Productions. Golden Era Productions, or "Gold" as it was called, was responsible for the worldwide dissemination of Scientology, including all films, videos, television, Internet, and international event production. It also produced the tapes of LRH's lectures and other materials, such as the E-Meter, training devices, and anything else needed to deliver Scientology to the public and staff. It was headquartered at the Int Base and staffed by several hundred Sea Org members, many of whom were parents to kids at the Ranch.

The first morning, we were driven by bus to the base after breakfast. The team was going to be assembling the new E-Meters in Building 36, Hubbard E-Meter Manufacturing, HEM. The place was buzzing, as we needed to get the machines ready for the May 9 launch date. Tons of staff were working there, even people from other posts who had come to help. We were divided into different sections along the line, so I was never in one section for more than a couple of weeks during the nearly year-long assignment during which time I got to work in every section.

I started off hot-stamping the plastic E-Meter casings with dial numbers and letters, and ended up in QC, Quality Control, where my job was to catch any glitches in the finished product. There were only three of us in QC, and we had to plug the finished E-Meters into all sorts of machines and do tests at different settings. HEM had a certain quota to make, and we were getting closer each day, as May 9 approached. Every time an E-Meter passed through the QC department, we would ring a bell and everyone would cheer.

Working in QC was sometimes exciting and sometimes nerve-racking. Throughout the day, senior executives would come through to inspect our work. There was a period of time when I was rejecting many E-Meters, so the execs brought in a technical guy to see if the problem was with my inspections or the meters. The tech expert concluded that the E-Meters were problem-free, so it must have been me. I stood my ground, insisting the meters were faulty based on the standard tests I had done. I even demonstrated the problem to several executives, and when it turned out that I was correct, I was praised for persevering.

The E-Meter assembly project went on for a few months. Mom

was often the inspector. She would give me a hug and check on me, then go on her way. I was impressed by how everyone seemed to love and respect her while also fearing her. In the Sea Org, this was called "Ethics Presence," which was essentially a combination of fear and respect, both of which were considered necessary to get compliance. Because we were already accustomed to working long hours, it really was no sweat, and working at a desk was much easier than deck work at the Ranch. When we worked at HEM, we stayed there all day, only going home in the evening in time for dinner, followed by studies. I was still in charge of the Children until they went to bed.

Once demand for the new E-Meters had subsided to a manageable level after the celebration of Dianetics Day, we resumed our normal schedules at the Ranch, but being a part of the E-Meters only added to the sense of progress that I'd built, a sense that came to a halt just as I was settling into things at the Ranch.

One day, out of the blue, it was announced that from this point forward all Cadets had to be higher on The Bridge before they could graduate from the Ranch and become Sea Org members. This was another part of the Church's plan to make perfect auditors. The problem for me was that it could take years to become a Class V Auditor, which meant it could take years for me to graduate. The news came as a huge surprise and disappointment for all the kids, but I had a particularly hard time with it.

Ever since I'd returned from Flag, I'd been making continuous improvements. I had more responsibility and felt like I'd been building momentum. For months I'd been taking comfort in my hat-in-life plan I'd put together to join the Commodore's Messengers Organization (CMO) after graduation. That plan had offered me a sense of direction, not to mention excitement about the future.

Having to become a Class V auditor changed things completely. Now it could be years before I'd get to realize that plan. It was a bitter pill to swallow, but as most every Scientologist learns at some point, these kinds of adjustments are all too typical. Just as I'd been getting into a rhythm and just when I'd figured out the rules, they changed them.

A few weeks later, at my brother Sterling's wedding, I had a chance to talk to Aunt Shelly about it. I told her I was very upset about the new graduation requirement. She explained to me that she thought that auditor training was the greatest thing in the world if you really wanted to learn how to help other people. She said that the finest CMO messengers were trained auditors, and Uncle Dave himself had become an auditor at a very young age. The way she framed it made it sound sensible, and her words calmed me down. At the very least, she'd made it sound more exciting. After all, the way to clear the planet was through Scientology auditors and our goal as Sea Org members was to bring everyone on the planet to a state of clear. Only then, could we be at peace. Still, it seemed like a lot of work and a lot more years.

Even though I was still frustrated, I turned my focus to Sterling and Suzette's wedding. Suzette was actually Aunt Shelly's half sister. My mother didn't like her very much for some reason. I got along with her better than I did with Sterling, as Sterling and I hadn't had a chance to get very close. He had left the Ranch to work in the Sea Org at Int some years earlier and prior to that, when he was at the Ranch, he had been much closer to his younger brother Nathan. I was the flower girl, and Justin the best man. I thought I was a little too old to be the flower girl, though.

The event was being held at the Celebrity Centre in Los Angeles, as were most Sea Org weddings. That Sunday morning, Justin rehearsed his best-man speech in the car during the entire drive down from Int. When we arrived, I went into the dressing room where all the bridesmaids were gathered. Aunt Shelly helped me get into my dress and put the floral wreath on my head. Her other sisters, Clarisse and Camille, were tending to Suzette. Sterling and

Suzette's wedding was a traditional ceremony, with the bride in white and an exchange of vows. There were about one hundred people in attendance. A Scientology wedding ceremony also included the ARC Triangle, the letters of which stood for Affinity, Reality, and Communication. The ARC Triangle was a fundamental Scientology concept of how to get along with people and build understanding relationships. It stressed the importance of communication, which was applicable to marriage, with the ceremony having the bride and groom promise that they will never go to bed without resolving an argument. After the ceremony, we all watched Sterling and Suzette open their gifts.

On a Sunday morning following the wedding, I told my mother that I really missed my friends at Flag, and that I was bummed about not being able to graduate until I did my auditor training. To my surprise, she said that she would let me visit there, and even stay long enough to do a course. Though I was intrigued by the prospect of this, I was over the moon when she suggested that I do my entire auditor training program at Flag. Flag, she explained, had the best auditor training on the planet, and this would probably mean spending a year in Florida. I had never intended to stay that long, but I figured I wouldn't be held to it, so I agreed immediately. My father didn't like the idea of me being gone for so long, saying he would miss me too much, but he didn't stop me from going. The next few weeks at the Ranch were just about counting the minutes until I could board a plane to Flag.

As I waited to leave, Mr. C got me even more excited about the auditor training. He told me I'd have a thrilling time, as the program led to personal miracles. Remembering the story of one course in particular, he told me that when he was finished, he was suddenly able to play the piano, something he had never been able to do before in this lifetime. The prospect of discovering a hidden talent was very alluring. After this course, I thought, anything might be possible.

CHAPTER FOURTEEN

CMO TRAINING

THINGS WERE ODD FROM THE MOMENT I LANDED IN CLEARWATER that June afternoon in 1996. Tom, who was supposed to meet me at the airport, was nowhere to be seen. I had no money, no phone number for him or anyone else, and I was starting to get really worried. There I was at Tampa International Airport without a backup plan. When Tom finally arrived an hour later, he looked happy enough to see me, but somewhat distracted. He apologized, saying he had gotten the arrival time wrong. He thought the flight landed an hour later than it did.

During the ride to the base, he seemed in a hurry and a bit preoccupied, although he was still nice. When we got to the Hacienda, he drove right by Mom's condo, where I thought I would be staying, and pulled up in front of the H-block, where the CMO dormitories were. I was not sure what was happening at first.

"I don't get to live over in L-block?" I asked, confused.

He laughed and said, "No, that is for senior execs from Int."

"Oh," I said, suddenly wondering what I had actually signed up for. The whole time I'd imagined living at Flag; it had never occurred to me that I wouldn't be living in Mom's old apartment. It had never occurred to me that I was going to be in a dorm.

We got out of the car, got my bags out of the trunk, and walked up to the door of apartment H-2 on the ground floor. I remembered this being Valeska's apartment, but even she wasn't there. In fact, Tom told me that she was no longer in the CMO, so she had a different berthing. He offered no explanation, and I didn't ask. He seemed to be in a rush to go somewhere, so he said I should probably unpack my stuff and get some rest, and then he was gone.

The H-block was a dormitory for girls in CMO; most of them were fifteen or sixteen, not twelve, as I was. Apartment H-2 had two bedrooms, with three girls in each one, one bathroom, and a small kitchen. Diane, my old twin from my first Key to Life course, now lived there and was going to be one of my apartment mates. The girls didn't seem to know why I was living in H-2, as I had told them I was only a Cadet, and the Cadets didn't live in CMO berthings. They were supposed to live at the Cadet Org. I said I didn't know why I was there, either. I thought I was going to be at Mom's apartment and had been looking forward to it. Now I was on my own.

I claimed the bathroom for a quick shower; a girl banged on the door five times and shouted at me to hurry up. When I got out, one of the girls was mouthing off at me for taking too long. It seemed pretty harsh for a new place; I just walked away without saying anything. When I went to lie down for a short rest, there were no sheets on my bed. Being too shy to ask, I almost burst into grateful tears when Diane saw that I needed linens and showed me where to get them. I still didn't know where I was supposed to go after this; Tom had told me nothing. Things were not off to a good start, and it was very possible that I had made a huge mistake by coming back to Flag.

I tossed and turned for thirty minutes and finally decided to walk over to Don's place in the H-block to see if he knew the plan for me; he was the only person whose location I knew. He seemed genuinely happy to see me and gave me a hug. He said he had no idea, either, but that he would take me to the WB and that someone there would certainly know. Don drove a white convertible Mustang, a cool car according to my mother, but I didn't know anything about cars.

At the WB, I went straight to Tom's office on the third floor. He greeted me warmly when I came in, then instructed one of his messengers to get me a uniform. I was taken aback when the woman returned with a blue uniform, the type all the Sea Org members wore. I thought I was here for an auditor course and had no idea why I was getting a Sea Org uniform. Before I could ask Tom, his messenger handed me the dark blue pants, light blue collared dress shirt with epaulets, cross-tie with a button snap, and flat black shoes. The name tag read Jenna Miscavige—Trainee, CMO Clearwater, so it became obvious to me there was no mistake with the uniform. I was going to be in the CMO training to be an auditor.

I had always dreamed of being in the Sea Org, and being in the CMO had been my plan for the future, but this had come on so suddenly. Not only that, I had wanted to join mainly so I could work at Int with my parents, friends, and family who were at the base, but now they were three thousand miles away. I was speechless.

The strangest thing about all this was that I knew I hadn't done the steps that were necessary to be in the Sea Org. Specifically, I hadn't done the basic EPF, the Estate Project Force, mandatory for all Sea Org members. The EPF was an introductory ritual for the Sea Org, and everyone who joined was required to do it as their first step to becoming a Sea Org member. The EPF was a rigorous boot camp of sorts, with some physical labor and a few intense courses. Even more baffling, CMO, where I was now going to be a trainee, had its own individual EPF requirement. I hadn't done that one, either. In every way, this was premature.

I changed into my uniform and went back to Tom's office. He laughed at the sight of me, saying, "Little Jenna is all grown up." When I told him how uncomfortable the situation was making me because I had bypassed the two EPFs, he told me not to worry about it, for now I was a Sea Org member. I wasn't sure if I should smile or burst into tears, but Tom didn't seem to notice my anxiety. He instructed me to go to the Coachman Building to start the course.

One of my first courses was called the "Student Hat." I saw several people I knew in the course room, which made me feel somewhat more at home. My first checksheet assignment had me sitting in a chair in front of a wall that had an LRH policy bulletin taped to it. I had to sit and look at LRH's words for one straight hour. If I moved, got tired, coughed, looked away, or fell asleep, the hour would start over. The idea was that I was supposed to learn to be a good student, and that this drill would force me to confront the policies I would have to study in order to achieve that. Several people in the course room had been on this drill for weeks. Because I was the restless type and used to being up and about, I knew it would take me forever, too. Sure enough, I struggled to sit still.

In terms of vocabulary, the entire course was so far over my head that it might as well have been in another language. I had to learn "The Ten Points of Keeping Scientology Working" verbatim, reciting it over and over to a wall and having it verified by another student. I also had to learn the 10 different ways a word could be misunderstood. Beyond that, I listened to twelve tapes of LRH's notoriously dense, wordy lectures filled with technical terminology about photography and printing, and read hundreds of his bulletins. After I had read a series of bulletins, I was put through rigorous testing of my knowledge with what were known as "Theory Drills" and/or "What Do You Do?" drills. This meant another student would ask me a series of questions taken from quotes in the policies. "What do you do?" he might ask. Or, "What are the ten ways in which a word can be misunderstood?"

I would have to respond correctly and without hesitation in order to pass the drill. The shortest one I ever took was twenty-five questions, but they were usually between forty and one hundred questions in length. If you answered a question incorrectly, you would first have to finish the series, then start again from the beginning until you could do a run-through without a single flunk. As was standard for any Scientology course room, we would receive daily meter and spot checks. I would count the seconds until lunchtime, both because I was starving (as I never could get ready in time for the bus from berthing to have enough time before roll call to eat breakfast) and because it was a much-needed break.

I ate lunch at the crew dining room in the newly refurbished Clearwater Bank Building, right across the street from the Coachman Building. I was so happy to see that Valeska worked there. We gave each other a huge hug and caught up. She told me she was no longer allowed to be in CMO, because her mom was speaking out against Scientology, which made her unqualified for the organization. She was now a staff steward, so she was responsible for serving food and cleaning up after the crew.

I was very uncomfortable in the crew dining room. Everyone had an assigned place to sit but me; all of the seats in the CMO section seemed to be taken. Whenever I asked if I could sit in an open spot, the CMO gals would tell me that someone else was there. I was so shy that instead of claiming one of these seats, I would just eat with Valeska and the rest of the galley crew at their table after mealtime was over.

I didn't really fit in with the CMO group. They thought it was strange that I hung out with kitchen staff, so they kind of shunned me. When the course was over at nine-thirty, I caught the bus home and went to Valeska's room, only going to my room to sleep. If I got too scared in the middle of the night, I could still run across the apartment complex to Valeska's room and crawl into bed with her. I had to do my own laundry now, but I had no idea how to do it, since one of the kids at the Ranch was always assigned to that duty. Valeska helped me wash and iron my uniform shirts and showed me how to do it myself. I didn't know what I would have done without her.

After a few weeks, Valeska suddenly disappeared without even saying goodbye. Her departure was so abrupt; I was really worried. I later heard that she had been sent to the *Freewinds*, which would make it much more difficult for her mother to get in touch with her.

Nothing about this return to Flag was panning out as I had envisioned it. My living situation, my routine, my courses, and my friends: none of it fit the picture that I'd created mentally, or the experiences that I'd had in the past. During all three of my previous trips to Flag, my enjoyment had stemmed in no small part from having access to my mom's lifestyle and leisure. Now, suddenly without that, I found myself at a loss, unsure of where I fit in and whether this was even where I wanted to be. In the past, Flag had reinforced my desire to join the Sea Org; now it was making me question if the CMO was what I wanted. Maybe I'd been wrong. I was twelve and making decisions that would impact the rest of my life, and there was no margin for error.

The course work was a source of anxiety because it was over my head. I did anything I could to get away from it. I preferred hiding in the bathroom stall or pretending I needed to look something up in the library.

One day at lunchtime, Aunt Shelly, who had just come into town with Uncle Dave, sought me out in the dining room and told me to come with her to the executive dining room. In the hallway on the way there, she asked what my days were like. I told her that I mostly studied, then hung out with the galley crew during mealtime and in the evening before bed. At that, she seemed appalled, but clearly recognized that I didn't know any better.

"You know, Jenna," she said, shaking her head, "you never should have come to Flag in the first place. From now on, you will be hanging out with CMO and CMO only, going to CMO musters and being a part of that group. CMO staff does not hang out with galley staff."

I took her words to heart. After the meeting, I was also pulled aside by Don's wife, Pilar, who was charged with getting me back on the rails. She told me point-blank that I looked like crap in my uniform, and that I needed to get one that fit. Right after my reprimand, she gave me a few of her own Egyptian cotton shirts, the special ones only for executives. It was a little confusing how she could be so mean one minute and so nice the next. Even though the shirts were hand-me-downs, they were coveted because they were considered to be the best, so I knew how lucky I was to have them. After those two meetings, I started going to CMO musters after each meal, just as Aunt Shelly had ordered. I was assigned a place at one of their tables, taking the pressure off me to find my own seat.

ONE DAY, NOT LONG AFTER I ARRIVED IN CLEARWATER, THE NEWS that Don Jason had "blown" swept through morning muster. Blowing was taking off and deserting the church, a scandalous act equivalent to Scientology treason. Nobody had heard from him, and like those around me, I was completely shocked. He was one of the highest-ranking executives at Flag. I had just spoken to him in his office a couple of days earlier, and he seemed completely normal. He had relayed that my mother wanted him to check on me, which I thought was really nice.

The flap this news created was enormous. It made me want to call Mom, knowing she and Don had been friends, but I didn't have permission to use the phones at the base. The phone system at Flag required a special code, which I didn't know, so I had been using my own system when I wanted to call home: I'd sneak into Tom and Jenny's apartment to use theirs while they were still at work in the evenings. I'd ask a Sea Org member who was in charge of the berthing for the master key, then let myself into their apartment. He trusted me because he knew me from my previous visits to Flag, having seen me with Mom, Sharni, and Valeska. He also knew I was in the CMO, so he thought that I was using the key for something like the laundry. Tom had once said offhandedly that I could use his phone any time and I knew I was really stretching this, but I didn't know what else to do.

The night we heard about Don's blowing, I sneaked into Tom's apartment and phoned California, reaching Mom through the RTC Reception. I only told her I desperately wanted to come home. She seemed to already know about Don. I told her how sad I was at Flag, and that I was unprepared to be in CMO. Mom was surprisingly sympathetic and said she would book a flight for me to come back to California at her first opportunity.

Two days later, on Wednesday, I got word from Mom that a flight had been arranged, so I packed and got ready to go. I sneaked into the galley, and with help from my friend, who was a galley cook, we made a special cake for me to bring to Mom. I had already said goodbye to my other steward friends and was waiting in the kitchen for either Tom or someone else to pick me up and take me to the airport when my friend's phone rang.

She looked a bit worried as she handed it to me. I instantly recognized the voice of Mr. Sondra Phillips, a high-ranking officer in CMO. She said I needed to come over to the WB immediately. When I explained to her that I was about to go to the airport to catch a flight back to California, she said there had been a change of plans, and I was to get over there right now.

Annoyed and worried, I dragged all of my bags down the block to the WB, went upstairs, and found Mr. Phillips, who took me into a small office and shut the door behind us. With her face bright red, she started screaming at me at the top of her lungs, spraying spittle in my face. I couldn't even believe this was happening. She yelled that I was unethical, or "out-ethics," as they said a horrible student, individuated from the rest of the group, and not abiding by the rules. She ended by saying there was no way I was going home, and that I needed to toughen up, because I was a Sea Org member now.

All of this had come out of nowhere. Just when I was about to give her a piece of my mind, Tom's wife, Jenny, came in and told Mr. Phillips to get out, that she was going to handle this. Jenny had been promoted to Commanding Officer of CMO Clearwater, and I was sure she was going to sort everything out. She would undoubtedly help me to get to my flight.

Instead, to my horror Jenny also told me I was staying and I could tell she meant it.

"Why?" I asked her, completely stunned.

"You just are," she said dismissively. "You came here to become an auditor, and so we are going to train you to be one."

I tried to protest, but she shushed me and proceeded to read me a quote from LRH's policy titled "Keeping Scientology Working."

"When somebody enrolls, consider he or she has joined up for the duration of the universe—never permit an 'open-minded' approach. If they're going to quit let them quit fast. If they're enrolled, they're aboard, and if they're aboard, they're here on the same terms as the rest of us—win or die in the attempt. . . . We'd rather have you dead than incapable. . . . The whole agonized future of this planet, every man, woman and child on it, and your own destiny for the next endless trillions of years depends on what you do here and now with and in Scientology. . ."

As dramatic as this sounds now, at that moment, I really believed that the future of the planet rested on my twelve-year-shoulders. Much as I wanted to protest, there was no arguing with her words. Begrudgingly I accepted, and my fate was sealed. I was not going home to see Mom. I was stuck here.

Chapter Fifteen

MOM

THE SUDDEN CHANGE OF PLAN THAT HAD ME STAYING IN CLEARwater was frustrating, but more upsetting was the fact that, in the days that followed, I couldn't get in touch with my mother. In the evenings, I'd use the master key to get into Tom and Jenny's apartment to try to call her at the RTC, but whoever answered the phone would say she was unavailable. Despite my asking when I might be able to reach her, the answers were always vague and unhelpful. Finally, my father called me. He told me I needed to stop calling the RTC Reception to reach Mom. When I asked him why, he said it was because she was on a special project that was keeping her busy. Even he wouldn't say what she was doing.

I was beginning to worry that all of the secrecy meant that she had been sent to RPF, Rehabilitation Project Force. The worst punishment the church dealt out, RPF was a type of reprogramming to bring people back in line. Often, they went to a segregated location on the base, usually for at least two years, but it depended on how fast they did their rehabilitation program. I couldn't imagine why she would have been sent to RPF; after all, Uncle Dave had recently promoted her to Lieutenant Commander and praised her in front of everyone at Sea Org Day. Still, she'd never been so inaccessible. I struggled to think of another reason for her absence.

The day after I spoke to Dad, an RTC Rep named Sophia Townsend pulled me out of my course room. When someone from RTC came for you, it was almost never a good thing. RTC was the most senior organization in the church hierarchy and played a huge role in enforcement of rules and standard application of LRH policy. Mr. Townsend took me into a room upstairs for what she called a "quick session" with me. When I asked her what she meant by a quick session, she said, in a very unfriendly tone, I'd have to wait and see.

She did the usual procedure of asking if I was tired or hungry, and if there was any reason not to start the session. I responded "no" to all the questions.

"This is the session!" she half yelled, staring.

She asked me several questions that were standard at the beginning of every session and pertained to whether I was upset or had my attention elsewhere. After a brief discussion of what was on my mind, namely everything going on with my mom, she moved on to the heart of the matter and the reason we were having a session in the first place.

"Has a withhold been missed?" she asked me. She was trying to uncover whether I had done anything bad that I didn't want people to find out about. After confirming with the E-Meter, she looked at me expectantly.

"No," I said, as this seemed like a reasonable response.

Mr. Townsend didn't like that answer. I tried to think of minor withholds I was guilty of, like the fact that I was using Tom's phone to call home without telling him. But I didn't want to tell Mr. Townsend that one, because she would tell Tom, and I would no longer be able to make calls from his place.

"No," I said again. Apparently the needle still indicated I was lying. For a third time, Mr. Townsend asked me about a "Missed Withhold"; again, my response was "No." I could tell she was getting really annoyed.

"Okay," she said, "have you robbed a bank?"

"What!" I asked in disbelief. "No! How in the world would I do that?!"

"Okay, did you kill somebody?"

The questions were preposterous. "Are you serious right now?" I asked.

"Yes, I am," she said with a hint of annoyance, even as she delivered the next question. "Did you have sex with your father?"

"What are you even talking about?!" I yelled back.

"Well, let's take a look, because you have something here."

"No, I don't," I insisted, adding I couldn't believe she would think that I could do any of these things.

Mr. Townsend wasn't quite done. "I will repeat the question, has a withhold been missed?" she said robotically.

It went on like this for hours—an interrogation for something, but for what I had no idea. I couldn't understand why this was happening or what it was all about. Did it have something to do with my mom? What did I do wrong? Finally, when it was clear that we weren't getting anywhere, I simply refused to talk to her. She said we were ending the session, so she could turn me over to "Ethics" for "no report," failing to answer questions that the E-Meter determined I knew the answer to.

"Fine," I said, relieved to be out of the room, but also aware that I was in big trouble. I next went to the examiner, protocol after every E-Meter session.

"Thank you very much, your needle is floating," he told me, as he always did. A floating needle was supposed to indicate that you were happy and relieved, but nothing could have been further from the truth—I'd never felt so on edge. Mr. Townsend told me to wait in the auditing room until someone from the Ethics Department could pick me up.

From there, I was escorted to the WB while being given a scolding for not cooperating with Mr. Townsend. Soon we arrived at the WB, where, in a few minutes, I was met by another more senior RTC Rep, Anne Rathbun. I knew her because she had worked in Uncle Dave's office for several years and was married to Marty Rathbun, Uncle Dave's top lieutenant. She told me that Mr. Townsend's session had been too harsh, and another auditor was going to administer a new session.

The next auditor, Mr. Angie Trent, also an RTC Rep, was much friendlier. She asked a series of questions from a prepared list, and if the E-Meter responded, she looked at me for answers. This session went much better. When it was over, she promised she would help me get some information about my mom's whereabouts.

Difficult as it was, I tried to settle back into my courses. Providing some comfort was the fact that I had a familiar face to help me. Claire Headley had been one of my supervisors at Int when Justin and I had been twinning, and even though I'd struggled, she had always been upbeat and encouraging. She was older, but soon we had become good friends. Since then, she had been promoted to RTC, had come to Flag as part of the team to enforce the new Golden Age of Tech, and was now referred to as Mr. Headley. Despite our friendship, I had to call her "sir," because she was now an RTC Rep who was to be respected and feared.

Still, she helped to get me back on track in my studies and calm me down. As weeks went by without news from my mom, Mr. Headley assured me she was really working to get information for me. One Saturday morning during "Clean Ship Project," the time allotted to clean our dorms, Mr. Headley came to my room and told me that she and I were going to take a flight that morning back to Int to find out what was happening with my mother. I was shocked but happy. Mr. Headley was going to have a chance to see her husband at Int, so she was excited, too, as they had been separated when she was sent to Flag as part of the RTC Rep team.

We flew to L.A. and drove to the base. Mr. Headley delivered me to my parents' apartment and left as soon as Dad walked in, giving us some privacy.

"How are you doing?" he asked, as he reached over to hug me.

I tried to maintain my composure but as I opened my mouth to respond, I felt the tears start to stream down my face. A jumble of thoughts and emotions poured out of me, as I told him how worried I was about Mom and how I still hadn't been able to reach her. I also shared my horrible session administered by Mr. Townsend.

"I'm sorry about that," he said, looking me in the eyes. "But what happened with Mr. Townsend was a standard procedure in a situation like this, uncomfortable but necessary."

I pulled back, irritated that he took her side but also confused: standard procedure for what? Before I had time to turn the question over I got my answer.

"Your mom has been having an out 2D," he said matter-of-factly. Essentially, this meant she was having an affair. As shocked as I was, I realized that this had been my fear all along. This was why I'd been afraid she was on RPF and why I'd become so upset about not being able to speak with her. This was why Mr. Townsend had been checking me for a withhold—to make sure I hadn't known anything about Mom's behavior.

"With who?" I asked.

"Who do you think?"

"Probably Don."

"Yep, that's right," Dad said. "Did you know this was happening?" The way he asked the question made me think he was accusing me of conspiring. I thought back to my session with

Mr. Townsend and how intensely she'd checked me for a with-hold. Only now, I could see that she'd been making sure I didn't know anything about my mom's behavior.

"No," I responded, "but they were really close, so it made sense to guess him."

Even to me, it had been obvious that they were more than friends. But I had no idea it had gone this far.

I had a mental panic about the consequences for Mom. Those who went "out 2D" were looked upon as the worst of the worst. My mother was someone whom I had always looked up to. Despite what others undoubtedly thought about her now, I knew she had done many good things for the Church and was still very capable. I wasn't about to forget that. But knowing she had done something as blatantly forbidden as out 2D made it difficult to rationalize.

I purposely blocked as many feelings as I could. I separated myself from my emotions and tried to act completely logically, and do what was right and necessary, not just react. Here was a situation where my TR Bullbait training became particularly useful. It had taught me how to suppress my feelings and react not emotionally but rationally. I had to disconnect my mind from my feelings. Even in regular situations, something way less significant than learning your mother has been having an affair, if you reacted or got upset, other people would tell you to get your TRs in. If you got into an argument or got upset, you were told to use your TRs to keep cool. With my father's news, I used my TRs to disconnect. At that moment, the approach was helpful.

While I attempted to keep my feelings in check, Dad proved unable to control his and started tearing up. He told me that he felt like the last two years of their marriage had been a lie, and that Uncle Dave had been nice enough to pull him aside to tell him about the affair himself. I gave him a sympathetic hug, as it seemed the right thing to do.

"Where is Mom?" I asked, knowing well that policy stated an out 2D resulted in getting "beached." The policy, written when the Sea Org was still on the ship, meant that the transgressor would be left on a beach. Now the person being punished usually went to the RPF.

Dad confirmed this was the case, "She's on the RPF, where she should be," he said without much warmth.

"Is she doing okay?" He seemed shocked by the question, as if it didn't matter.

"I think so, but her well-being hasn't exactly been my concern. She completely betrayed me," he told me. "But, don't worry. In the RPF, they get meals and have a place to sleep, so I'm sure she'll be fine."

I had always been a compassionate person who felt for people when they got in trouble, even if it was of their own doing. It only made me feel worse knowing that wherever she was, she was likely being treated very poorly, without any of the importance or amenities to which she was accustomed. Dad, however, and somewhat understandably, seemed to think she deserved it. He must have put out of his mind that their relationship had begun with their committing an out 2D before they were married.

Dad told me he was in the process of going through Mom's possessions and packing them to send them to storage, as she wouldn't be needing them again, and asked me if I wanted to help. People sent to the RPF usually spent years there. Even two years was considered a short stay. As we started going through her closet, Dad would hold up a piece of clothing and say, "Do you want this? She'll never need *that* again," insinuating that she was going to be gone for a long time.

It was hard to know how I should react to all this. If I were following Scientology, the proper response would have been to hate her immediately, not because she'd jeopardized our family but because she'd broken Scientology rules. What worried me, though, was that I didn't hate her; sure, I was upset with her, but I didn't *hate* her; in fact, I still loved her. I knew that this wasn't the proper feeling to have, so I kept my feelings to myself.

My silence didn't stop Dad from asking why I wasn't crying. He told me that Uncle Dave asked him how I would respond to the news, and Dad had told him that I would go apeshit. It annoyed me that he thought he knew me well enough to make such an assumption. Also, telling this to my uncle and making me sound like some sort of child, when in fact I was a Sea Org member now, just as he was, irritated me equally.

After an hour of going through Mom's belongings, Dad had to return to work, at which point Mr. Headley came back, giving me a hug and telling how sorry she was. Her sympathy made me tear up a little, as I felt as though she really cared.

A few minutes later, Aunt Shelly opened the door.

"Hey, I heard you took the news like a champ!" she said. "Good for you!" She gave me a hug, and we walked outside to talk.

"Your mom is okay, and she's going to be okay," Shelly told me. "She always claimed to be the strongest woman on the base, so she will be fine with the MEST work they have to do on the RPF."

When I told Aunt Shelly that I was worried about my mom and that I didn't want her to be sad, she became much less complimentary.

"Did you know," Shelly continued, "that the reason your mom wanted to send you back to Flag for your auditing classes was that she was looking for a way to stay in touch with Don?" Those words landed hard. I didn't know if they were true, or just an exaggeration on Aunt Shelly's part. While I was still stomaching that news, wondering whether it was true, Shelly tried to explain why the RPF was the right place for my mom, stating that she had a history of this, and making it clear that she strongly disapproved of my mother's behavior.

Aunt Shelly and I also talked about my future. She said she

was excited about me becoming a messenger, because she wanted me to get through my training so I could come back and work at Int. I loved that she envisioned me working where I had always dreamed I would be. We talked for an hour or two. She told me stories of growing up and working for LRH and what it had meant to her to be a messenger for him at the age of nine. Our time together ended and we hugged and said goodbye.

For the next couple of days, I spent time with Mr. Headley at Int. She took me around the base and showed me all the cool things that had been happening since I left. The Int Base was spread out over five hundred acres. It had been a resort before the church purchased it in 1978, and still had a huge man-made lake, a castle, and an irrigation system that kept everything lush and green in the hot California desert. The entire property was surrounded by razor wire and hundreds of security cameras, some hidden but many in plain view. The recently added structure Mr. Headley showed me was a mansion called Bonne View. It had been built for the day LRH returned and was ready for occupancy. "Like in another body?" I asked her, wondering how and when he would be returning.

"I guess so," she replied, not seeming sure of the details, either.

We were given a tour of Bonne View's interior by Stacy Moxon, a member of the household unit. This small section of CMO was on standby to take care of LRH's personal needs the moment he came back. The house was gorgeous, with brick walls and fireplaces, was surrounded by elaborate landscaping. It was by far the nicest building on the base.

Taking in the full scope of Int was eye-opening, but I quickly grew tired of being there, reminded of the news of my mother's indiscretion and my father's grief. A few days before, I'd wanted nothing more than to escape to Flag; now, after everything that had happened, I was relieved when it was time for Mr. Headley and me to return to Clearwater. It didn't matter to me what was going on in Clearwater or what my complaints had been with the CMO; I just wanted to leave Int and all those problems behind.

Nonetheless, Dad insisted I return to California for Christmas; I did so reluctantly, staying at the Ranch for most of the week. At first, I was annoyed with staying at the Cadet Org because I was supposed to be a Sea Org member, but my dad didn't view me that way. But after a while, being there made me long for my days before the CMO. I felt a connection to my friends at the Ranch. They were the people who really knew me. I had grown up with them, and they implicitly understood who I was.

At the annual Christmas Beer & Cheese Party, I was with some of my Ranch friends when Dad came up to me and quietly pulled me aside.

"Uncle Dave wants to see you," he said, his voice brimming with urgency. "He is in the billiards room."

I nervously found my way across the dining hall to Uncle Dave's private room. When I arrived he started asking me questions about how I was doing, not really seeming to listen to the answers. After few moments he apologized.

"I'm sorry, Jenny, for being so distracted. But I wanted to talk to you about something important." He let a pause pass between us as though he wanted to see how I'd react to his words. As they settled into the air, he continued, "Your mother has been asking me to see you."

I was a bit surprised, as I hadn't heard anything from her in months. But when my dad said Uncle Dave wanted to speak to me, I figured it was somehow related to my mom. Uncle Dave seemed to be the only one who had access to her. Even though I was not angry with her, I could not get over the awkwardness that I would have to endure by listening to her confession about her affair with Don if I saw her.

Turning over Uncle Dave's words, the truth was that I didn't want to see her. It wasn't because I knew that's what Uncle Dave wanted to hear, but because I didn't want to have to see her and talk about everything. I didn't want to sit around, rehash what she had done, and have to confront all the confusing feelings that this conversation would inevitably produce. I wasn't mad at her; I just wanted to avoid the emotion of the situation, as I'd been taught. I wanted things to be normal.

"I honestly don't really want to see her," I said to him. "I hope she's well, and I want her to just get through the program. Once she's done with the program, we can put this whole ordeal behind us. And none of us will ever have to think about it again."

"You're right, Jenny," Uncle Dave said, seeming relieved. "She does need to get through the program—that will be best for her. Maybe hearing that you think so will motivate her. At this point, she hasn't been cooperating."

I wasn't surprised that she wasn't cooperating. On one hand, she was a senior level executive who'd risen through the ranks and knew that following orders was the easiest path; on the other, she was a tough, often headstrong woman. The question was how far she'd be willing to go in her resistance. She knew as well as anyone that there were few alternatives. The only options were completing the RPF or leaving the Sea Org for good.

"I want you to write her a letter," Uncle Dave instructed, "so that she can see that this refusal is coming from you and not me."

He gave me some paper and I started with, "*Dear Mom . . . ,*" but I didn't know what else to write. Uncle Dave gave me some suggestions, but he didn't want the letter to sound like it was from him. In the end, I kept the correspondence short, telling her that I still loved her, but I just wanted her to get through her program, as that would be best for both of us.

"Thank you, Jenny," Uncle Dave said with a smile when I'd finished writing, "I'll make sure she gets this."

The day before Christmas I became extremely ill, and wound

up spending Christmas day in bed. I had a high fever, swollen glands, and vertigo. Dad came to visit me and brought me a packet of Emergen-C and some cough drops. He even brought me an enema bag, telling me that Aunt Shelly said it was a good idea. I thought it was disgusting and told him as much.

The day after Christmas, Dad said I was booked to fly back to Clearwater. He wanted me to come to the base to say goodbye to Uncle Dave and Aunt Shelly, even though I was still sick. We waited in the reception area of their office for a long time until they came out to meet us. Uncle Dave hadn't known about my illness, so there was a bit of an uproar about the possibility of his getting sick. With that, he hurried back into his office, and only Aunt Shelly said goodbye, but not before insisting that my flight be rebooked for a few days later, so that I had time to get better.

CHAPTER SIXTEEN

ON THE EPF

NINETEEN NINETY-SEVEN BEGAN WITH ME RETURNING TO FLAG just shy of my thirteenth birthday and determined to forget about the previous months. For the first time, I didn't want to see either of my parents; I just wanted to push through my duties at the CMO and find my place.

Of course, that was easier said than done. It was hard to simply put aside what had happened. I knew that it was best for me to separate myself from my emotions, but I couldn't bring myself to do it completely. Rationally, I still found myself worrying for my mom and hoping that she was being taken care of—I couldn't force myself to detach completely like a good Scientologist would. While I should have been able to block it all out, somehow the past always managed to force its way in. And it might have stayed that way had it not been for a bright spot that helped get me through this and refocus my energy on the Sea Org.

More than ever before, I found myself relying on the weekly graduation ceremonies at Flag to inspire me and keep my spirits high. Whereas, when I was younger, I was simply caught up in the spectacle of these events, I now found myself paying more attention to the words that were spoken and the stories of what Scientology could accomplish.

I was particularly drawn in by the wins that graduates would speak of every week. Wins were the big reveals, the prizes at the end that kept people coming back for more, and I was no different. These testimonials always demonstrated the power of Scientology, providing everyone with a clear sense of the potential that it could unlock. It was almost like I needed something to throw myself into at this vulnerable time, to get my mind off of things and focus on something positive. The wins came in all shapes and sizes. People would talk about how, at first, they were unsure if they could afford the fees for the courses, but, by the time they were done with the classes, they had turned their companies around and become so successful that they were now earning ten times their previous income. Other people would say that they were so *exterior*, meaning outside of their bodies, that when they got up after an auditing session, they'd realize their body was still in the chair. At one point, I witnessed actress Juliette Lewis sharing her wins after achieving the state of Clear, and although I don't remember what she shared, the fact that celebrities like her endorsed Scientology impressed everyone, myself included.

No matter who it was sharing, though, the wins always got everyone motivated. The more wins you shared, the more you were telling other people that it worked for you, and the more invested you became, making it harder to turn back on that investment. It was hard to listen to these stirring, emotional stories of transformation and not feel that Scientology had the power to change lives and change the world.

Riding this wave of excitement, I started to take the auditing courses, for which I'd come to Flag. With me in CMO and in the course room was a girl my age, Luisa; we became fast friends. Her family was from Denmark, and while her dad had also been posted at Int, she had been raised in L.A., first at the PAC Ranch at the L.A. Cadet Org. Luisa was painfully shy but with a good sense of humor, and I could tell right away that she was trustworthy.

Luisa and I tried to be serious in the course room, but sometimes we'd let loose. We would often find ways to escape to the bathroom, where we'd have a toilet paper war between our two stalls. Other times, we'd chase each other up and down the stairs. We lived in the same dorm, so before bed or during meals, she'd tell me stories about growing up on the PAC Ranch, which made it seem that those Cadets did less work than we did. Still, listening to her stories, I learned that they too were treated badly, perhaps even worse than we had been at the Ranch.

The new course I was on was Professional TRs. The training routines I was going to be tackling now were the "Pro TRs," and though there were some similarities with the TRs I'd done at the Ranch years earlier, these were much more rigorous. I needed to do them to become an auditor. After several days of reading the policies and theory behind the TRs, and watching films and listening to LRH lectures on tape, I moved on to the practical section of the course: the TRs themselves. From the start, they were grueling. I focused on just getting through them as best I could. The way out was the way through.

I had to be able to sit comfortably in a chair in front of another student for two straight hours without speaking, moving, twitching, coughing, or blinking excessively. Many people, including me, stayed on this training routine for weeks. At one point, I had been motionless for ninety minutes when a fly landed on my nose. I blew it away with my lips, which caused me to flunk, and I had to start over again. It was excruciating, several times bringing me to tears. I found it almost impossible not to move. My legs felt like they were going to walk away on their own, and it took everything I had to stay still.

The TR Bullbait was much worse than the kids' version. We had to endure two hours of being yelled at, made fun of, and even sexually taunted. One of the supervisors specialized in creeping people out, saying suggestive things to which we weren't allowed to react. A good friend of mine, who was also thirteen, was being bullbaited by a male student, who went on and on for hours about her blooming breasts being like tiny rosebuds. She had succeeded in not reacting, but the whole thing had disgusted me.

When we were done with the Pro TR course, we moved to the Upper Indoctrination TRs. Here we learned about Tone 40, which was a state of mind at which point you were absolutely 100 percent positive in your thought, with no room for opposition or anticipation. LRH believed that all humans could be put on a scale according to their emotional state. The Tone Scale began at −40, defined as total failure, at the bottom of the scale, and ended at +40, the serenity of beingness.

The tone scale applied to your tone of voice, delivery and emotional state. A Tone 40 delivery was so powerful and precise that the person getting the command would follow the order no matter what. My twin and I took turns practicing our Tone 40 deliveries in the routines that were laid out in LRH policies. We'd sit at a wall and say a command to our twin, who then had to follow that command. Each command was always followed by a thank-you.

"Look at that wall, thank you."

"Walk over to that wall, thank you."

"Touch that wall, thank you."

"Turn around, thank you."

It continued like this for hours.

The next exercise was geared toward helping us control the people we were auditing. As auditors, we would have to use any means necessary to prevent the pre-Clears from leaving a session before it was over. Our job was to keep them in place until we had given them permission to leave; this exercise taught us to do that both physically and verbally. I'd always heard that this was the most fun. You used the same patter: "Walk over to that wall, thank you." This time, however, your twin would do everything physically possible to disobey, running away, pulling away, shouting, refusing to move, anything. You had to physically force them to follow your command in order to succeed.

I twinned with my burly friend Buster on some of these exercises. Because he was so large, it was more of a challenge. As it was with all others who did this routine, if I wanted him to look at the wall, I had to pry open his eyes and twist his head. Getting your coach over to the wall was the hardest part, since you had to drag, push, or even carry him. To top it off, you would be bullbaited the entire time, so you couldn't laugh or get upset. You passed when you could get your twin to comply with the commands, regardless of any physical and verbal obstacles.

Next, we had to yell at square glass ashtrays at the top of our lungs. The idea was to train ourselves to express absolutely clear intentions, and by mastering this, we'd be able to guide our future pre-Clears to successfully confront things.

And it didn't end there. Directing our intentions into particular parts of the ashtray, we'd ask our ashtray very specific questions. The belief was that whenever you asked a question, you had the intention of getting that question answered, as you should when you asked a question of a pre-Clear in session. The ashtray was required to be square; we were to direct questions into each of its four corners.

"Are you an ashtray?"

"Are you a corner?"

"Are you made of glass?"

The same principles that we were trying to learn and understand as auditors were the principles that prevented us from questioning these ridiculous tasks. We'd been trained to follow instructions, just as we were now learning how to make others follow ours.

Outlandish as all these tasks were, none of them ever struck me as odd, but remembering the scene now, they were. We'd stand there for hours, next to our twin, packed into a room full of other twins, each pair doing a different part of the course. Some would be barking orders to go to the wall, while others sat silently, as they stared deeply into each other's eyes. In another part of the room, someone would be yelling insults as part of a Bullbait session, at the same time that someone a few feet away was screaming instructions to an ashtray.

All these courses were supposed to be about training auditors to be smooth with their communication and less distracting to pre-Clears in session, but the result was that it made all of us more robotic. It automated our responses, turning everything we said into a script. Furthermore, the exercises themselves encouraged us to see the people we were auditing not as people with feelings but as reactive minds that needed to be bent to the will of the auditing session for their own good. The dialogue was designed to dehumanize; the fact that we spent time practicing on an ashtray only emphasized that. The Tone 40 commands in particular were about getting people to follow orders without questioning.

With courses like these, it was often hard to tell what real progress looked like. Sometimes I'd work hard to follow the instructions but only have frustration to show for it; other times, I was rewarded with success. There wasn't much consistency, and it could be difficult to get a definitive sense of what improvement was. Even if you were a natural at something, it seemed like they would keep you in place just to make you put in the time. Much of it seemed subject to the whims of the course supervisor, but no one thought much of it as long as we moved up in the TR levels.

The training was hard work, but being an auditor was a glorified position, and I wanted to prove that I could do it. In the back of my mind were Aunt Shelly's words about the importance of being a good auditor. She'd always told me the best messengers were auditors, and while I was at Flag, she continued to encourage my training. I saw her every few months when she came to town; she would speak to me for at least an hour, always pushing me, saying I could do it, reminding me that auditors were the only ones who could save people.

When I wasn't taking my auditor classes, I worked a few hours a day in the CMO department responsible for making sure people were ethical. People who worked in this department wielded a lot of power. They had the authority to be the enforcers, and they used their power to make sure people towed the line. Because I was training to do this job at CMO Int, this job was good practice, although I didn't have to dole out punishments.

As it turned out, I knew my co-workers, Olivia and Julia, through Valeska. Because of her, I had been friendly with them even though they were at least three years older than I, and was glad they were in CMO and in my department, because now I could fraternize with them without getting in trouble. They were both really nice and very pretty. Apparently, my uncle had been impressed with their abilities and had promoted them both.

One of my duties was to give the mail that had been sent from relatives of people in the CMO to Olivia and Julia, who served as the screeners. In CMO, they had passed around a slip that we were required to sign, allowing our mail to be opened and inspected. Every piece of mail had to be read before it was distributed. If there was any sign of anti-Scientology sentiment, the letter was not passed on.

JUST AS I WAS SETTLING INTO A ROUTINE WITH MY AUDITOR TRAINing at Flag, the fact that I had not completed all the prerequisites to be a Sea Org trainee began to nag at me. Though I'd raised the issue with Tom when I'd first arrived at Flag that I hadn't done the Sea Org's boot camp (known as EPF), he had told me not to worry. I tried to put it out of my mind, but I felt like I was just a Cadet dressed up as a Sea Org member, and I wanted to be a real member.

Concerned, I wrote a letter to Aunt Shelly. In the letter, I told her I hadn't done the EPF and thought I should have. A week or so later, I was called to the office of Mr. Sue Gentry, the head RTC Rep at Flag. When I arrived, she handed me a letter Aunt Shelly had written me. In it, she scolded me about not wanting to do the boot camp, saying that everyone had to do EPF, even senior executives, and I was no exception. Clearly, she had misread my letter to her and thought that I was trying to get out of my obligation rather than trying to fulfill it.

Apparently, Aunt Shelly had instructed Mr. Gentry to make sure my complaining was addressed, so Mr. Gentry said I was going to do a little cleanup. I was nervous when another RTC Rep, Mr. Wilson, came in and told me we were going to have a session immediately.

He began with the two standard questions, was I tired and was I hungry? I was prepared for what always came next, the booming Tone 40 command, "This is the session!" Instead, I heard him say, "I am not auditing you." My stomach dropped. This indicated that I was not receiving auditing, but rather a security check: in other words, a confessional. Unlike auditing sessions, your confessions were not confidential and could be used against you for disciplinary actions.

My confessional stretched out over several weeks. I was asked everything from had I stolen anything, to had I done anything unethical on the Second Dynamic, to had I done anything I didn't want my parents to find out about. The interrogation procedure still relied on the needle readings of the E-Meter. If my E-Meter didn't show a floating needle, my auditor asked variations of the question until the needle gave either a negative or an affirmative. The E-Meter's answer always trumped your own. If the meter said "yes," the answer was yes, even if yours had been "no." If your needle was dirty, it meant you hadn't revealed everything. On every transgression you gave up, you had to tell when and where, an extremely detailed what, how you justified it, and who almost found out. As with auditing sessions, each security check session ended with a trip to the Examiner. If your needle didn't float, you would be required to go right back into session to find out what was missed.

What made all this particularly arduous was not just the invasive nature of the questions, but how relentless the people asking them always were. They wouldn't ask you a question once and be done with it; they'd ask the same questions over and over, your fear mounting each time that the meter would contradict your words. They were like detectives investigating a murder, and once the meter gave them the reading they were looking for, you were guilty.

While this questioning itself was stressful, the real impact was something much more deeply psychological and unsettling: the repeated nature of the questions made you doubt yourself in ways that were hard to describe, especially when the E-Meter indicated that you did have an answer to the question. At first, you would know the answer, but, as they asked the same question over and over again, with increasing levels of intensity, suddenly you'd start to doubt yourself. These were confessions for things that you knew for a fact had never happened, and yet after hearing the same question for long enough, you'd start to think that maybe your answer was wrong. Maybe you had done this in some alternate universe and somehow didn't know about it. Maybe you were withholding something.

Every question was a conflict of interest—if you admitted to doing something wrong you would be punished, but if you told the truth and the meter questioned your answer, you'd get asked the question over and over again, until you gave the answer that they were looking for. So many times I'd end a session not having done any of the things I'd admitted to, just because it was the only way to make it end. Mostly, though, I just prayed for my needle to float.

When Mr. Wilson was finally finished, he wrote up a "Knowledge Report" of anything that had come up in my sessions. He turned this over to "Ethics," and I had to address each transgression and prove that I was now taking responsibility for it by correcting it or making the necessary amends. Once that was completed, Mr. Gentry informed me that I would be starting the Sea Org EPF the next day.

Everybody did the EPF at his or her own pace. Some people took two or three weeks; others could be on the program for months. It all depended on how long it took people to get through their life history, various security checks, and required courses. The required courses all had to do with the history, structure, and attitude of a Sea Org member. They included such courses as "Welcome to the Sea Org," "Introduction to Scientology Ethics," "Personal Grooming," and "Basic Sea Org Member Hat." We also listened to various LRH tapes and learned our code and purpose: "The basic purpose of the Sea Org is to get 'in-ethics' on this planet and universe."

For EPF, I was moved into a different dorm in the Hacienda with twelve other girls, who were also just joining the Sea Org. Every morning we woke up early, donned blue shorts, blue T-shirts, and boots, and did military close-order drills. None of these bothered me, because I was already accustomed to them from the Ranch.

Next, we took the bus into the Flag base, where we were assigned to clean the various restaurants and hotel rooms in Fort Harrison and the Hubbard Guidance Center, where the public Scientologists received their auditing. We had fifteen minutes for breakfast; then we had to bus and clean the entire dining room after hundreds of staff and public had eaten there before us. After this was completed, we had study time followed by cleaning everything from stairwells to galley floors to any public spaces that needed attention.

There were about twenty people on the EPF with me, and nobody was over the age of eighteen. One small boy was only nine. He had come with his mother to Flag to take services. He wound up being recruited into the Sea Org, much like everybody else on the EPF. There was always a huge recruitment drive, and there was always at least one person recruited each week.

Our taskmaster, Dave Englehart, played the roll of drill sergeant. He was a longtime Sea Org member who had worked with LRH. He had a reputation for being tough and ruthless with a touch of crazy, and he lived up to every word. He would take us out on a sailboat to give us the whole Sea Org experience, but, while he was supposed to be teaching us to sail, instead he'd just shout out random commands at the top of his lungs, then get angry that we didn't know how to sail a boat. At uniform inspections, he would sniff the air and say, "Someone here stinks!" We would all look dumbfounded, but he'd scream out in a rage, "What is that smell?" One time, he dove down to the ground and pulled a Russian guy's foot, causing him to fall over. "It's you, you fucking pig!" he fumed. "Go wash your goddamn feet, and don't you ever, ever come to one of my musters smelling like shit again!"

Even though I was only thirteen, I had to fill out a "Life History," a form that asked a lot of personal questions, many of them very adult oriented. I was asked to provide my name, birthplace, Social Security number, other ID numbers, credit cards, and bank accounts, as well as their numbers and expiration dates. I also had to fill in the names of all my relatives and how they felt about Scientology, and if I had ever been connected to someone who was critical of the church. There was a space for me to list what Scientology courses I had done, as well as any auditing I had received;

whether I had ever committed a crime or been in jail; or if I had been part of the government or any type of intelligence organization. I was also supposed to detail every single sexual experience, including masturbating, that I had ever had; if I had ever engaged in anything homosexual in nature; any and all medications I had ever taken; any hospitalizations; illegal or abused drugs; and the dates.

I knew I had to do it, but it was hard to understand why the Church needed this information. The theory of confessionals made sense to me, but this was not standard confessional procedure, and what did my relatives' names have to do with my eligibility? I was too young to have a credit card, but why would they need that info? Even though I had nothing to hide, I felt like the Church was asking me for information just for the sake of having it, almost asking for material they might blackmail me with that served no Scientologic purpose. I felt like I was handing over a piece of myself. I did it anyway, of course, rationalizing that, if I had nothing to hide, I shouldn't have a problem with it.

Once I'd completed EPF for the Sea Org, I had to do the EPF that was just for CMO. The uniform I was given was a pair of dark blue pants paired with a white polo shirt. My day started off with an early morning bus to the WB to clean the executive offices. We had to follow the Basic Sequence for Cleaning a Room, as laid out by LRH, a very thorough cleaning indeed. Our morning studies included a lot of basic courses, including "Keys to Competence," "Basic Cleaning," "Basic Computer," and "Basic Messenger Hat."

This EPF had a lot of cleaning. We would clean the berthings of the CMO executives and RTC Reps, and had to do it perfectly. We also made their beds, turned down their sheets, and left snacks, usually fruit, cheese, and crackers. We would even clean their cars if they asked us to. When all that was done, we did their laundry, following a very precise procedure. We had to iron their clothes using starch, and could not leave train tracks along the seams. We had to steam their pants and polish their shoes and put them away, so that they were ready to wear. Any items that went in drawers were folded impeccably before we stacked them. To complete our CMO EPF, we had to pass our cleaning as well as laundry skills. The execs received vote sheets and graded each of us for our services in housekeeping and laundry.

The laundry room had about twenty washers and dryers for the thousand-plus crew at Flag. Two washers and dryers were dedicated to executives and were not to be used by anyone else, even if those machines were idle. The crew could only do their laundry on Friday night and Saturday morning, which meant there were always huge lines, many people staying up past four in the morning to use a machine at all. The execs could get shirts whenever they needed them, but general crew members only had one or two shirts, which meant they had to hand wash and iron theirs daily.

My friend Luisa and I were often on assignment with our little friend Charlie, the nine-year-old boy who was now on the CMO EPF with us. Charlie was an impish troublemaker who needed constant monitoring. He had an uncanny ability to intend to clean a berthing, and then turn what was already relatively clean into a disaster. One time, we all got in trouble because instead of doing the dishes like he was supposed to, he had shoved them all into the oven, where they sat for several days before an executive found them. Even though our nine-year-old wild card was the one who had hidden the dishes, we all got yelled at.

Though he was a nuisance, it's only in retrospect that I can see Charlie for what he was: a neglected young boy. He was often lost in whatever he was doing. His hair was always unbrushed. He never washed his clothes and probably didn't even know how, so he had giant stains all over his uniform. Once, when he was ordered to go clean his shirt by an executive, we found him five minutes later in the bathroom, trying to clean his shirt in the toilet.

Lost as he may have been, it was easy to get annoyed with him for his unusual behavior; after all, Luisa and I were punished because of it. However, for me, he was as much a curiosity as a source of annoyance. I didn't realize it then, but he was the first child I'd encountered who actually acted like a child. At the Ranch we didn't have kids like him; kids at the Ranch were too busy being little adults. In Charlie, I was witnessing how a kid was supposed to behave at this age. He seemed totally foreign, as though his brain was wired in a way that I'd never encountered, with an absence of logic and unique ignorance of instructions. Never before had I met a child this impulsive, and only now can I see that *I*, not he, was the strange one for expecting him to follow orders.

CHAPTER SEVENTEEN

"HANDLING" FAMILY

WITHIN A COUPLE OF MONTHS, I HAD FINISHED BOTH MY EPFs and was back to studying five hours and working the rest of the day with Olivia and Julia, but, just as I was starting to get comfortable back in the CMO, problems with my family threatened to complicate things once more.

It started with my brother. One day, at lunch, my friend Jessica, who had briefly been with me in my early days at the Ranch, told me she had just seen my brother at the Hacienda. I told her this was impossible, because Justin was in California at the Int Base, so she must have mistaken someone else for him. She said she was sure it was him, and that he was on RPF; like my mother, it seemed he had broken the rules and received the worst punishment in the Church.

The RPF lived, ate, and worked separately from other staff, but we still saw them every now and then when they were doing projects around the base, and, of course, they were always running everywhere they went. They lived at the Hacienda, in separate quarters.

I couldn't believe that Justin was on the RPF. I hadn't seen him since I left California for Flag in June 1996 and had no idea that he had even been in trouble. Why hadn't anyone told me? Later that afternoon, Mr. Wilson came into my office and closed the door, as he had been told I was asking questions about Justin.

"So, you heard about your brother?" he asked. "Well, yes, he is on the RPF, and there is not much more I can say."

My eyes started tearing up. The fact that I now had two family members on RPF was almost too much to take. In the Church's eyes, we were probably becoming a family of criminals, but all I could think was that my family was coming apart at the seams.

"Why are you crying?" Mr. Wilson asked. I tried to find a reason that was not purely emotional, but I couldn't figure out a logical, excusable justification for my emotional display. "This is the Sea Org, and that is just the way things are," Mr. Wilson continued unsympathetically. "I haven't seen my own sister in years. She was an RTC trainee. Now I have no idea where she is. It is nothing to cry about. I haven't even seen my wife in a year and have no idea what is going on with her."

"Yes, sir," I said, trying to contain my emotions. The next day, I received a letter from Aunt Shelly, explaining that Justin was being sent to Flag to do the RPF, and apologizing in advance if I found out before her letter reached me. She seemed sorry to have to be the one to tell me that Justin had supposedly gone out 2D with my friend Eva. He had also "blown," which meant he had taken off from the Int base without permission. Aunt Shelly asked that I not be hard on him, as he had already been through enough.

Once I knew Justin was at Flag on his RPF, I started to see him in passing. On occasion, I was able to give him a hug and talk to him briefly. He would sometimes send me a list of anything he needed, like shampoo, and I would do my best to get it for him. He was only being paid fifteen dollars per week, which made it hard for him to afford the Aveda shampoo he liked, so I'd use some of my twenty-five-dollar weekly pay to cover the difference. Money was tight for me, too, though. There were no meals after five in the afternoon and, by ten-thirty, when I got home, I would be starving, so I always bought myself Frosted Flakes at the canteen, an expense that added up.

I heard through the grapevine that my brother was doing his Purification Rundown while on the RPF. The idea of the Purification Rundown, or "Purif," was that a person could get rid of residual toxins and poisons from chemicals or drugs in his body by intense sauna treatments. The basic routine was to ingest a bunch of minerals and vitamins, run for thirty minutes, then sit in a sauna set at 160 degrees for five hours a day, with occasional breaks. The point was the first step on LRH's Bridge to Total Freedom.

People had supposedly seen Justin in the Purif area in the early morning, and my plan to see him more was to do the Purif, too, even though I had already done it at the Int Base when I was nine. When I'd done it back then, we had to take several thousand milligrams of niacin, an extremely high dose, which was supposed to help dislodge the toxins. Next were the handfuls of vitamins and minerals to replace those lost in sweating. At nine years old, I naturally didn't like swallowing pills, so I'd fake it and hide them in my bag. Then we had to drink a quarter cup of vegetable oil, as this helped to put in the good fat, which then pushed out the bad fat, where the toxins usually resided. This was absolutely vile, and I would gag trying to get it down. Finally, we drank cal mag, but I was used to that.

Before we got in the sauna, we had to run for thirty minutes to get the niacin circulating in our bloodstream. The thirty minutes was way too hard for me, so I'd end up walking most of the time. I'd still get a niacin flush, which was an uncomfortable red prickly rash, then I would sit in the sauna for hours. I was in there with older men, who would be dripping with sweat, but because I was young, I would hardly sweat at all. Whenever I was out of the sauna to cool off for more than a few minutes, a staff person in charge of the Purif would usher me back in, telling me I was taking too many breaks. The Purification Rundown went on like this for a few weeks and, by the end, I was ready for it to be over. My young body wasn't prepared for temperatures like that.

The Purif could be a pain, with all of the vitamins and high temperatures, but you were required to take at least five hours in the sauna where you could chat with the others, read your favorite book, and even play board games, which was much more fun and exciting than being on course. More important, though, it now offered a way for me to see my brother.

I used whatever I could to get on the Purif. I confessed that when I'd done the Purif at the Ranch, I hadn't taken the majority of my vitamins. In addition, I mentioned that I wasn't sure I had achieved the end phenomena and brought up how I'd had a bloody nose after it, which wasn't a good sign that the Purif had been successful. After hearing this, my case supervisor agreed that I could do this next step, and I started almost immediately.

Unfortunately, it was all for naught. Though I had requested it solely in order to see Justin, after a couple of days I found out that RPFers did their Purif at night. My plan had backfired and, as usual, the sauna was too hot for me. I took a lot of breaks or lay on the floor, where it was cooler. The thirty-minute run prior to the sauna was the worst part. Thankfully, Lisa Marie Presley happened to be on the Purif at the same time, so my exercise time would often get cut down. When she was in the gym, nobody else was allowed in. She would run on the treadmill while listening to Madonna.

While I'd never seen Lisa Marie before, like most Scientologists I knew that she was part of the Church. She appeared in many Scientology promotional pieces, and some of her Scientology projects were announced at the church events. The Celebrity Centre even published a magazine that often featured success stories and testimonials from celebrities about their belief. Every celebrity had a code name used on their pre-clear folders to protect their privacy. Lisa Marie was referred to as "Norma" or "Norma Darling." I assumed the celebrities had made-up names so that people wouldn't snoop, or in case their folders ended up in the wrong hands.

On the Purif, Lisa Marie was in one sauna, while five or six of us were in the other. I would sometimes see her in the changing room or pass her in the hallways. She was shy, but friendly. She had seen my name written on something and asked me if I was related to David Miscavige, so I told her I was his niece. From then on, she said hi whenever she walked by.

One afternoon, when I was finished with the sauna I was approached by Anne Rathbun, who was now the Head RTC Rep. She told me that my brother wanted to leave the Sea Org, and she wanted me to help talk him out of it. I agreed to meet with Justin in the security offices, which were in the garage of the Fort Harrison Hotel. Those small rooms were fitted with cameras, where we could be observed while we spoke.

From the start, I felt strange. I tried to convince Justin to stay, but speaking to him and knowing that we were being recorded was awkward. I hadn't spoken to him in nearly two years, and I just wanted to talk to him off the record. But, when we were in those rooms (and even when we were outside them), Justin simply refused to talk to me about the Sea Org. He knew as well as I did that we were being filmed. I could tell he was really troubled, because he was the type of person who always puts on a comedic face, and now he didn't.

I was also confused as to why he was suddenly going by the name Justin Tompkins, rather than Justin Miscavige. Ever since my dad had married my mother when Justin was two, he had gone by Justin Miscavige. I asked Mr. Rathbun if she knew, and she said it was for PR reasons: the Church didn't want people to know that a Miscavige was leaving or on the RPF. Mr. Rathbun told me that I was not to speak about Justin's situation with anyone.

Things only got worse when I learned from the RTC Rep, Mr. Rodriguez, who was auditing my brother, that he had been classified as a "List One Rock Slammer." This meant that, while Justin was in session and talking about Scientology, his needle did a "Rock Slam," a wild slashing back and forth in a crazy motion. A Rock Slam signified that someone had an underlying evil intention against whatever he was talking about at the time and, in his case, it was Scientology itself. LRH said that List One Rock Slammers had done no good in their entire past, lifetime after lifetime, and had only brought harm to people. She then showed me the LRH policy on List One Rock Slammers. One of my friends had been assigned to the RPF on the grounds of a List One Rock Slam alone. When I told Mr. Rodriguez that I didn't believe he was a Rock Slammer, she told me it had been verified by the video of the session.

The next time I saw my brother he seemed genuinely hurt by being named a List One Rock Slammer. I tried to console him by telling him I didn't believe it. However, it was clear that I wasn't getting anywhere trying to convince him to stay. Mr. Rathbun eventually said she didn't want me to talk to Justin anymore, as it wasn't panning out and violated a policy called "Leaving and Leaves," which forbade staff to talk to each other about leaving the Sea Org or Scientology.

While I was disappointed that I couldn't help Justin more, and help the Church more, there was also a small part of me that was starting to see that maybe all this was happening for a reason. I never would have admitted it to anyone, but little by little I began to see that maybe the only way for Justin to be truly happy was for him to leave, as he had apparently wanted to for a long time. Until then, I hadn't really thought about his leaving in terms of what would be best for him. I'd only thought about what was best for the Church. But as I listened to his reasons and arguments, it seemed to make sense why he would be considering departure.

• • •

ONE AFTERNOON SEVERAL WEEKS LATER, I WAS CALLED OUT FROM the sauna and told to go to the WB right away. I protested at first, concerned because you weren't allowed to cut your five hours short. However, I was told that I absolutely had to, because someone very important needed to see me. I put on my uniform and took off for the WB in one of the vans.

I wasn't sure if I should be worried or excited. At the WB, I was directed to the upstairs auditing room at the end of the hall. I was surprised when the Inspector General RTC, Marty Rathbun, himself, walked in. He was the second in command of the Church of Scientology. He was one of the few executives who worked with my uncle whom I had never really known, so I didn't know what to expect.

"Hi, Jenna," he said, flashing a smile and introduced himself. "Have you heard anything about your mother over the past year?"

"No, sir," I said, which was the absolute truth. I had no idea how she was progressing. I had received no calls, letters, or updates from anyone, not even my father. Dad had been writing me several times a week, but he never mentioned her. He had also been very insistent that I call him, even sending me a calling card to use at the pay phone, since I couldn't dial out on the Org phones. When I asked about her, he always said he didn't know anything and assumed she was simply doing her program. Unfortunately, Mr. Rathbun only had more bad news.

"Your mom is going to be declared a Suppressive Person," he said, very matter-of-factly. "She wants to leave the Sea Org. She has taken off several times without permission, she still is not following orders, and at this point, she's started accusing the Church of ridiculous things.

"I've done everything I can, and so, at this point, we are probably just going to let her leave." He let that sink in for the briefest of moments before continuing. "However, before she leaves, I want you to visit her, so that she can't make a legal claim against the Church and say she was forbidden from seeing her daughter."

There it was. I sat stone-faced, but I felt like my world was unraveling. The thought of her leaving was overwhelming enough on its own, but coming so soon after I'd been forced to think about Justin's possible departure, it felt like too much. It never occurred to me that someone from my own family would be declared an SP, and yet here I was, confronted with that possibility on two fronts. The prospect of my already fractured family suddenly disappearing entirely was unnerving. But I managed to maintain my composure.

"Mr. Rathbun, I'm pretty sure that if I can see her, I can get her to stay." It wasn't a job that I wanted, but I knew it was a duty I had to try to perform. Hearing everything that Mr. Rathbun had to say made me think that perhaps my decision not to speak with her had played a role in her wanting to leave, especially since she'd apparently been asking for pictures of me. I didn't really want to be in the role of arbitrator and I never wanted to be caught in the middle of all this, but I honestly thought I could make her stay. And, if she really was going to leave the church, I wanted to see her before it was too late.

"Really?" he asked, as if he was considering it. "Let's see what happens."

With that, he told me we were flying to L.A. together that night. We were even flying first-class, and Ray Mithoff, another senior executive in the church, would be joining us. The fact that I was sitting in first class beside these two senior executives, my feet barely touching the floor, was hard to believe. I slid down in my wide, soft seat, and planted my feet firmly on the carpet, thinking about how, a few hours earlier, I'd been following my routine at Flag and now was on a plane flying across the country to see my mom. I truly hoped that I would be able to deliver on my promise, and was nervous about what would happen. I felt worried about all the responsibilities I'd assumed on behalf of my family members and what would be the consequences if I failed. I was only fourteen, but I had to negotiate with my brother to try to make him stay, respond to my dad's letters, which felt a bit needy and obsessive at times in my mom's absence, and now travel to California to convince my mother to stay in the church.

After we landed, the three of us drove to the Int Base, where I was to meet Mom. Mr. Rathbun had me wait in a room in Building 36 while he arranged everything. About thirty minutes later, he came in.

"She is waiting in the next room," he said. I got up slowly, not excited about starting this process. "You know, Jenna, I should probably be there when you speak to her. Would you prefer that I be with you guys as part of the conversation, or would you prefer that I stay at the other end of the room, away from you?"

I looked at him, considering his offer. In truth, I didn't want him anywhere, because I didn't even want to have a conversation with her, much less have someone watching. I didn't want to confront her about any of these issues, but I felt obligated.

"Honestly, Mr. Rathbun, I'd prefer to go in there by myself."

He seemed surprised by my response, but nodded his head in assent.

"Okay, if that's what you want, Jenna, I'll allow it."

As the door swung open, I caught my first glimpse of her in over a year. She looked thin and somewhat haggard, with tanned skin and sun-streaked hair, like someone who had been working outside. She stood up and started crying as I walked into the room. And that's when I realized just how much I had missed her. All at once, I felt awful, as though I should have made more of an effort to find out what was happening with her, as though I'd been neglectful of how much she needed to speak to me. I hadn't even thought of what this would mean to her own healing process. We hugged each other for a long time. She wasn't saying anything, so I started the conversation.

"Look, Mom," I began haltingly, "I don't want to make you feel horrible" I tried to avoid using words like "out 2D" as much as possible, as I really did not want to get into that discussion. "I don't think that would be helpful, and that's not why I came here. I just want you to figure out why it happened, resolve it, and move on."

"I've done so much bad; I feel like can never make up for it," she stuttered through her tears. This was a bit surprising to hear, as Mr. Rathbun had told me a few hours before that she was being uncooperative. Seeing this strong woman, a woman I'd admired and respected my whole life, so upset, I started to fall apart, too, but I did my best to compose myself.

"Mom, you have to remember that no matter what anyone said, did, or implied, you are a good person. LRH would not have put the technology out there to help people if they didn't deserve to be helped. Anyone making you feel guilty or unworthy is guilty and unworthy himself." My mom choked back sobs before I continued, "If you can make it through your program we can be together again."

"Yes, I'd like that," she replied, nodding her head as though she was already on board. "I'd like for us to be in touch. That would help with the tough parts."

"Mom, of course I will write," I said trying to use this opening to get her a bit excited. "I'll send you anything you need; just let me know what it is."

She smiled as I spoke. The role reversal wasn't lost on either of us. Was it really that horrible or even unnatural that after being separated from my father, her spouse, for years due to her commitment to the Church that she had craved and found solace in a human relationship? This was the perfect recipe for an out 2D. Despite her mistake, she had dedicated her life, worked rigorous hours, and given up so much for the cause that I didn't see how an out 2D wiped away all the good she had done. It felt like she had sacrificed a lot for the Church, and although the punishment was expected and even standard, it just felt so unforgiving.

"How's Justin?" Mom asked, changing the subject. When I told her what had been happening, and that he would most likely be leaving, she didn't seem surprised. "Maybe he'll be happier that way," she said her voice sounding a bit more hopeful, "he always wanted to get out."

"Yes, I think so," I agreed.

And, with that, we hugged for a long time and said goodbye.

In the next room, Mr. Rathbun was waiting for me. He looked at me expectantly and gestured for me to come in. When I gave him the news that Mom wanted to do her program now, he looked shocked.

"Are you serious?" he asked, taken aback.

"Yes," I said.

Stunned as he was, he was clearly very pleased about Mom's decision. He went to speak to her himself, then came back and told me he couldn't believe that I had taken care of this whole problem for him. He was astonished.

The next morning, Mr. Rathbun came to see me again. He told me that he thought I was such a good Ethics Officer that he wanted me to talk with my father, who hadn't been doing well on his post since Mom's out 2D. I wasn't sure if he was right about me, but I would if he wanted me to.

However, the conversation with Dad was really awkward. When I asked him how he was doing, he said he could be better. I told him things similar to what I had said to Mom, that I believed in him, that he was capable, and that he would be able to pull himself together. He was happy to see me but not at all interested in my opinion or advice. He was closed off and didn't want to talk about it, which, to a degree, was understandable. Apparently, my Ethics Officer skills were not quite as good as Mr. Rathbun had thought they were.

CHAPTER EIGHTEEN

THE QUESTIONS BEGIN

I RETURNED TO FLAG WITH MY FEELINGS IN A TANGLE—PROUD OF the work I'd done in convincing my mom to stay, but concerned that I hadn't done enough to help my dad. I'd barely settled back into my life when the news I'd been dreading landed: one of my family members was leaving the Church. It wasn't my mom; it was Justin.

After everything I'd been through with him, I wasn't surprised that he was finally leaving. My lack of surprise, perhaps more than anything, showed how far I'd come in a short period of time. I remembered how shocked I'd been that first time Taryn had told me that Justin had even considered leaving the Sea Org, how nervous I'd been just to hear someone mentioning the thought of leaving the Church. At the time, it had been nearly impossible to fathom that a member of my family wouldn't be in the Church. Now, not only could I fathom it, his decision made sense to me.

My acceptance didn't make it any easier to say goodbye. For my entire life, I'd been saying goodbye to people—friends, my parents. People moved out of my life, often just as I was getting to know them. But, at least when people left, I always had a sense that they were staying within the Church, that somewhere down the line, I would get to see them again. As I watched Justin prepare to go into the Wog world by himself, I had none of that optimism. I didn't know whether he would be declared an SP or not, but there seemed a good chance that he would. The rule was that anyone from Int who left the Sea Org was declared an SP, and, prior to his RPF, that's where he'd been stationed. I knew I had to recognize the possibility that we would never again speak to each other.

Making things harder was that my other brother, Sterling, was not much of a presence in my life; in fact, I didn't even know if he was aware that his own twin brother was leaving. Sterling was stationed at Int and we didn't really keep in touch. While we'd never been terribly close, in recent years, before I left for Flag, Sterling had become very caught up in the hierarchy of the Church and his own status. As a result, there was a distance between us. I knew I couldn't rely on him for comfort.

Finally, I got word that it was time to say goodbye to Justin. I went to his berthing at the Hacienda, and from the moment I walked in, I was struck by how happy he seemed. Despite my sadness, seeing him smile was a relief. I gave him my Discman and a magazine that he had asked to borrow. He didn't even consider trying to convince me to leave with him. He didn't think what he was doing was right for everyone; he just knew it was right for him.

We chatted a bit, hugged for the last time, and then I left. I barely made it out the door before I burst into tears. Upset as I was about losing my brother, my feelings were more complicated than that. My family was getting smaller with every step. Justin had been a much more frequent presence my life than my parents; at the Ranch I used to see him every day, something that hadn't been true of my parents for more than a decade.

Seeing him leave the Flag base for good and knowing the

trouble that he and Mom had been in, I realized all at once that the people I loved could leave me behind, that maybe, someday, I would find myself the last one here—the final believer among us.

In early 1999, shortly after I turned fifteen, the church celebrated the rerelease of LRH's *Volume Zero* of his eight-volume *Organization Executive Course* set. It was met with much fanfare, but that also meant that all staff had to buy it, read it, and complete its accompanying checksheet. The price was eighty dollars, which was several weeks' pay. I was being paid half pay, only twenty-five dollars per week, and sometimes I'd go three weeks without any pay at all.

When I did have a little money, I wanted to buy food with it, not an eighty-dollar book. We were told not to share or borrow *Volume Zero,* either, as we were each supposed to have our own copy, likely to help boost book sales. I was one of the last people on the base to get mine, but luckily I didn't have to buy it. My father mailed me his marketing copy, which he had received due to his post, which was a huge relief.

Having recently finished a course on learning to operate the E-Meter, I was able to switch my attention to the study of *Volume Zero. Basic Staff Hat* was grueling and eight hundred pages long. One day, I was studying it with my friend Marcella in the public course rooms of the Coachman Building. At one point, I started reading a piece called "The Structure of Organization: What Is Policy?" It was an eleven-page policy letter replete with seven hundred word paragraphs, and, at fifteen, I couldn't understand any of it. In the usual LRH style, it was full of multisyllable words and referenced obscure subjects and people from the 1940s through the 1960s. It went on and on about how some fellows named King, Nimitz, and Short were idiots and allowed Pearl Harbor to happen. I might have understood it, if I concentrated really hard, but it was so boring and verbose that I couldn't stay focused.

Marcella and I took a trip to the library where there were extremely large dictionaries, and we hoped to find a correct definition for one of the words in the text. When I came back, a kid about my age was sitting next to our seats, and he was wearing my glasses.

"Excuse me, those are my glasses!"

"Oh, they are," he replied with a grin. "I'm sorry."

Clearly not sorry, he kept them on and bounced them on his nose. I was surprised at his cockiness. People were usually afraid of CMO members, and even if they weren't, at least they were usually reserved with us.

"So, what's up? What course are you doing?" he asked looking right at me.

I looked behind me to see whom he might be talking to, but apparently he was talking to me, even though conversation was not allowed in the course room.

"We are on Vol Zero, Martino," Marcella said, answering for me in a condescending but familiar way. She and Martino had grown up together at the Flag Cadet Org, which was in the old Quality Inn on Highway U.S. 19. Unlike at the Ranch, Sea Org members at Flag who had children were allowed to spend nights there with their kids and were provided bus service to and from the base. Some of the motel rooms had been converted into course rooms, so the Cadets could do their schooling. Sea Org members who were under eighteen took the bus there once a week, usually on Sundays, to do our schooling, returning to the Hacienda by ten-thirty that night.

Due to the way that Martino was acting, I almost took my stuff and moved, but he was sitting with Tyler, a boy I thought was cute, so I stayed. The rest of the morning, Marcella and I endured their ridiculous antics. When they were clearing words, they used our names in all of their sentences. They called the supervisor "Sarge," when his real name was Sergio. They kept passing my glasses between them throughout the morning, using them to do impersonations of us. Much as we tried to ignore them, Marcella and I couldn't help but laugh.

Over the next few weeks, I went to the course room with my friend Cece. We had become friends when she was in CMO with me, but she had been demoted to the Cadet Org when she got in trouble for something stupid. Even though it was forbidden for CMO staffers to fraternize with Cadets or other Sea Org members, technically, we were just studying, so I was able to get away with it. During one drill, I got stuck, so I asked the supervisor for someone to word clear me, and he paired me with Martino. I was a little hesitant. I remember thinking Martino was nuts, but at least he was a Cadet and not a public Scientologist. They were always awkward to work with.

We went to the practical course room and sat across from each other. Martino asked me the standard first question for any worksheet, "How do you spell your name?" As soon as I told him, he abruptly asked me a second question—one that was not part of the patter: "When do you see your parents?"

I was a little startled, because I realized he was asking me this on account of seeing that my last name was Miscavige. Nobody had ever asked me that before. I could have ignored it, but I found myself wanting to answer.

"I see them whenever they come to Clearwater," I said honestly and candidly. "My dad was here once last year, and I saw him for a few minutes."

Martino's face went from jokester to disbelief. "Wait, so you don't see your parents except once a year if you are lucky?"

"Mm-hm, yeah," I said, somehow feeling like I had to explain why it wasn't as bad as it sounded.

"But you're just a kid."

"No, I'm a Sea Org member; that's just how it is."

"You're a Sea Org Member," he said sardonically. "What does that even mean? You're a kid. How old are you?"

When I told him I was fifteen, he continued with his observation. "Yeah, fifteen, the same as me. Just because you are in the Sea Org and wearing a fancy CMO uniform . . ." To emphasize the point, he puffed out his chest trying to demonstrate a pose of someone important. I burst out laughing, but that didn't stop him. "Seriously, I would die if I didn't see my mom," he said quietly, waiting for me to respond.

"I don't know, I just . . . we are Thetans," I added haltingly, ". . . and Thetans can't really be the parent of another Thetan, and so family isn't really real, or that important." I was reciting what Aunt Shelly had told me in her office all those months earlier after I had returned from visiting my mom.

"Yeah, but don't you miss your mom?" he asked, almost pleading to my true self.

His genuine concern almost made me cry. Just earlier that day, Mr. Anne Rathbun had pulled me into her office and shown me an opened letter from my mother. In the letter, Mom, who was still on RPF, told me how well she was doing in getting through her program. She talked on and on about how much she loved the gardening and how certain things reminded her of me. She had enclosed some pictures and told me how much she loved me. I dared not show my emotion in front of Mr. Rathbun. I wanted to take the letter home, so I could put it under my pillow and read it over and over again, but when I got up to leave Mr. Rathbun picked it up. I looked at her, and she told me she would be keeping it, as it had confidential photos of Int in it. Of course, I should have expected as much.

It was weird that Martino would have any interest in my relationship with my mother, but I was drawn in by his curiosity, as well as by his honesty. He didn't seem to be putting on airs, and he certainly wasn't trying to pretend that he was more ethical than I was. There was something very natural about him that I hadn't encountered before. I didn't even know him, but somehow he seemed to think like me. Whereas, for years, everyone had been telling me that the way I missed my parents was wrong, that I should be accustomed to not having them around, he was the first person who seemed to acknowledge how strange the situation was. Everyone else simply said that the way I was thinking was wrong. Listening to him talk was the first time that it had even occurred to me that maybe they were the ones who were wrong, not me.

Over the next few weeks, Martino and I started working together all the time, although we hardly did any work. We talked about everything. He told me about his early boyhood in Italy, and how his parents split when he was young, and he moved to Florida with his mother. He was really close to his mom and would have been lost without her. He spoke about growing up at the Flag Cadet Org, and I described life on the Ranch. Apparently, there was a huge discrepancy between the two when it came to labor and enforcement. The Flag Cadets weren't required to work, and if they were asked to do so, many of them would simply refuse. Instead, they might walk to the movie theaters down the street, because the Flag Cadet Org wasn't in a remote place like the Ranch. Unlike us, they were not considered Sea Org members, although almost all of them also ended up in the Sea Org.

As much as we shared stories from our past, we were also fifteen-year-olds who liked each other. Sometimes we would supposedly work in the library, which had more space. We loved picking out random encyclopedias and reading about different subjects. Not surprisingly, Martino's favorite subject was sexual behavior. I thought it was funny how open he was about it.

When we spoke about Scientology, it wasn't just the usual patter; instead, we actually spoke about belief, something we never did in any of our courses. We talked about Thetans, and how he wasn't at all convinced that he actually was one. I couldn't believe he was saying that. I told him that I unequivocally knew that I was one.

"But how do you *know*?" he asked.

"I just do," I replied authoritatively.

But the truth was, I really didn't know. This was what I had been told since my earliest childhood, and I believed it; however, I couldn't say why I believed it. I'd never thought of myself as just a body. I'd never thought of myself as *just a piece of meat*, the phrase Scientologists always used to refer to the human body. The idea that Martino believed differently made me think about the whole concept of a Thetan with a scrutiny that felt foreign.

Other times, we found ourselves talking about Scientology's most precious secret—the OT Levels. Because Flag was one of the few bases where the higher OT Levels could be administered, there was an air of secrecy about them everywhere. Frequently, the higher ups briefed the staff about the increased security around the OT Levels, taking pride in the fact that the levels were safer than ever. They'd make announcements listing out the various measures that had been taken to make the delivery of the OT Levels completely secure—some parts of the base that dealt with the OT Levels were only accessible through a combination lock and special key card, and there were other special security measures as well.

Not surprisingly, all of this secrecy only made me more curious about the levels themselves and the secrets that they held. I can't say whether it was deliberate strategy by the Church, but the end result of this security talk was a powerful desire to learn the truth. I couldn't wait to climb the Bridge and find out what the OT Levels were. I figured they had something to do with how we all came to exist, which was something I often wondered about. Occasionally, I'd try to get the librarian to reveal information about the levels to me or at least hint at it, but not surprisingly she refused. She knew as well as I did that there was a risk I could be physically harmed if I learned the levels out of order.

Compelled as I was by the mystery of the levels themselves, this concept of physical harm also perplexed me. Talking all this over with Martino, I kept coming back to this simple question: how can information hurt you physically? It made sense that information could upset you emotionally—but physical harm was a different story. I tried to imagine what that harm would be. Something about the whole idea seemed wrong, but the threat of pain and even death inspired fear nonetheless.

My discussions with Martino always possessed an openness that I hadn't encountered before; they weren't regimented or scripted, they just sort of unfolded depending on how comfortable we were and what we felt like sharing. It wasn't long before I confided in him that my mom was in trouble and on the RPF. As I told him the story of what had happened, he was visibly moved by my words. From then on, he would always ask for updates about my mother, often becoming as excited as I did when a letter from my mother arrived. Since Mr. Rathbun always kept the letters, I could never show them to him, but he was enthusiastic about them nonetheless.

More than anything, it was this sincere concern that made me feel more comfortable with the skepticism he displayed about the Church. Because he was so good-natured, I could see that it didn't come from some sinister desire to be troublesome or get me in trouble. He wasn't a bad person and he wasn't trying to undermine the entire Church. He was just trying to understand the world he had grown up in, and in doing so, was asking some uncomfortable questions.

It wasn't just Martino's earnest approach that opened me up to these ideas; after everything I'd been through with Justin's departure and my mom almost leaving the church, I was also at a point where I'd started to acknowledge that plenty of people, including those I cared about most, had these kinds of thoughts. If I'd met Martino just a year earlier, I probably would have dismissed his questions as invasive and dangerous. Now, in part because of what had happened to Justin, I found his preoccupations becoming my own.

It wasn't one big issue he raised, just a lot of little ones. Why had I been separated from my parents? What did these courses really mean? Why did we all have to work as we did? What does it really mean to be a Thetan? It was a lot to take in, but it was also energizing to think about these issues in such a different way. Of course, the tricky thing about these little questions was that, once I started asking them, it was hard to stop.

AFTER A FEW MONTHS, MARTINO WAS BY FAR THE BEST FRIEND I had. He knew everything about me, and I about him. He understood things in a way that my friends in CMO didn't. Now they all seemed so fake and so robotic. I became friends with his friends. Tyler was in that group. He was cute, a goofball, and a good friend, but by now I'd fallen for Martino. The best part was that he clearly felt the same way about me.

The only problem was that because he wasn't in the Sea Org, he and I weren't supposed to even talk outside the course room, so we had to do our best not to let others know what was going on. Neither of us let the fact that we were not supposed to speak get in the way of our friendship, but it certainly complicated life. Being friends with Martino made it much harder to relate to other people in the CMO. People in the CMO didn't think like he did and didn't have discussions in the same way. It was hard to go from being open and honest to stifling everything. This was especially true with Olivia and Julia, with whom I worked.

I'm less than a year old in this photograph of my mother and me in New Hampshire. Behind us are the beginnings of the dream house my parents were building.

This is from my first Christmas. I can't believe how much I looked like my own daughter does now.

This is also in New Hampshire, shortly before my parents decided to give up the life they had started and the house they had just built, to move our family to California and dedicate our lives to service in the Church.

Rainbow Brite, pictured here on my shirt, was my all-time favorite cartoon character. I loved that she was a heroine whose mission was to bring color into the world.

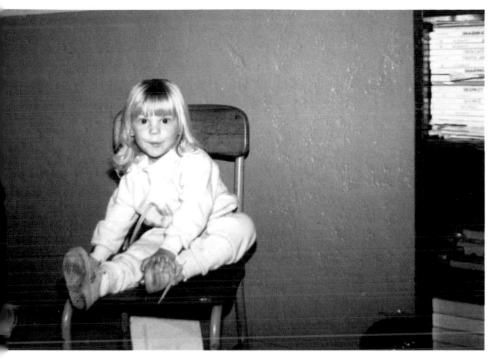

This is in the Church's L.A. nursery school. There are "value books" that teach things like sharing, imagination, respect, and truth on the bookshelf to my left. You can see that our education in Scientologist thought started at the very beginning of our lives.

During this time, my brother Justin would pick me up from the bus stop after nursery school and we would walk back to the apartment together.

I've always been a girly-girl at heart, even though I went through a long tomboy stage in order to fit in at the Ranch.

I loved my baby doll and carriage, and wouldn't go anywhere without them for a while.

I cut my hair short in order to be like my mom, who I missed when I lived at the Ranch. Here I am in front of the Motels, the austere dormitories my fellow Scientology kids and I slept in.

We couldn't keep pets in our rooms, but some roamed around the Ranch. I'm petting my cat Bella in this picture.

This was on a Sunday, since I'm not wearing my uniform. You get a sense of the remote desert environment we lived in here.

On a mini-golf outing with my great-grandmother, who I met three times in my life. David Miscavige, the leader of the Church and my uncle, is in the corner.

In my parents' Vista Gardens apartment in Hemet, California, on a Sunday morning—the one time a week I got to visit them.

My husband, Dallas, and I had the opportunity to go to Australia on a mission to raise money for the Church. It was a great experience, in part because we had the opportunity to be more self-sufficient and independent than in our daily lives at home.

When I look at this photograph of my husband, my son, my daughter, and me, it all seems worth it. Having a close-knit family is an experience I may have never gotten the chance to have if I had not left the Church.

They'd always been intense about their work, but, after I began to spend time with Martino, I started to see they weren't just intense; they used the power of their positions to intimidate the rest of the group. The policies for our department instructed that we were supposed to *help* people do their jobs—help them find a disturbance or down statistic in any part of the organization, investigate that disturbance, and root out anyone who was causing it. Instead, Julia, in particular, became obsessed with enforcing the rules and checking people's mail, and Olivia often went along with her although I could tell her heart wasn't really in it. They would walk around with swagger sticks—sticks carried by Sea Org members to add an authoritative presence—which they would slam on someone's desk if that person was resistant when asked to show his daily statistic graph. Julia would yell at anyone whose statistics were down, leading many people, including myself, to falsely report their statistics. If you were found to have done this, of course, you would get into even more trouble and be assigned to a lower condition. People who flunked meter checks would be put into a metered ethics interview, during which Julia would yell at them to come clean with their transgressions, while she loomed behind the E-Meter operator.

Around this time, members of the CMO staff were chastised in front of the entire group for going to the canteen at night and fraternizing with Flag staff. Some were brought up in front of the group for daring to wear tank tops, which were considered too skimpy. The CMO group as a whole was put in a condition of "Danger," and movies, outings, and libs were canceled until that changed.

Prior to that, my libs day had been a cherished part of my schedule. I only had one or two a month, and I would usually spend them with my dad's mother, Grandma Loretta, or his sister, my aunt Denise. They were the only family I had in Clearwater, and they would bring me shopping, buy me what I needed, and take me out to eat. Sometimes, we went to the beach, and I would hang out with my cousins, Taylor and Whitney. I'd see my cousins when they came to the base for courses. Because they were all public Scientologists, not Sea Org members, their lives seemed amazing and fun.

It was awkward that I could not tell them that Mom was on the RPF. In retrospect, I wish I had. They were the few actual support people I had, and they would have given me the help I needed. However, Mom had been a top executive at Flag, so telling them would have been seen as "out PR" for Flag, Int, and my family name, even though they were Miscaviges, too. When it came to matters of ethics for Sea Org members, it was not the business of people in lower orgs or outside the Sea Org to know about them. Mom's case was even more classified, because she was David Miscavige's sister-in-law.

The risk of embarrassing people and my family was too great and I was afraid of the consequences, but I should have trusted my grandma. She was very human—probably one of the most compassionate people I knew. There were a few times when I was on libs that she had broken down and told me that she wished she could see my dad more. He was at Int and rarely had time off. She also complained about Aunt Shelly, who had made my cousin Whitney cry by criticizing her because Whitney wasn't in the Sea Org.

It wasn't just Aunt Shelly who Grandma Loretta had a problem with. She didn't understand some of her son's own rules. A medical nurse by training, she didn't like the fact that the local RTC Reps oversaw her exercise program, and she couldn't understand why she wasn't allowed to be a nurse herself. According to her, Uncle Dave didn't allow it, but I had no idea why it wasn't allowed or if it was even true. I assumed that Uncle Dave didn't want his mother working as a nurse because the medicine field was looked down upon for often prescribing drugs. Nursing work was also an admission of the power of the body. Regardless, I didn't ask questions, because the stakes were too high. Delving into Grandma Loretta's disagreements with my uncle could put me in dangerous territory, and I might be questioned as to why I didn't defend Scientology's leader, who was so hardworking and doing so much for us. I sympathized with her, though, since there were so many things I too had to give up because of my Miscavige name.

Instead of being a nurse, Grandma worked as an assistant/bookkeeper for Greta Van Susteren, the Fox TV anchor, and her lawyer husband, John Coale, both public Scientologists. Not being allowed to watch television, I had no idea who they were, but on some of my libs days, I'd go to their beach house. It was gorgeous, right on the ocean, three stories high, with an elevator. They also had a yacht, which I went out on a few times. They were both very nice to me. John was sarcastic and self-deprecating, like my grandma. Greta was tougher and hard-nosed, somewhat like my Aunt Shelly.

While not having libs days was hard, my grandmother was in the same course room with me, so I would get to see her and chat with her throughout the day. My friends met her, too, and we would all joke around together before class. I could tell that Grandma really enjoyed it. She was happy knowing that I had friends, as it provided a degree of normalcy in my life. Because she was a public Scientologist, normal was actually something that mattered to her.

Looking back, I think that's one of the reasons why my libs days with her meant so much to me: She showed me that there was this other existence outside the walls of the Sea Org. She showed me that while people like Olivia and Julia and Mr. Anne Rathbun became obsessed with the implementations of rules and punishments, there was a way to be a Scientologist without having to have so much responsibility. For all Loretta's belief, and the fact that her son was in charge of the entire Church, she'd managed to keep her feet on the ground throughout her life.

Unlike other people in the Church, she didn't take herself so seriously, a quality I loved about her, and one that I saw and admired in Martino.

Chapter Nineteen

"THINK FOR YOURSELF"

PEOPLE WERE STARTING TO NOTICE THAT MARTINO AND I WERE seeing a lot of each other. Some said that we were in love. Cece, who had once had a crush on him, told me that he had completely changed since we started spending time together, transforming from the kid who was always the jokester and pest to someone who was a real person with feelings and compassion for other people. Her comment made me happy.

Unfortunately, people at all levels began to notice, including adults. Martino was told that he should be spending less time with me, and more time working on clearing his misunderstood words. So we started working with each other only a few days per week. On those days, we often didn't have to say anything to make it clear how much we missed each other. It was apparent just from how he would lean in close or wrap his legs around mine and covertly take my hand. I desperately wanted to return the gesture, but I knew it would mean serious trouble.

I found myself increasingly resentful about being in the CMO and having no control over my friendships or love life. I'd been dealing with rules, regulations, and requirements my entire life, but never had it been so difficult to obey them. Since becoming friends with Martino and his friends, I had gotten back into music, which I had always loved. I'd even started drawing in the evenings before I went to bed. I used to do this during the five minutes before lights went out at the Ranch or during meals, but in the years since then, all of the rules I'd encountered seemed to have stifled my creativity. The rules in Scientology all forced us to act as if we were the same: They didn't encourage people to have their own thoughts, despite Scientology's new slogan, "Think for yourself." When I got back into drawing and music, I realized how much I missed them and how I hated being so confined; it felt natural to let my creative side show.

With Martino, I felt I didn't need to have the responsibility of being a role model all the time. I just wanted freedom to be myself, but I knew how impossible that was. I became conflicted by the whole situation: on the one hand I wanted to spend as much time as I could with him; on the other I feared that our friendship was unsustainable. And I wasn't the only one who saw the risk. Friends who saw us together would warn us under their breath, telling us to be careful.

I decided to write a letter to Aunt Shelly requesting a transfer back to the Ranch. In my petition, I didn't say anything about Martino but made it clear that I wanted to rejoin the Cadet Org at the Ranch and finish school. I knew that asking to leave the CMO and the Sea Org to become a Cadet again was a big deal—if it happened. I'd be taking a big step backward in the eyes of the Church—but there was precedent for it. It had happened before. It all depended on how my aunt Shelly decided to apply the Church law to my situation. If my request was accepted, I would not see Martino again, but at least I wouldn't have to worry about getting into trouble for so much as kissing someone who wasn't technically a Sea Org member, which would be an out 2D and could land me on the RPF like my mom. If I wasn't allowed to go back to the Ranch then maybe I could be with Martino, as well as my other friends, at the Flag Cadet Org. Both scenarios meant quitting the CMO and the Sea Org for the time being. The way I figured it, it couldn't hurt to ask, because LRH policy stated that you weren't allowed to get in trouble for writing a petition.

Sending the petition was bold, but I convinced myself it was the only way I could stay out of trouble and do the right thing. As it was, I was already dangerously close to crossing a line—in love with Martino, fighting hard against my teenage urges, and fearing I would lose. I was afraid that if things kept going the way they were, I would end up in an even worse situation. I was very torn, as was Martino, who was shocked that I'd written my aunt.

Confusing as my situation was, there was also turmoil at the base, which complicated everyone's life even more. Every day there were demonstrators in front of the base, intensifying the air of paranoia that usually surrounded us.

The whole mess started when the church had been charged with two felony counts in the death of Lisa McPherson, a public Scientologist who had died on December 5, 1995, while under the care of church staff at the Flag Land Base. It had all begun with a minor car accident on November 18, 1995, in the Tampa/Clearwater area. Paramedics determined that Lisa, who was thirty-six at the time, was unharmed physically, but was exhibiting unusual behavior, like trying to take her clothes off. The medical team wanted to admit her to the hospital for psychiatric observation, but she refused on the grounds that she wanted the religious care and assistance of fellow Scientologists. People from the Church came to help her with her discharge and brought her back to Flag for rest and relaxation. Having been a Scientologist since the age of eighteen, she trusted them with her welfare. Instead, she was put on a so-called isolation watch, essentially 24/7 monitoring. This was despite the fact she had attested to a state of Clear a few months earlier.

The word was that she had been extremely mentally agitated during the last few months of her life. The coroner's office had initially called the cause of death "dehydration." A subsequent investigation led two criminal charges against the Church, "abuse and/or neglect of a disabled adult" and "practicing medicine without a license." However, the Church fiercely denied any wrongdoing on its part.

The fact that Lisa had been under the care of Scientologists at the time of her death incited outrage. There were even accounts that my uncle had been directly involved in the auditing that led to her being declared Clear, so there was a stain on his name too. Lisa McPherson's family filed a civil suit against the Church in 1997, alleging wrongful death.

The anti-Scientology sentiment really got fired up in 1999 when multimillionaire businessman Bob Minton created the Lisa McPherson Trust with the purpose of "exposing the deceptive and abusive practices of Scientology" and "helping those victimized by [the Church of Scientology]." It had a staff of five, four of whom were former Scientologists; the fifth was Minton.

To mark the four-year anniversary of Lisa's death, Minton organized a huge picket line in Clearwater, demanding the Church be held accountable for Lisa's death. Due to all the protesters on the base, we got regular briefings from the Office of Special Affairs explaining to us what was being done to handle the crowd of people who called themselves the Lisa McPherson Trust.

I knew a little bit about what was going on. Uncle Dave had briefed the whole Flag crew. He had sounded angry when he told us that the whole thing was happening because we, the base staff and those who had been responsible for delivering the services, had allowed someone (Lisa) who was a PTS, a "Potential Trouble Source," access to Scientology, which was strictly forbidden. Supposedly, Lisa had been a PTS Type 3, which was essentially someone who was crazy and saw Martians, as defined by LRH.

After the briefing, I tried to talk to Aunt Shelly about the case, but she blew up at me. "Of all the things we could talk about, you have to ask me about *this*? Weren't you at the briefing? Do you know that if the Church loses this case, we will have a criminal record? We will be the first church in history to have a criminal record," she said angrily.

Later on after the criminal charges against the Church were dropped, it was explained to Scientologists by my Uncle Dave that a conviction in this case would have endangered the Church's tax exempt status, and thus its hold on the copyrights themselves, which would have been catastrophic to the Church.

Office of Special Affairs (OSA), which handled external public relations for Church matters, said they were on top of the protesters and the situation. In reality, they were trying to get the protesters removed by having OSA members bait the protesters into acting out, at which point the OSA person would act as though they had been pushed or hit, when, in reality, they had not. They would then call the police and try to get the protest called off or have the protester arrested. OSA also put up mug shots of all of the protesters all over their neighborhoods, alleging that the protesters were sexual perverts and deadbeat dads. They did the same inside our buildings as well, posting the protesters' photographs and lists of their alleged crimes in case anyone started wondering about them.

As if all that weren't enough, OSA also warned us not to read the protesters' signs, saying the signs might contain OT Level III material. They reminded us that if you were not at that level on The Bridge, having it revealed to you prematurely had serious consequences. After all, encountering knowledge of this magnitude out of sequence was said to cause serious harm or even death.

The Office of Special Affairs said the best way to keep us from inadvertently reading about levels that were beyond us was to put restrictions on travel. An order was passed that we were no longer allowed to walk between buildings because of the outrage. Instead, we had to take vans everywhere, even just across the street. The windows of the vans were covered with blurry contact paper, so that we couldn't see what was happening on the streets or read any of the posters. Sometimes the protesters would try to film us as we were getting off the vans. It was unnerving to get out of a van or a bus and see cameras recording our every move. Sometimes, because of the filming, the buses would have to go around the block several times, causing us to miss breakfast. All this fear of the protesters made our lives even more claustrophobic, since we were only allowed to go outside to pass from the Church vans to the door of our destination.

The whole situation often put a monkey wrench in my already short time with Martino. CMO people were always waiting for the vans, so when I was in Martino's vicinity, I had to act as though I didn't know him. He didn't seem to like it, but he'd understand soon why it had to be that way.

ABOUT TWO WEEKS AFTER I HAD WRITTEN THE LETTER TO AUNT Shelly, Tom, who was now the acting CMO, made an announcement at the lunch muster; much to my surprise, it was about me.

In front of the entire group, Tom announced the details of the petition that I sent to Aunt Shelly, informing everyone that I was requesting to return to the Cadet Org. For an instant, I felt I could hear a pin drop. Everyone was looking at me. Aside from Aunt Shelly, the only other person I'd told was my auditor, but I was supposed to tell her everything. I had also told Martino, but I knew he would never tell on me. Now, suddenly, my private life had been made public; even Julia, the last person I wanted to know something like this, now knew.

After muster, I went to see Tom, whom for the last three years I had had to call Mr. Devocht. At that moment, I wasn't thinking of his status, though, I was fuming. I couldn't believe that he would have gone out of his way not only to humiliate me but to do so over a petition, which was not supposed to get anyone in trouble. As I started to explain myself, Tom cut me off, frustrated by my lack of respect. He blew up and started yelling at me.

"Jenna, you are in big trouble," he began. "You have been fraternizing with Cadets, and you just boss me around like you own this place. You are rude and disrespectful and you belong on the RPF. Now, get out of my office."

With that, I was taken to my apartment at the Hacienda under house arrest. His rebuke was a slap in the face, and as I walked into my room, I was still reeling.

In truth, I probably should have seen my punishment coming, not just because of Martino, but because there had recently been a crackdown on girls in the CMO for flirting and related behaviors. It had all started with Olivia and Julia, of all people, the rule enforcers themselves. They had been temporarily working for my uncle, and even though they were already married, they got in trouble for flirting with some of his staff. Ironically, I am pretty sure the main reason both Olivia and Julia were chosen to work for my uncle was that they were beautiful, more so than anyone else in CMO. He often worked with attractive women.

Like Olivia and Julia, my roommate Mayra had also been in trouble because of a guy. She was a few years older than me and had been having a relationship with an RTC Rep with whom she had been in the Cadet Org. For years, they had talked about getting married, but it was forbidden because he was in RTC and she was in CMO. When their relationship came to light during a security check, she faced a harsh reprimand, too.

In response to these violations, the Church had started embarrassing people who were "out-ethics" at muster. The idea was to "put a head on a pike," as LRH wrote in one of his ethics policies, so that it would discourage others from being out ethics as well.

Though I'd watched it happen to all three of these girls, somehow I didn't think it would happen to me so publicly.

Based on Tom's words to me after the muster, he clearly knew I was doing something unethical. Despite the fact that there was precedent for people going back to the Cadet Org, Tom's reaction made it clear that they weren't going to consider it favorably; in fact, I would likely be punished for wanting to leave the Sea Org.

Still, I couldn't believe that Tom was threatening RPF simply because I'd written a petition. After everything I'd witnessed with my mom and Justin, simply hearing the letters RPF triggered a visceral response. Whatever I was guilty of—whether it was my time with Martino or my desire to become a Cadet again—a punishment of RPF did not fit the crime. After all, I'd been trying to do the right thing.

Collapsing on my bed, I found Mayra in our room as she, too, was under house arrest. In addition to the relationship she'd been having, she'd even tried to take off a few days earlier, resulting in full-time watch and our rear sliding-glass door being bolted closed. She'd tried to blow the Sea Org and had been caught in the process. Escape attempts like hers were a rare thing and a big deal. The punishment was always swift and harsh. Because I hadn't seen her trying to leave, I'd been considered suspect as well, though now I had bigger problems to worry about.

A short while later, news came that I would be doing MEST work with Mayra and several others who were also in trouble, but I refused. I knew what I was doing was wrong, but I didn't believe that forced labor was a punishment that I deserved. Lower conditions maybe, but not labor. I had written the petition to Aunt Shelly in an attempt to do the right thing. I had also told my auditor about my fraternizing with Martino, and she had assured me I wasn't doing anything wrong. Yet, I was being harshly punished.

Mayra tried to convince me, telling me that she knew how I was feeling, but I was defiant. By now, it was evening. I was scared, and worried about what was going to happen to me, but not ready to comply. I wanted to call my dad. I knew that calling him was not the proper procedural way to handle my upset, but after hearing Martino say how important his mom had been in his life, I thought it was worth reaching out to my dad to see if he could help. It was not either of my parent's post to take care of me. This was to be dealt with on Org lines. It could also be considered to be enturbulative for my parents at their jobs, which could cause me to get into more trouble. If I was upset, I was supposed to write a report, which they would then consider to be "nattery" or "complainy," which would then mean I had withholds, which would mean I would get a security check, which was going to happen anyway. This was the cycle, the endless feedback loop of disobedience that, once it began, was hard to break.

At this point, though, I didn't care about that cycle or the consequences. I knew I didn't deserve MEST work, but my biggest fear was that Tom would have me shipped me off to RPF and that soon, contacting my parents wouldn't be an option at all. My dad was the one person who I could think of who could advise me and might even be on my side.

There was an authorized phone in our apartment for her one of my roommates' use only. It was there in case anyone tried to take off in the middle of the night and she needed to call security. I picked up the phone and dialed the receptionist at CMO Int. Shocked, but delighted that my call had gotten through at all, I was disappointed when I was told that my dad wasn't there. However, the receptionist said I could talk to my mom, which *really* confused me. The last I had heard, she was on the RPF. The receptionist put me on hold, then came back saying that Mom wasn't available at the moment, but that I could try her again in a little bit. Amid all my frantic dialing, I sat there stupefied for the briefest of moments: after everything we'd been through how could no one have told me that she was done with RPF?

I tried dialing out again a little while later, but this time, Mayra noticed. She quickly ran and got Olivia. I wasn't surprised that she was ratting me out. Even though we were both being punished, we could redeem ourselves by reporting a bad behavior in the other one and proving your own loyalty. This is one of the ways that the Sea Org encourages snitching on fellow members, and keeps paranoia high.

"You cannot call your parents," Olivia said as she entered the room.

"Go fuck yourself," I shot back, not caring anymore what the consequences were. I picked up the phone again, but she held down the button. No matter how hard I tried to get her to stop, she wouldn't.

"Fine, I'm going to the pay phones." I started out the door, but Olivia blocked me. I tried pushing to get through, but Mayra joined in and wouldn't let me leave.

"Sorry, Jenna, I just can't let you do this," Mayra apologized, but I easily broke free of the two of them.

A girl, from next door joined in trying to stop me as well, yelling how unethical I was. Each of them had a hold on one of my limbs. I was struggling and fighting, trying to break free, but they wouldn't let go. When I finally escaped, my old friend Melinda Bleecker raced in and jumped on me, too. I spit in her face, which made her let go for a second. I might have managed to bolt out the door but for the security guard who had arrived on a bike after being summoned. He told me I was not going anywhere, and he meant it.

By now, I was flailing my arms and legs, just trying to get away. All I wanted was for them to let go of me, but they were pulling me in four different directions. Even when I got away from one or more of the girls, though, I couldn't get past the security guard. I knew the back door was bolted shut from Mayra's attempted escape a few nights before, so that was not an option.

Apparently, capturing me was Mayra's chance to redeem herself, because she was relentless.

Several times, I almost got away. Then I saw Tom standing outside the door, obviously alerted by Olivia. He was going to use the firm, rational approach to get me under control. I was so angry that I refused to speak with him, but I quickly realized that he was my only way out.

"If you calm down, Jenna," he said, "I will talk to you upstairs to my berthing and see if we can work this out." Tired of fighting, now apathetic because I couldn't get away, I reluctantly agreed.

When we got up to his room, we each took a seat. "I hadn't intended for things to go this far, but I don't understand what's happening with you. It's like you've become a different person. What's going on?" he asked.

Stupidly, I tried to be honest. I told him the full story about Martino, how I felt about CMO, and why I had written the petition to Aunt Shelly. As I finished, he paused for a moment as though still taking it all in.

"I understand, Jenna. I'll try to get things back to normal tomorrow."

The next morning, I went to course, where I saw Martino and told him everything that had happened. He was disturbed and worried for me—to him the whole situation sounded crazy. An hour or so later, Tom showed up at the course room and said that Martino and I had to go with him. I begged Tom to leave Martino out of it, and he did, at least for the time being.

After driving for a while, I could see that we were going to the Hacienda. He told me I was going to do MEST work at the Hacienda and get through my program. Apparently, my words had no impact, other than trying to spare Martino. Now I was just supposed to be contrite and accept my punishment? I refused to accept a punishment that was beyond what I deserved.

My anger arose all over again, and once more I refused to do the MEST work. Mayra tried various ways to convince me, yelling at me, talking to me, begging me, but I didn't budge. Even though I was scared, I didn't want to be in CMO anymore, and I told Mayra as much. I even said I wasn't sure I even wanted to be in the Sea Org. As any good Sea Org member would do, she reported all this back to the top.

That night, Tom came to my room. "Your parents are on the phone demanding to speak with you." Tom sat right next to me as I spoke to them. They said that they heard I was in trouble, but reminded me of my merits, and how I was strong, and I could get through this. To comfort and inspire me, they added that Mom had succeeded in her program and that Tom had promised he would make sure I was all right. Tom had been my guardian the whole time I was in Florida and, for the most part, had always been very nice to me, but with this last incident, everything was different.

"Be sure to call us and keep us updated," they said.

"I'll call you tomorrow if I can."

I was still determined not to cooperate. I simply dug in my heels further. This wasn't about being afraid of hard labor; it was about principle. I'd done my share of MEST work at the Ranch and could do it with ease again if I had to. But I wasn't going to accept an unjustified punishment.

Eventually, someone was sent out to the Hacienda to begin security-checking me. In the past, I had always been obliging with my security checks, but now I had had enough. I deliberately challenged the sec-checker by trying to leave the room. I knew I would be denied, but I did it anyway. I just didn't care. Sure enough, my auditor/sec-checker was bigger and stronger, and she prevailed, keeping me in the room for hours.

Finally, I agreed to give some withholds and pretended to be happy, so that my needle would float and she could end the session. Auditors were under tremendous pressure to make sure they didn't miss withholds and could not end a session without getting what they were supposed to get. A lot of times, I cooperated solely out of my empathy for the auditor.

The next day, Mr. Anne Rathbun came to see me. I thought there might have been a slim chance that she would come to my defense, but that was not to be. She told me that I was so far off track and out ethics that saying she was disappointed in me was an understatement. She said I really needed to get my act together and frightened me with her emphatic delivery. At my next auditing session, I tried cooperating with my auditor to see if that helped anything, but I didn't feel better. I just felt I had agreed to something against my will.

When I awoke in the morning, I was told that I had to go to the base immediately, as someone urgently needed to speak to me. It was an emergency, just throw on whatever clothes I had and get to the base. I was terrified.

The driver, a guy I knew from CMO who was driving like a maniac, brought me to the WB. Upstairs, Mr. Rathbun met me and curtly told me to write my overts and withholds, while I waited in the auditing room. I was already writing when a few minutes later, in walked Uncle Dave, looking very unhappy.

"What are you doing?" he asked.

"Writing my overts and withholds, as I was instructed by Mr. Rathbun," I told him.

"Hmm, I see," he said very distantly. "Are you in ethics trouble?"

"Yes, sir" I said, almost bursting into tears.

"What for?" he demanded.

"I was trying to call my parents and I got into a fight and—"

He cut me off with a low-pitched, "Unbelievable, just unbelievable." Then he raised his voice significantly, saying, "There will be no more special treatment for you." With that, he left the room. He hadn't even heard my whole story, not that any of it would have made him less angry.

Seconds later, Aunt Shelly came into the room, accompanied by the CO, Olivia, and Mr. Anne Rathbun. They all stood at the side of the room, crossed their arms, and looked at me. Aunt Shelly was especially furious.

"Jenna, I have been like a guardian . . . no, a guardian angel to you," she began. She continued describing her generosity. "I have given you my time, looked after you, and all you have done is take advantage of it." Next, she started with her opinion of me. "You have been completely outrageous. What do you do? You find some loser and start acting like *him*?" Apparently, she was referring to Martino.

She went on and on, telling me how the only person on the planet allowed to call the Int base was Uncle Dave. She cited my long history of running to my parents whenever I felt like it, violation one—distracting them from their jobs and violation two—being so needy and entitled.

I tried to say that I had only seen them both once in the last three years so how could this be true, but she cut me off.

"Don't you dare backflash me!" she commanded.

She continued with her grievances, using my petition and anything else she'd heard about my behavior. I was grossly out ethics for flirting on course, just one step down from having sex in an auditing session. I had always been unethical and uncooperative with my auditors; and now I was even getting into physical fights with them, punching Olivia and spitting at Melinda. Throughout her rant, she had been looking at me with fury, and I finally began to cry.

"Yes, acting like a baby," she said angrily. "Just another one of your tactics. So stop it, now."

I sucked it up with all of my might, but she wasn't done.

"Everywhere you go gets ruined. The Ranch was created because of you, and now it is because of you that it is a giant mess that I have to handle."

At this point, she could have been saying anything, her claims were so ridiculous. No matter what, though, her next threat was even worse. "If you continue this way, you are going to get your name changed to something else, as it is completely out PR." She was referring to the fact that I was a Miscavige, so as a representative of my family, my conduct had to be exemplary. "You are going to get through a program and you better cooperate. You'd better be good, and you'd better do it."

Her words were grave. "Yes, sir," I said, growing anxious as she turned to leave.

"Will *you* still talk to me?" I pleaded, trying not to cry again.

"I don't know, Jenna," she said with a twinge of heart and just enough manipulation underlying her words. "Maybe if you get through your program." With that, the whole group filed out of the room.

I couldn't believe how I had come to this, how unethical I had been. I had risked losing everything I had worked for and dreamed about my whole life for some guy I just met a few months ago. I knew that I had to make up for this, that I had a long road ahead of me, but I vowed to myself I would. As I was finishing my thought, Anne Rathbun returned to the room, closed the door, glared at me, and told me to pick up the cans.

CHAPTER TWENTY

PUNISHED

MR. ANNE RATHBUN GAVE ME A METERED ETHICS INTERVIEW, essentially a one-session security check, then immediately demoted me to the CMO EPF. With everything that had gone down, and the fact that my uncle and aunt had gotten involved, I was just happy the punishment wasn't worse. I could not believe that I was back there. I had been demoted, and had to wear a different uniform to show it. Because of the crackdown on flirting, Mayra, Julia, and another girl were all with me.

While not nearly as strict or isolating as the RPF, it was nevertheless demeaning, as it was intended to be. We were all put on rice and beans for every meal. I was subjected to security checks and assigned the laundry and cleaning duty. We still lived in our berthing at the Hacienda. At first, I'd go to sleep every night beating myself up about my flaws, thinking I was the most worthless person in the entire Sea Org. I didn't regret meeting Martino, but I was disappointed in myself for being unethical. I didn't know how I could have betrayed my family in this way, or why I had put up so much resistance. I knew I had a long way to go to be the nice, respectful, and conforming person that I expected to be.

I'd wake in the morning totally discouraged, no end in sight, with a dark cloud hanging over my head. I was told that Cece, Martino, and Tyler and the others were only my friends because of my name, and not because I had anything likable about me. I wasn't allowed to speak to them. I had no life and nothing to look forward to. I had to gather all my strength to get up each morning and do what was expected of me to get out of this mess. All this was exactly the reaction they wanted. In many ways, this was how I felt when I'd first come to Flag at age twelve; only this time it was much, much worse.

Mayra was assigned to watching me and had to keep me in sight at all times. Even in the bathroom, she had to wait outside my stall. I was forbidden to use the phone to call anyone, including my parents. Our laundry chores were downgraded, as we were now not trustworthy enough to do the laundry for the executives. Instead, we had to do it for the CMO staff.

My daily schedule revolved around Mr. Rathbun's security-checking me. I was beginning to realize that any niceness she had ever shown me had been a façade, because she clearly hated me. Now that I was on the outs with Uncle Dave and Aunt Shelly, she wasn't compelled to be nice to me because of my family ties. She was now liberated to tell me just how big a piece of shit I was. She told me continually that I belonged on the RPF and was lucky I was saved. Sometimes I was bold enough to tell her she should just do it, instead of wasting her precious time on me. "Maybe I will," she'd snapped in response, but she never did.

Our sessions were ridiculous. They all went the same way.

"Have you used your name inappropriately to get what you wanted?" she'd ask, then look at me expectantly, as if the meter had indicated that I had.

"No," I'd respond, and she'd turn red and tighten her lips, while seemingly exercising the utmost restraint not to slap me across the face, for not bursting with answers to her question.

Twenty minutes would go by with her asking the same question, and, finally, I'd make something up.

"Okay," I'd begin, and continue with something like, "the other day the crew steward came to our table and asked us if we needed anything. I asked if he could please get some butter. He did so really quickly, and I think he did it so fast because he knew who my uncle was, and I felt guilty about that."

Inevitably my answer would cause Mr. Rathbun to spin it into something even more evil. "Okay, did your request cause him to not serve the others as well as he could have?" followed by "How many others did he not serve because he was busy tending to *your* needs?"

The meter thought the correct answer was fifteen, so I just agreed. This was how security checks went. If you didn't have anything to confess, you needed to be clever enough to fluidly make stuff up to get you out of there.

When I wasn't cleaning/doing laundry or in session with Mr. Rathbun, I was at the staff college listening to the "State of Man Congress Lectures" by LRH. In true LRH style, the lectures took you through topics ranging from various Greek philosophers to the story of ancient Rome and how its downfall was because of out 2Ds, to all of L. Ron Hubbard's purported past lives along the way. They were essentially about how honesty and clean hands were important. Anyone who didn't like Scientology or spoke badly about another person or matter, regardless of how right they might be, was saying those things only because they had done something harmful that they were hiding.

In other words, if you ever disagreed with anything and spoke up, you were told that *you* had something to hide. And if you had nothing to hide in the present, then your transgression must have stretched into a past life. I never knew if I felt this way because I had the worst hidden crimes of anyone in the world, crimes so bad they were hidden deep inside. If I had hidden crimes, as everyone kept telling me, what were they?

ONE AFTERNOON, IN THE MIDDLE OF ANOTHER MONOTONOUS day, I was in the staff college, listening to my tapes, when a girl whose face I knew walked in. It was Kiri, followed by about twenty other kids from the Ranch, including B. J. I was shocked. I couldn't imagine what they were doing here. They all saw me and smiled and waved excitedly, but when they tried to approach, the supervisor told them to move along, as this was strictly forbidden in the course room.

Ever mindful that Mayra was always watching me, I was also aware that she wasn't obligated to follow me into the bathroom when we were both on course. I just hoped that Kiri would use the same strategy. Sure enough, about twenty minutes later, Kiri and my friend Caitlin gave me a silent signal stare and walked into the bathroom.

I waited at least forty-five seconds, then got up myself. "Where are you going?" the supervisor wanted to know. I told her I needed to go to the bathroom, and she allowed it on the condition that I'd be meter-checked afterward. *Give me ten meter checks*, I thought. I didn't care; I just wanted to see my friends.

They were waiting for me there. I gave them huge hugs and was so excited to see them. I asked what they were doing there.

"We're on the EPF," Kiri said. "We're going to be posted at Flag." I was shocked.

"What about the Ranch?" I asked.

"Your mom and dad have been on some special project at the Ranch to find guardians for all of us and send everyone to Flag, or if they were unqualified for Flag, to PAC. There is nobody at the Ranch anymore."

I was speechless. It was hard to believe that the Ranch was empty of kids. No one knew for sure why it had closed. But, years later, my mom mentioned how Uncle Dave had told her that the Ranch was not only a waste of money, it was a distraction to the parents at the Int Base. The kids needed to learn Scientology and learn a real job.

Shocked as I was, I could barely contain my excitement that they were in Clearwater, but I could see the fear on their faces. They had all just been sent three thousand miles away from their parents, who were at Int. At least they came together. When I made the trip three years earlier, I was all of twelve and all alone. I hugged them again and told them it was going to be okay, that they would like it here. They could see from my CMO EPF uniform that I was in some kind of trouble, and I briefly told them what had happened.

Just then, Mayra walked into the bathroom, obviously knowing what was going on but not being in a ratting mood, thank goodness. She seemed to be willing to keep our bathroom rendezvous secret, but she did give us an "Okay, wrap it up" look. Kiri, Caitlin, and I grasped hands, then went back to study.

For the next few days, the highlight of my day was when they would all walk into the course room and smile and wave. I would always try to get a seat facing the door, even though it wasn't always possible. Another time that week, I went to their course room under the pretense of cleaning up. Kiri was in tears, telling me how scared she was to be so far away from her parents. I tried to reassure her, telling her how I'd be there for her.

Later that day, I decided to try to advocate for my friends, who were definitely struggling. Since my own experience had been very similar, I was in the perfect position to help. I wrote a letter to my CO, telling her that some of the transferred Cadets might be upset or distressed because they weren't going to be seeing their parents anymore. I told her that Kiri was downhearted, and maybe there was something we could do, like give them a session to make them feel better. I even offered to meet them and give them a pep talk.

My plan backfired. The next day my CO pulled me aside and screamed at me. "The kids from the Ranch haven't even been here a week, and you are already poisoning them!" she yelled. "I spoke to Kiri, and she is totally fine!" With that, she told me I was forbidden to speak to or see them again.

I felt my face flush with anger, but one more backflash and I was off to RPF. Julia was already on my last nerve, with her frequent and purposeful personal attacks. Not only was she the ultimate tattletale, but she now hated me, which was a lethal combination. She would be excruciatingly sweet and kind when any execs were nearby, then look at me with disgust the moment they left. She started getting more and more in favor with the execs, mostly by kissing butt and putting others down. On the contrary, I was told to take different routes into and out of the WB so that I would never have to cross paths with Uncle Dave and Aunt Shelly, as I would just enturbulate them.

It was hard enduring weeks of hearing all the negative labels being attributed to me by Julia, my CO and Mr. Anne Rathbun, who would launch personal attacks on me after every session, calling me "out ethics," a "criminal," and finally an "SP." All of these instances of people telling me how bad and evil I was forced me to look at myself and examine my feelings, intentions and what I really knew to be true. As a result, I underwent a mental shift. I came to see that all of these people telling me that I was bad were just a bunch of hypocrites. They claimed to care about other people but, in reality, their selfishness was quite transparent. All you had to do was look for it and trust yourself. I knew I'd done things wrong, but I also knew that my transgressions, despite what people around me were saying, were not evil.

Suddenly, I wasn't afraid to call things what they were or trust my own judgment about other people, as well as myself. Previously, I'd compare my actual feelings to whatever Scientology said I was supposed to feel. If I felt anything else, then surely the problem was with me. As a result, I doubted myself constantly. I doubted whether I was a good person; I doubted whether the people around me were good people; I doubted whether my emotions were appropriate—all because Scientology made me feel that *I* was the problem.

Now, for the first time, I was able to see myself for what I was: Someone who made mistakes and was trying to make up for them. I might not have made great decisions, but that didn't make me bad and it certainly didn't make me evil. "Evil" was where they made their mistake—I might have had doubts, but I came to recognize that I was not evil. If there was one thing I was certain of, it's that I cared about other people. I cared about my friends tremendously and would have put them before myself at any moment. I knew I was not an SP, because SPs did not feel that way. I knew without a doubt that I was a good person, and, no matter what anyone else thought or said about me, no matter who they were or how important, I didn't care. When I realized this, down to the moment, the clouds opened up.

This realization was the beginning of personal integrity, when, instead of dismissing my feelings or my intuition, I found myself following them, even if they led me to a place that Scientology said was wrong.

It was amazing. Now, when I got yelled at, I would just say, "Yes, sir" so flatly, unconvincingly, and meaninglessly that I was starting to piss people off. I wouldn't let them get to me. I would even smile a little bit, because I knew that I wasn't listening and they were getting so worked up. At staff meetings, I would get called on in front of the whole group to tell them my "flap," which was stuff that had come up in my sessions. Maybe it was that I had smiled at my friend, which was the same as not concentrating on my studies. Or I might have chatted for one minute with Mayra instead of working like a slave. Anything I did wrong had to come up in my sessions.

"Jenna, do you have a flap?" the CO would demand from me in front of everybody.

"No, not other than the one that everyone already knows about, and that I already announced last week," I'd offer.

This would undoubtedly be an opening for an attack on me. "Oh, real smart, Jenna! Be a smart-ass to your CO in front of everybody! Change your attitude, or you will go straight to cleaning pots and pans in the galley!" She used me as an example for the entire group of how *not* to act.

Tom's wife, Jenny, was at Flag now and was holding my mom's old post in the Watchdog Committee. I still had fond memories of the time I had spent with her when I had come for my Key to Life course. She asked to speak to me alone, hoping to get me to see things differently. She told me that she had been in trouble a few times and didn't always agree with what she had to do as a result, but she had pushed through it by reciting LRH's two rules for happy living: one, "be able to experience anything," and two, "Cause only those things which others are able to experience easily."

I wasn't sure I totally got her point, but I thought she was on my side. But the next day, in front of everyone, she directly told me that I had been given so much, and I needed to be grateful and show compassion.

I was dumbfounded. "Compassion?" I asked. "Are you serious?"

The reason I was in trouble wasn't that I needed to show compassion, it was that I'd shown too much compassion. I had befriended people that they considered too far below them to be worth befriending. I couldn't help but think how contradictory and pompous a respected authority was sounding.

All I had done was try to make Kiri feel safe, because I had once been scared in the same way that she was. I was trying to advocate for the greater good and, instead, I was made to feel like a selfish, entitled brat. At the moment, I wasn't under the impression that the CMO was all about serving mankind. It seemed like it was more about tightening the clamps.

Jenny just dismissed my outburst with a laugh, "That was so Jenna." I had no idea what she meant by that, but at least I didn't get in trouble for backflashing.

After a couple of months, Mr. Rathbun turned my sec-check sessions over to Jelena, a CMO auditor. In our sessions, Jelena would wear a headset and a mic. Many times, I could hear people yelling directions at her through the headset, telling her questions to ask me, which resulted in many eight-hour sessions. The only way I got through it was by answering as quickly as I could and by trying to float the needle by thinking happy thoughts—a task that, of late, had gotten increasingly difficult.

ONE DAY, AFTER A COUPLE OF MONTHS ON THE EPF, I WAS FI-nally allowed to go to school on a Sunday with everyone else; it was there that I saw Martino. For the day, I was now under the watch of Steven, a little CMO boy, as Mayra was too old to go to school. I saw that Martino, who was doing MEST work, was under watch, too. One time, when Steven was lagging behind, I ducked into the room that I knew Martino was in.

He looked very wary as I approached. I beckoned to him so that we could talk, but he glanced at the two people watching him, who were eying me suspiciously. I signaled to him to come anyway. His guards looked at each other, and then looked away, meaning they would pretend that they didn't see. They were just Cadets, after all, not as hard-core as the people in CMO who were watching me. My tears started welling up as he came over.

"I am so, so sorry," I whispered to him. "I never meant any of this to happen. I begged them to leave you out of everything, and I feel horrible that I got you into this."

He cut me off, taking responsibility. "Oh, my gosh, this is not just your fault," he said. "Don't even say that. I feel like I've ruined everything for you. You are on the CMO EPF now," he said apologetically, gesturing to my uniform.

Just then, little Steven walked up. "What is going on here?" he asked with the seriousness of a police officer, but the voice of a little boy. He was only ten and about a foot shorter than me. It would have been hard to take him seriously in any situation but, as my guard, it was downright disturbing how authoritative a little boy could be when given a little bit of power. Martino put his hand on mine briefly before he turned to go. The two boys watching him were his friends, and he was likely to be safer after this brief chat than I was.

Now that Martino had left, I looked at Steven pleadingly, hoping he would not say anything. Steven had been my friend prior to all of this. I had even saved him from the wrath of Julia once, and hoped that he would return the favor, but no such luck. A few minutes later, he was on the phone reporting what had happened. About thirty minutes later, someone had driven the Org car to the Quality Inn to get me. School was over before it had started; I was no longer allowed to go there.

The cycle felt impossible to defeat. Even if I behaved perfectly, things would keep coming up that pulled me back. It was exhausting.

Finally, after months of me being a stain on the face of the universe, my CO asked me what was stopping me from getting through my program. I was honest. I told her that I couldn't get over some of the claims that had been made about me: that I ran to my parents on every whim and that I had been the cause of the closing of the Ranch. I also took issue with the amount of flap my using the phone had created. I told her that, from what my Ranch friends were telling me on the down low, they called their parents at Int all the time.

I requested a conversation with Aunt Shelly. She agreed to talk to me, seeming both reluctant and relieved, as if she had wanted to talk for some time. The meeting took place in one of the auditing rooms in the WB. Shelly was curt and standoffish when she came in, greeting me with a hello instead of her usual hug.

After telling her about my progress, I got into my disputes of the claims against me. When I began getting specific, she became very angry.

"I took time out of my day to talk to you, and now you just want to tell me I was wrong? Even if some claims against you aren't absolutely accurate, plenty of things in your ethics file *are*." She let that sink in before continuing in a softer tone, "In my opinion, your troubles stem from misunderstood words on course, specifically those in *Vol Zero*, and you just need to go back and clear them." This was her way of acknowledging that it wasn't all my fault or simply because I was a bad person.

I thought she would leave it at that, but she had a warning about men, too: "Many guys who are hungry for power and eager for information marry CMO girls for this purpose and wind up bringing the girls down. You need to watch out for that, because it's been proven in history."

Although she didn't say as much, I could tell that I would be somewhat pardoned now. The part about men suggested that she thought some of this was Martino's fault, that I was his unsuspecting victim and should stay away from him and clear my MUs. Shelly even gave me a hug after we talked.

Miraculously, the next day, the attitude about me had changed. Aunt Shelly had obviously been receptive to at least part of my self-defense, because she seemed to have had a change of heart that quickly spread to everyone around her. Initially, she had wanted to make it known that it wasn't acceptable to disagree with her and get away with it. On the other hand, I thought her anger might have been obligatory, as though, perhaps, my uncle was the one pissed about my fraternizing and Aunt Shelly had to display the anger or she'd be in trouble herself. Whatever the underlying cause, she must have been tired of being mad at me, because she certainly calmed down.

Now, instead of being viewed as the enemy of the group, I was seen as having made huge steps toward recovery and on my way back to being in everyone's good graces. At the time, I simply accepted the change for what it was—a welcome relief—but looking back, it represents as clear an indication as anything about just how much sway Uncle Dave and Aunt Shelly had over people. For months, I'd been tormented and insulted. I'd been embarrassed and harassed. I'd been put in my place and told that I was the lowest of the low. Yet, in spite of all that, it took just one conversation with Aunt Shelly to put things on a path to improvement. While the situation worked to my benefit in this case because Aunt Shelly clearly had a soft spot for me and decided to forgive me, it also made me afraid of what could happen if Uncle Dave or Aunt Shelly simply didn't want to forgive someone.

None of this forgiveness meant I was excused from having to repeat the CMO EPF; however, I was allowed to have brief conversations with my friends from the Ranch, although I was still not allowed to fraternize. Soon, many of the kids from the Flag Cadet Org came on the EPF, including Martino, Jasmine, and Cece. It was cool, because my Flag friends made great friends with all my Ranch friends, especially B. J., who had been struggling since coming out from the West Coast. They took him under their wing almost as a favor to me. I was finally allowed to graduate in November 1999, having been on the CMO EPF for five months.

• • •

BACK AS A GOOD-STANDING MEMBER OF CMO, I WAS GIVEN A new post, Flag Crew Programs Operator. Flag Crew was five hundred people strong and responsible for running the five hotels and four restaurants that the public Scientologists who had come to Clearwater for services used. Each hotel had its own maids and maintenance, and the restaurants had hosts, servers, cooks, dishwashers, and busboys. As programs operator, I ran programs to resolve organizational dysfunction.

I loved this post far above and beyond being on full-time study. I had a job, which was all that I had ever wanted. I wasn't holed up in a course room all day but had freedom to walk around the building. I got to meet new people, make friends, and feel like I was producing something. My boss, the operations chief, was a really cool guy. He was smart, helpful, and reasonable and appreciated that I was a hard worker. Occasionally, I was scolded for wearing my civilian clothes inappropriately. For PR purposes, we were allowed to wear civilian clothes on Sundays, but my CO often had to tell me to put on something less tight and better suited for my position, as I was not a little girl anymore. For my part, I didn't think my clothes were out of line.

I hardly saw Martino anymore. After he graduated from EPF, he was posted as someone who carried pre-Clear folders to and from the case supervisors, but that was not my area, so I rarely went there. Once or twice, I did try to go through the hotel to see if I might run into him, but I never did. In spite of everything that had happened, I was still in love with him and still thought about him all the time. I heard rumors that other girls liked him, so I figured that he was probably caught up in that. I also knew that he had been threatened with the RPF if he messed up again. Still, I remained close with our mutual friends.

Christmas 2000 came and went, just another Christmas spent

away from my family. Gone were the years of flying out to Int for the Beer & Cheese Party and the ski lodge trip with the Miscavige family. I hadn't spoken to my parents since July, before I'd gone on the CMO EPF, although I did get occasional letters, more from Dad than Mom. I don't know why, but them being back together gave me a sense of stability, making me feel like things were a little bit more like they had been before Don and before Mom's RPF. I guessed they both saw Mom's affair as something that had happened as a result of them being separated for so long. For all practical purposes, it didn't really matter, because I saw them so rarely.

As time went by, I became more successful at keeping Martino out of my thoughts. I switched my school day so that I wouldn't run into him on Sundays. During course time, I started sitting near a kid named Wil, who was tall and cute. I could tell he liked me, because he always saved me a seat. Cool and funny, he also played guitar, which of course impressed me. I liked talking to him, because he always listened. He hadn't grown up in the Sea Org, so I was fascinated when he would tell me about his life in the Wog world.

I never felt the same way about Wil as I had about Martino, however, even though I was moving on. It was all good until one day after school when I was waiting for the bus back to the Hacienda with everyone else. Wil, waiting with me, was holding my hand to see me off. All of a sudden, I saw Martino race by, clearly trying to avoid the sight of us. We no longer had the same school day, so it was really weird. I hadn't seen him in ages. The following week, I was walking into the course room and over to my seat near Wil. Sitting on the other side of him was Martino, a huge grin on his face. I had deliberately changed my school day to avoid him and stay out of trouble, and now he was sitting at my table. I was annoyed and even a little angry with him. I felt that he had just become disinterested in me, and I was hurt by that, although it could have been that the reason he was avoiding me was that he was trying to stay out of trouble. Whatever the case, I was trying hard to get over him, and I believed I was.

Martino seemed to be enjoying all the discomfort he was creating by being there, which made me even more annoyed. I grabbed Wil, and we moved next door, but Martino moved, too, again sitting right at our table. I wanted to strangle him, but even Wil seemed to think it was a little funny but awkward. I just couldn't figure out why Martino was doing this. I had finally moved on, and he was intruding. I decided to act as if he wasn't there.

The next week, things got worse. I had recently gotten word about Justin, whom I hadn't heard from in well over a year. A Ranch friend visiting Flag had recently spoken to him and had his number. I decided to call him during lunch.

The area code was L.A., so I figured he must be living there. While he was out of the Sea Org, I thought he might still be a Scientologist to some degree. Some girl who answered the phone put him on. When he said, "Hello," he was not excited in the least, even though I was practically giddy. At first, he acted as if he had no idea who I was. Eventually, after prodding and probing, he came clean.

"Look, I don't give a shit about my family. They don't mean anything to me. You're with Ronnie and Bitty doing their thing and I don't want anything to do with them, either."

"But, Justin, I'm not with them. I haven't spoken to them in forever. What does your problem with them have to do with me?"

It was no use, though; he couldn't be reasoned with.

"I don't give a shit about them; I don't give a shit about you. I don't have a sister."

And, with that, he hung up the phone.

I was devastated. I had no idea what had just happened or why, and I had taken a risk by calling him.

When I got back to class, I was barely holding it together.

Though I hadn't spoken to Justin since he'd left the Sea Org, I never expected our first conversation would be like that. I never expected the anger that he had. His words confirmed my worst fear when he walked out of Flag almost two years earlier: that he was lost to me. Worse, it was of his own choosing.

Wil was oblivious, but Martino, who was back to sitting at our table again, could see I was upset and asked me what was wrong. I tried as hard as I could not to cry as I told him about the phone call. Martino was empathetic and said, somewhat jokingly, that he was going to kick Justin's ass, which made me laugh because my brother was so much bigger than Martino. For his part, Wil sat quietly, not even part of the conversation. When he went to the bathroom a few minutes later, Martino put his hand on mine. I could have moved it, but I didn't.

The rest of the day went by quickly. When it was time for the bus, Wil tried to kiss me goodbye, but I dodged it, causing him to ask me outright if it was because of Martino. I lied and told him it wasn't; I just wanted to slow it down.

For the next week, I tried to avoid Wil, but he simply could not be avoided. Wil kept paging me and cornering me. Finally, he had a libs day and was not in school, which left Martino and me alone to talk. We were back in sync in no time, talking about everything and commiserating. Now that he was a Sea Org member, he wasn't scrutinizing Scientology in quite the same way, but that was fine with me—I wasn't, either. And that difference didn't change how comfortable we were around each other. When we walked around, he leaned into me, just as he always had, and all of my feelings rushed back. Later that week, I just had to tell Wil that I still had feelings for Martino. He was sad and had suspected as much. He was really upset when I broke it off with him, but I preferred to tell him rather than string him along.

After that, Martino and I went back almost to how things had been before everything fell apart. At school, we'd sit next to each other in the course room with our legs intertwined under the table, and during breaks we'd talk to each other. Once again, school day was my favorite day of the week.

One afternoon, while we were waiting for the bus, we talked about how not being able to date was such a drag. We were both in Sea Org, so we should be allowed to. The issue was that Aunt Shelly and Anne Rathbun forbade it. It was all unspoken, but she essentially had determined that he was bad news, so I was constantly being watched. I had already done bad things with him, so for me to go back to him would show that I hadn't changed.

"Look, Jenna," he said, catching my eye but then looking down at his feet, "I'm—I'm at the point where I'm not sure I even care about the trouble we might get into."

And, with that, he pulled me close and kissed me.

CHAPTER TWENTY-ONE

SECURITY CHECKS

THAT NIGHT, I WENT HOME AND TOLD ALL THE GIRLS IN MY DORM that Martino had kissed me. I was so happy; I couldn't stop myself. Despite the risks, Martino and I began to see more of each other. Because he was no longer a Cadet, technically we were allowed to see each other; however, from the reprimands Aunt Shelly and Mr. Rathbun had given me, I knew that they forbade the two of us from being together. During the week, we would talk, but always had to hide. Someone would inevitably walk in, so we would just have enough time to quickly grasp hands before I slinked away.

By the end of September, I was in a better place than ever before. I loved my job. I had a ton of friends both inside and outside the CMO, even if it were on the down low, and all my childhood friends from the Ranch were now at Flag. Best of all, I was finally going to be with Martino. I should have known it was all too good. More important, I should have listened to my friend's when he warned me that Martino and I should be careful, as it was the same time of year we had gotten in trouble the first time.

A few days later, Mr. Rathbun called me into her office. She said we were going to do a metered interview. She had all sorts of weird questions, some about my parents' old coin collection and others about a bunch of photographs, and if I had seen them before. Mr. Rathbun said the photos were on a roll of film that I had sent to my dad. One was a photo of my roommate, Mayra, which I'd taken without realizing she was in her underwear with a shirt on. Over the course of several months, I'd taken a bunch of other photos and sent the whole roll to my dad so that he could have them developed. I was a bit confused as to how she'd gotten hold of the photos, but odd as the questions were, I was more focused on the fact that she had yet to ask me about Martino. I figured I'd cooperate in any way I could so that I wouldn't draw her attention to him.

Still, the interview went uncharacteristically smoothly, and Mr. Rathbun said she would let me know if she had any other questions. Perhaps best of all had been the fact that she hadn't asked a single question about Martino.

Unfortunately, the next day, she called me in again. This time, she started asking more personal questions and if I was hiding anything, exactly the questions I'd been thankful to escape the previous day. She didn't seem to know anything that was happening with Martino, but she was also asking questions about my parents. I tried to sidestep her questions, but she wouldn't have it, and, apparently, neither would the E-Meter.

"I am going to find out what you're hiding," she said, in an ominous tone.

Finally, after several hours of intense questioning, I broke down. I told her the truth about kissing Martino. First, she wanted to know why I felt the need to hide it, which I thought was a really stupid question. Then, she made me tell her every single detail, from how close we were to each other when we kissed, to how long it lasted, to what my intentions were, to what led up to it, to every minuscule thought and action. Revealing all those details about such a private moment was excruciating. They were the kinds of personal details that should have been insignificant to everybody but me. Not to mention that, had it not been for Aunt Shelly and Mr. Rathbun's stance against Martino, he and I would have been allowed to kiss. Out 2Ds only applied to heavy petting and sex, so I wasn't sure why I was being subjected to this detailed interrogation.

When it was over, I was sure I was in serious trouble, but instead, Mr. Rathbun said I could return to post. Unsure of what to prepare for, I told Martino about the session, and he seemed worried for me but also acted as though he didn't care what she thought. In his opinion, we weren't doing anything wrong, so there was no reason to be afraid. Two days went by, making me think I was in the clear, until I was summoned again. This time, Mr. Rathbun informed me that I was getting another security check, which, again, would last several weeks.

The first withhold I gave up for this sec-check was my confession that I had gotten my belly button pierced a few weeks back, during my first libs day in months. I had it done for my sixteenth birthday in the company of my cousins, some of their friends, and Aunt Denise, who signed the consent form as my mother. My grandmother had warned me that it would get me in trouble, but I had done it anyway.

Bizarrely, Mr. Rathbun seemed to be cool with it, but her news about Martino was even better.

"Just put things on hold with him for a bit, Jenna," she told me. "Just while this security check is going on. After that, you guys can pick up where you left off."

I couldn't believe she'd actually said those words. Painful as it would be not to see him for a bit, if it meant that, in a few weeks, Martino and I would no longer have to sneak around, it would be worth it. The next time I saw Martino, I told him the news. He was bummed and annoyed that we had to wait, but I told him that I would get through it quickly. He wasn't thrilled but decided to trust me.

A few days later, I saw him when he was with his mother, a boisterous Italian woman with a huge personality, who I liked in her own right regardless that she was Martino's mother. She leaned toward me to whisper that I should be strong and not feel bad, because bad people only pick on the good people. She gave me a hug, and Martino grabbed my hand, smiled sadly, told me to hurry and get through this, and walked away. It was the last time I ever saw him.

THAT AFTERNOON, MR. RATHBUN HAD A SURPRISE FOR ME. IN her office were my two superiors, my CO and the Ops Chief. In the same fashion as Aunt Shelly, she castigated me, saying I was grossly out ethics and that I belonged on the RPF. I couldn't understand what had changed since my last session. She was totally hurtful. She told me in no uncertain terms that my so-called friends only liked me because of my name, and that I was a Rock Slammer at heart; I just hadn't Rock Slammed yet. She was so completely different than she had been the last time we met. I felt betrayed.

Immediately, Mr. Rathbun ordered that I be put under full-time watch and back into a CMO EPF uniform—though I wasn't actually on EPF. I had to clean the bathrooms and stairwells endlessly. The new head of our department had to stay with me. He would stand around in the stairwell or the bathrooms for several hours while I cleaned. She was pulled from her duty and replaced, however, when word got out that she had warmed up to me and was even telling me Harry Potter stories to help pass the time.

Upset as I was about this, I found myself much more in control of my emotions than I had been after I'd submitted the petition to Aunt Shelly to rejoin the Cadet Org. In part, because I'd been so happy with how my life was going, I was interested in simply fulfilling my tasks and getting things back to normal. I simply did what I had to do, so that sooner or later they would let me go back to Martino and my life.

Different as my reaction was this time, something still bothered me about my punishment: I wasn't sure what I'd done to deserve it. Sure, I'd been hiding things with Martino, but, again, it was a situation where the punishment didn't fit the crime. I hadn't broken a Scientology law; all I did was go against what Aunt Shelly and Mr. Rathbun had said. I honestly had no idea why I was punished to this degree. Yes, I had been with Martino, and yes, I got my belly button pierced, but those weren't against policy. Sometimes I slacked off a few times when I should have been working, but no more so than anyone else. Other offenders didn't have RTC waiting to sec-check them anytime they looked sideways. Why was this the case for me?

When I wasn't cleaning, I was going through grueling security checks with Mr. Rathbun. They were laden with questions tailor-made just for me: Have you used your name inappropriately to get your way? Do you have an evil intention against your uncle? Security checks were the Church's ultimate control mechanism and the sessions were all videotaped. In most cases, they used security checks to keep you cleaned up to get you back onto the Bridge. However, in my case, they were used to keep me in line. I got sec-checks because I nattered, disagreed, was difficult, or because I was frequently upset, which was considered "ARC Breaky." Between the ages of twelve and fifteen, I had at least eight security checks. No other staff member that I was aware of had this many in such a short period of time, unless, of course, they were on the RPF. I hated the security checks and never understood why I had so many.

Anytime someone was upset or disagreed with something in the organization, the Church said it was because you had withholds. Any criticism you had, anything you didn't agree with, essentially any dissent you had, was because you had done something bad. That was how they shut people up. In addition to looking at my life in search of withholds, I was encouraged and expected to look into my past lives to find answers about earlier, similar withholds that had caused me to act out.

I wasn't allowed to jump right into past lives. I had to get there slowly, answering all my auditor's questions as they were presented. If my E-Meter indicated I was on an earlier similar path, I was encouraged to continue. This emphasis on past lives always made me feel as though I were making up answers, but it also made things easier. When I couldn't come up with any real withholds, which was more often than not, it helped to be able to delve into a fantastical world of past lives where anything was possible. Sometimes I would feel better, but it could have just been because I was getting off the subject of my current life withholds and was able to talk about some imaginary life, which was easier and a huge relief. As long as the auditor said the E-Meter showed that I was on the right track, there wasn't any skepticism about what I was saying. Nobody was verifying any of my stories with actual science.

Many people would make up all kinds of exaggerated stories. They would come up with overts, in which they would confess to blowing up planets with bombs and outlandish things like that. They would come up with elaborate plots and detailed characters that were often hard to believe. I was more restrained. I never created fully realized characters or in-depth stories; I wasn't bold enough to act as though I knew it all for sure. I used my past life memories strategically, when I thought they would help move a session along.

Often my past lives were some alternate version of myself.

Usually, I was just some girl in a scene, a piece of a larger past life that I would never see. I would supposedly remember being a girl hundreds of years ago, who was poor and had to steal something. Another time, I remembered being a girl being chased down the street by an evil, scary man, and I wound up killing him. At the time, I imagined that this bad man was an image from a past life and was the reason I was scared at night, or anxious and paranoid that I was being followed. Often, it was something taken straight out of a movie I had seen or a book I had read, but I made it my own. My needle would always float at the end, so I wasn't about to argue with that. I was never fully convinced that the needle had to do with my story's accuracy. I was always told that as I moved up the Bridge, my recall of past lives would improve greatly.

Faking my way through the past lives didn't make me skeptical about the whole practice, though. I'd known about past lives my whole life, and while I felt like a bit of a fraud for not experiencing them fully, I sometimes managed to convince myself that they were indeed past lives, especially if convincing myself meant that I could get out of session more quickly.

Past lives aside, the sessions themselves were miserable, lasting upwards of six hours. Several times, I seriously considered throwing the E-Meter out the window. Mr. Rathbun was constantly putting words in my mouth and forcing me to confess to things that I hadn't done, just to give her any answer to her questions. If my needle wasn't responsive enough, she'd make me eat, whether I was hungry or not, likely because the E-Meter is supposed to respond better when you are well fed.

What I found weird was that sometimes, during session breaks, Mr. Rathbun would talk to me like a friend. I got the sense that she thought my biggest problem was entitlement; that because I was from Int and my family name was Miscavige, I thought those things allowed me special treatment. Nothing was further from the truth. In my mind, my family wasn't the Miscaviges; it was my friends in the Sea Org. I was also home here, at Flag.

AFTER A FEW WEEKS OF SEC-CHECKS, MR. RATHBUN GOT TIRED of the whole charade, telling me, in her most hostile voice, that I had so many withholds that our time would be better served if I just wrote them on the computer. That way, she could print them and send them to whoever it was that got them. It was much easier to confess to a computer than it was to her. At least, I could write things that actually happened without being hounded and harrassed. However, I would have to get meter checks along the way. When the printer wouldn't print fast enough, she would have a giant fit and scream at how much of her time I was wasting. Before long, the sec-checks resumed without the computer.

Besides sec-checks, I had to listen again to the dreaded "State of Man Congress Lectures" or scrub the toilets and the tile grout in the bathrooms with a toothbrush. If Uncle Dave or Aunt Shelly were in the building I was cleaning, I was directed to eat my meals in the bathroom so they wouldn't run into me in the hallway, because I might enturbulate them and thus hinder Scientology.

Everything about my life made me feel trapped. I was confined to the bathroom in the WB, unless I was in the auditing room with Mr. Rathbun or in another office listening to LRH tapes. I was not allowed to take the bus home, instead being driven home in a car to keep me from my friends. I was allowed a five-minute shower, then had to go to bed. Most nights, I couldn't sleep, but I couldn't go anywhere—someone was always posted outside my door. Even the letters I received from my friends were confiscated.

One evening, after I'd been cleaning bathrooms for months, Mr. Rathbun came to my door to give me important news. As usual my CO was standing right behind her.

"You are done with your ethics program," she said. "You have seen the error of your ways, and so, tonight you are going home." The statement was off because I was already home, here at the Flag base.

"Where is home?" I asked, thinking maybe she was referring to a different berthing.

"Int," she replied. With that one syllable I felt all excitement drain from my body. Flag was my home. My grandma, Aunt Denise, and my cousins all lived in Clearwater, so I finally had blood relatives nearby. All my friends were at Flag, and, perhaps most important, Martino was here. As much as I'd struggled here over the years, I'd also found a happiness that I'd never known before. Now they were asking me to leave all that behind, along with the hope that I might ever again be that happy.

"Am I coming back?" I pleaded. "Do I get to say goodbye to my grandmother?" I didn't dare even mention saying good-bye to my friends, and I definitely knew better than to ask about Martino.

"We'll say goodbye for you," piped in my CO from behind her.

"Okay," I said, stunned. I thought I would probably be back in a few days, so I took solace in that. Abruptly, the two of them came into my room and helped me shove everything I owned into some bags. I told them that I didn't need to bring everything, but they said I should, just in case. I didn't know what that meant, but it scared me. They hugged me as if we had always been great friends and said goodbye. Tom took me to the airport. I asked him to say goodbye to Martino for me, and he promised that he would.

CHAPTER TWENTY-TWO

L.A.

I ARRIVED IN LOS ANGELES, MY EYES SWOLLEN FROM CRYING throughout half the flight. Though I hadn't seen my parents much in the last four years, I had made this three-thousand-mile flight quite a few times. However, I had never been this upset about it.

A woman I vaguely recognized picked me up at the airport and, on the drive into the city, I quickly became mesmerized at how vibrant Los Angeles was. Stuck in the mass of morning traffic, I saw huge fashion billboards everywhere, hills in the distance, and people in droves talking to each other or hurrying along the streets. I felt like I was in a different world.

I settled in for what I thought was going to be a brief pass through L.A. before picking up Route 60 East for our two-hour drive to Int. Instead, the car turned into a parking lot, its gate closing automatically behind us. We crossed the street and entered a huge building I did not recognize, the Hollywood Guaranty Building. The lobby had marble walls and a soaring ceiling with a mural around the top. I still didn't know why we were here, but I decided not to ask, as the woman I was with was likely just a driver. There were other Sea Org members around, but they seemed different. They were in the old Sea Org blues, which we hadn't worn in a while. The updated uniform was less navy style, with a different color shirt and scarf. Everybody in the dated Sea Org blues looked out of place with the rest of the Sea Org world, like I had stepped back in time.

We walked past a security guard who greeted my escort, then took the elevator to the twelfth floor, where I was led into a boardroom outfitted with a green carpet and a large reddish wood table with several chairs. When I looked out the window and had a chance to evaluate my situation, I felt as though I were in a bad dream looking down at an unknown world. Twelve hours earlier, I might have had Mr. Anne Rathbun to deal with, but at least I knew where I was and who the people in my immediate vicinity were. Now I had no idea what would happen next.

"Take a seat," my driver instructed me. "Someone will be right with you." I waited anxiously. Even though my hands were cold, my palms were sweating. I hadn't slept, and I was tired, but I felt wired with worry about what was happening

Thirty minutes later, in came Anne Rathbun's husband, Marty, accompanied by B.J.'s father and our old apartment mate, Mike Rinder, who was the head of the Office of Special Affairs. I was totally surprised to see them, but this type of twist wasn't that uncommon in my life. They smiled and asked me if I wanted anything, and I said no.

Mr. Rathbun spoke first. "Look, Jenna, I don't know how else to say this, other than to be direct. Ronnie and Bitty," he said, speaking of my parents, "are out of the Sea Org."

His voice was blank and without emotion, and he waited for my reaction. It took me a few seconds to comprehend what he had said. I worked hard to conceal my own emotions.

"What happened?" I asked coolly.

"I can't really get into the details," he replied.

He started to talk about where things would go from here,

and as he spoke, two things became clear. First, I realized that everything I'd just been through—the months of security checks, bathroom cleaning, the CMO EPF uniform, and separation from Martino and my friends—was not because of something I had done, but because my parents were leaving the Sea Org which surprised me, and pissed me off. All that time that I had spent basically confined to the bathroom, wondering what I had done to warrant such punishment had not even been because of something I had done. Second, I realized that the only reason I would have been put through all that was because I was being sent off, forced to accompany my parents wherever they were. I had been receiving a leaving staff sec-check, which is given to members *leaving*, and I hadn't even known it. The stated purpose of a leaving staff sec-check was to help unburden the person leaving staff of their overts and withholds. But more likely, it was to collect personal information that could later be used against the person if he spoke out against the church.

I waited for Mr. Rathbun to finish before I asked bluntly, "So, now I am supposed to leave with them?"

Mr. Rathbun looked guilty, but he quickly affirmed my suspicions with a small nod. "You are going to join them. The plan is that you will do online Scientology courses, and when you are eighteen, you can come back if you want to."

So much was coming at me at once that I couldn't even think. I had just come out of a nightmare, but now I was supposed to leave everything I had ever known, all my friends, my whole life, to go be with my parents, whom I had hardly seen in years, whom I spoke to infrequently, and who seemed to know nothing about me. And all because *they* had decided to leave the Sea Org. They were going to turn my whole life upside down, right when I had just started settling in.

Mr. Rathbun and Mr. Rinder were trying to be very nice and watched me as I made an effort to think. Gentle though they were being, their approach set me on edge. Through the cloud of confusion, one thing stood out clearly: the situation was not normal. Sea Org members were not usually so forgiving to family members of departing Sea Org members. It didn't matter who was to blame; leaving was not something that was looked upon kindly. I knew that my parents were likely going to be declared SPs, so I decided to be blunt.

"If I leave, I am in the same boat as they are, aren't I?" I asked.

Mr. Rathbun smiled at my quickness. He'd said I could return when I was eighteen, but we both know that was a lie to placate me. He looked at Mike Rinder, who looked unsure, and then said, "Well, yes, to be honest."

I looked away and thought about it more. I thought about Martino, and how Anne Rathbun had told me we could pick up where we'd left off and how I still held out hope that was possible. I thought about my grandmother Loretta. I thought about how things had been a few months ago before Anne Rathbun called me into her office, before I started getting the sec-checks, when, at long last, I'd finally been building a life. I thought about how strongly I felt in my commitment to help others and how I believed that doing that through Scientology was the mission I had been born to do. I thought how Mr. Anne Rathbun might have known this all along and hadn't even let me say goodbye to anyone, and now I would never be able to speak to my friends again. I hated her, but none of her actions made me blame the Church; I simply blamed her and the way she was personally applying Church policy.

Then I thought of my parents' leaving. I grew angry just thinking about how selfish they were, that they didn't even consider or care that I had my own life now, a life that I'd been forced to create because of their choices for me. I thought about leaving all that behind. I thought about the prospect of going to a public school, and being called stupid and mocked, since I was so far behind. I thought about how I was all too familiar with being alone.

I knew I only had a moment to say what I wanted to say before these two men would start talking for me. I had to make a decision quickly, and I went with my overwhelming gut response. I looked right at them and said, "I don't want to go."

Tone 40. I was *not* going to take no for an answer.

They looked at each other in quiet astonishment. Finally, Mr. Rathbun spoke.

"What do you mean, Jenna?"

"I don't want to go," I repeated, adding for emphasis, "I would rather be on the RPF than leave." Admittedly, I was kind of twitchy about that, because I certainly didn't want to go on the RPF, but I wanted them to understand how serious I was. I wanted my response to be definitive.

They looked at each other again, half shocked and half amused. "Someday, you are going to be a huge asset to the Church," Mr. Rinder said, beaming at me.

Both of them had to think about what this meant and if it was even possible. They told me to wait while they discussed it outside. After about an hour, Mr. Rathbun came in and gave me a fatherly look. He told me that they were dealing with church issues other than mine, and that they wanted me to use my waiting time to study *Volume Zero*, the church's bulky administrative policy guide filled with strategies, rules, and orders, my least favorite course.

For the next several hours, I pretended to be reading it, but in reality I was just staring at its green print and thinking of my future, wondering if I was going to be allowed to stay and imagining myself in a public school if I weren't. At least eight hours went by until, finally, Mr. Rathbun came back in looking flustered, accompanied by a woman. With regret, he said they had gotten tied up with some other stuff and had lost track of time, and had forgotten they had me in there. "Since it is one o'clock, we're just going to have you leave now," he said. "We'll deal with this in the morning."

He flashed a forced smile as I said, "Okay," but there was nothing else I could do.

He introduced me to Linda, the woman with him. Standing there in her Sea Org blues with a sweater, she seemed nice enough. Mr. Rathbun told me she was going to take me to a place to sleep. She smiled, and I followed her out. "See you in the morning!" Mr. Rathbun exclaimed as he waved to us both.

We drove back to the same complex at the PAC base that my family had stayed at some fourteen years earlier when they were joining the Sea Org. It hadn't changed, although I couldn't re-member where anything was. Inside, the Sea Org members who were still wandering around at this hour stared at us, especially me. We took the elevator to the third floor, where two women coming from the shower, wearing nothing but towels, walked by us, saying, "Hi, sir," to Linda as we walked past.

The room I was staying in was at the end of the hall. Linda showed me in. "Oh good, this room has a shower," she said. "I'll meet you outside at nine tomorrow morning." And with that, she left, as I stood there gazing at myself in the mirror, wondering why so many weird things always happened to me.

I didn't know that having a shower was special, but my private shower had no soap or towels, so I couldn't have been that special. I washed my whole body and face with the shampoo I brought and dried off with a shirt from my luggage. I ignored the large cockroach crawling along the bathroom floor when I came out, closing the door behind me rather than confronting it.

I sat on the bed, the dirt on the floor sticking to my feet. Someone next door was blasting music and more people were chatting loudly outside my door. When I tried to lock it, I found it was not possible—there was no lock. Even if there had been, security and a million other people would have a master key that fit all locks, so it didn't make much difference. I opened the door to find a couple of teenagers looking back at me as though I were an alien, so I shut it as abruptly as I had opened it.

There was a window in my room that kept rattling. The bright light from the Scientology sign on the roof was shining through, but there was no curtain I could close. When I finally lay down on the bed, I left the light on because I was scared. I set the alarm clock and stared at the ceiling, unable to sleep. I didn't doubt my decision or the Church, but I found myself picturing what life on the outside would be like. I considered what it would be like to have my own room with no post responsibilities and not having to work.

Despite those thoughts, I kept getting stuck imagining myself in a public school, having to tell them that I was behind and being mocked for my ignorance. I remembered movies in which they always called on someone to answer questions in front of the whole class, and I imagined how humiliated I'd be. Then I thought about being sent to the school psychiatrist and what I would do.

I cried until the light in my room went blurry and I finally fell asleep.

In the morning, it took me a few minutes to find my way back to the lobby where Linda was waiting for me. We drove back to the Hollywood Guaranty Building and went into the same boardroom. Mr. Rathbun came bustling in, as though he had been awake for a while. "Hi, Jenna!" he said in a friendly tone. "Did you get a good rest?"

"Yes, sir," I lied.

"Good, because you may need it today," he muttered with a smile. I half smiled back, hoping that this didn't mean that I would have another session.

Mr. Rathbun informed me that Ronnie and Bitty did not receive the news that I wanted to stay in the Church well. Mr. Rathbun and Mr. Rinder had been working on handling them, but it was not looking good. He said that my dad in particular was starting to get threatening, and he let me know that they could only do so much for me.

I told him I understood, but I was amazed that my parents thought they had any sort of claim on me after they had missed so much of my life. Sure, there had been moments when I'd relied on them, more often when I was younger, but also more recently when I'd called them in the aftermath of my first EPF punishment and there was no one else to turn to. And, even then, they couldn't do much to help. Besides, I could count on one hand the number of times over the last four years that moments like that had happened.

Now, after all these years of leaving me on my own, forcing me to fend for myself, and being absent from my life, suddenly they thought they were going to start making decisions for me. Now they finally wanted to be involved in my life. Now that I was sixteen and finally growing comfortable with my role in the Church. Now that they wanted to leave and take me with them. I had only seen them four times since I was twelve. They weren't strangers, but in some ways, they might as well have been.

"I can try talking to them myself, if that would help," I offered. Maybe my parents thought the Church was making me stay against my will, and I could that get straightened out.

Mr. Rathbun left the room and returned a few minutes later, saying, "You're going to be allowed to talk to them. I'll be listening on the other line, so don't worry."

I wasn't worried, but I realized when Mom came on the line that maybe I should have been. She was fuming and I could hear Dad in the background sounding much the same—polite but clearly pissed-off.

"Jenna," my mom began, "what's going on? We were told you were coming with us. What's happened?"

Before I had a chance to answer, my mom continued. "They told me that even if you didn't want to leave you would be leaving anyway. This just shows that they clearly don't care about you or your feelings."

Hearing this got me conflicted all over again. She could have said many other things if she wanted to convince me to leave; this seemed too simple to be a lie. Why would Marty and Mike have told my parents that I was going before they'd even spoken to me, then told me that they were trying to allow me to stay?

Answering my question with her own speculation, she continued, "Marty and Mike have tricked you into thinking that you're going back up to Int and getting you all excited. What they really planned is dropping a bomb on you: you are just being thrown out. They are only playing with your head."

Those words made me angry. I was pissed that Mom was acting like she knew anything about the way I thought. The fact that she thought I wanted to be at the Int base just showed how much she didn't know anything about my life; I didn't want to be at Int, I wanted to be at Flag. I believed she was using manipulative tactics and twisting things to make Mr. Rathbun and Mr. Rinder the enemies, when, in fact, she and my dad were the ones trying to make me leave. Finally getting my opportunity to speak, I held firm.

"I don't know, Mom, maybe you're the one who's paranoid and assuming everyone is against you." I also threw Scientology at her as well by informing her that her generalities were not accurate: one of the characteristics of an SP was that they spoke in generalities.

Right after I said them, I could tell my words hurt Mom, which made me feel bad. Her response was defensive and even kind of desperate.

In some ways, my wanting to stay in the Sea Org should not

have come as a surprise to my mother; after all, I was learning for the first time during this call that she had been around my age when her parents had tried to get her to leave the Org, and she had refused. Hearing this, I realized just how little I knew about my mother. Now she was seeing her story play out in my life, only this time she was the adult who wanted out.

"You know Jenna, people like me who leave the Sea Org . . . we're not . . . we're not just dog meat."

"I know that, Mom," I said quietly, beginning to regress a little. I always felt responsible for my parents' happiness. As much I resented them for wanting me to leave my friends and my world, I still felt guilty about making them upset. "I'm sorry, my life is here, and I want to stay."

All three of us were silent for a moment, until I broke it.

"What is that music in the background?" I asked.

The whole time we were talking, weird Mexican music was coming in and out through their phone.

"We're living in Cabo San Lucas, Mexico," she said. I was in disbelief, although I quickly concluded it was obviously an effort by the Church to keep them off the radar, so that news that the brother of the leader of Scientology had left the fold didn't become a PR issue.

After the confrontational tone of our conversation eased, I talked with my father for a while. He continued in the same vein as my mother, expressing his concerns, but also letting me explain why I wanted to stay. He was being careful about what he said about Mike and Marty, most likely because he didn't want to alienate me, and he probably knew they were listening. Finally, both Mom and Dad agreed they would not put up a legal fight to make me leave, convinced I wanted to stay. Painful as it had been, I breathed a huge sigh of relief.

When we said our goodbyes, we said we loved each other, but the one thing we didn't say was the one thing we were all thinking: none of us knew when I'd see them again. They knew as well as I that whenever it was, it would not be for a long, long time. In fact, it would be forbidden now that they were out of the Church.

When I hung up, I felt both relief and guilt. I felt relieved that I had won, but guilty that I had hurt my parents. Mr. Rathbun seemed happy it was all resolved, even though he was defensive about my parents blaming him and accusing him of trickery for my desire to stay.

"So, where do we go from here?" he exclaimed, more of a statement of our current situation than an actual question.

"I don't know," I responded, hoping he had forgotten that I had mentioned I would be willing to do the RPF just the day before. I was sent back to the boardroom, where I waited a few more hours until Mr. Rathbun fetched me, saying we were going to do a metered interview.

He put on an intimidating sec-checker's demeanor, which always brought out the opposite effect in me. I was not easy to intimidate. He asked me the usual barrage of session questions: was I hiding anything, what my true intention was for staying behind, how I felt about my family, my uncle, on and on for at least three hours. In the end, he could see that I wanted to stay because of my desire to be a Sea Org member, although he did discover that I had lied to his wife, Mr. Anne Rathbun, about having taken out my belly button ring, when in fact I hadn't.

Chapter Twenty-Three

MY CHOICE

I WAITED IN THE BOARDROOM FOR SEVERAL HOURS BEFORE Mr. Marty Rathbun finally returned, accompanied by two female RTC Reps who were now going to be my guardians. The good news was that I was not being sent to the RPF. The bad news was that, apparently, I was not going back to Flag, either. Instead, after completion of a program, I was going to be posted in CMO in the services division at one of the two L.A.-area CMOs, either at CMO PAC or CMO IXU. The two bases were only a few miles away from each other. Mr. Rathbun explained that I needed to keep a low profile, and that my new guardians were going to help me with that. He also made clear that I was not to discuss the situation with my parents or their departure with *anyone*; he was particularly emphatic on this point.

While he was detailing all of this, I was still stuck on the only thing he'd said that really mattered. "So, I am not going back to Flag?" I said, trying to clarify, hoping I'd heard incorrectly. He responded dismissively before he even realized why I was asking, "No, we can't have this kind of security risk at the Flag base with everything that is going on there." Then he seemed to realize that I might be upset by his words. "Don't forget, Jenna, this was *your* choice," he added, sounding a bit annoyed by my ungratefulness.

I sank down in my seat, crushed. It might have been my choice but I never thought I'd lose everything. It was one thing to lose my parents; fraught as our relationship was, I was prepared for that. But losing my friends and my family in Clearwater was not something I'd anticipated. I thought I'd be allowed to go back to Flag, back to my life. Instead I'd been labeled a security risk and was once again being taken away from all the people I cared about, making me feel completely alone in the world yet again.

Nonetheless, I said what I needed to say for the greater good: "Yes, sir."

With that, he smiled at me, shook my hand, and wished me well, then I followed my new guardians, Mr. Laura Rodriguez and Mr. Kara Hansen, out the door. I knew Mr. Rodriguez from Flag, and Mr. H, walked in RTC, but I didn't know either of them very well. We were barely to the parking lot when Mr. Rodriguez started ribbing me. "Hell on wheels!" she exclaimed. I looked at her a bit confused. At Flag she'd audited Justin—she'd been the one who'd told me he was a Rock Slammer so I already didn't like her. As I looked at her face, I realized that she was talking about me and that "hell on wheels" must have been what the RTC Reps had called me. "We are going to keep you in line!" she told me with a grin as she dropped me off at my room for the night. Given everything that had happened that day, I wasn't as amused as she was. She seemed to be personally offended by my lack of amusement.

The next morning I was still sleeping when she busted into my room yelling, "Rise and shine!" She was carrying a pair of pliers and headed right for me. "First things first, we are going to get that belly ring out once and for all!" She demanded I stay put as she took the pliers to the stone on my ring, cracked it in half, and pulled the ring out.

"Ouch," I said, more out of indignity than pain.

Next, she got out her makeup box and said that I was no longer going to be wearing my blue eyeliner, it wasn't becoming of a Commodore's Messenger. Mr. Rodriguez also wanted me to wear concealer in an effort to cover up my teenaged skin. It was highly embarrassing. I put on the uniform she gave me, dark blue pants and a bright blue shirt, and she told me I looked much better.

We met Mr. H outside by the RTC minivan that was going to take us to the Hollywood Guaranty Building for breakfast. Her "good morning," was uttered with a sarcastic smile, as though she was not overjoyed to have me intruding on her morning routine. On the way to the HGB, the two women played a Harry Potter book on tape, which, although not intended for me, was a good reprieve from conversation. I really didn't know how much more of Mr. Rodriguez's ribbing I could take.

As I walked into the marble lobby of HGB, I saw two people I knew from Flag. Excited to see them, I paused to greet them. Mr. Rodriguez grabbed my arm and yanked me away, leaving them both standing there, looking surprised. "Move along," Mr. Rodriguez said, urging me forward and scolding one of the people from Flag about butt kissing.

We took the elevator to the sixth floor, where the crew dining area was located. It was a large hall with folding tables, much uglier and smellier than the one at Flag.

At least five other people who knew me started to say hi, but I waved them off, silently implying that I wasn't allowed to talk. With everyone looking at us, Mr. Rodriguez, Mr. H, and I sat at the big round exec tables, toward the back of the room. Executive tables were round, while the tables for the rest of the staff were rectangular.

As I looked around and saw people I knew at the various tables, I felt a little better about being at this base, though the reality was still difficult to accept. Knowing that I was with RTC Reps, most of them were smart enough to keep their distance.

"Miss Popular," Mr. H commented, sardonically.

After a bit, a German woman came over and asked us what we wanted for breakfast. When my guardians ordered cereal, I did, too. I was feeling too shy to eat, but they told me I had to have breakfast, as I had to be "studentable," an adjective meaning sufficiently rested and fed to study. I reluctantly ate a little as the two of them spent most of the meal chatting. Occasionally, they'd make a comment to me but I was so unhappy to be there, I was sort of disconnected from them. After breakfast, we went downstairs to the fifth floor. Mr. H led me into a suite with three auditing rooms. These were the RTC auditing rooms where I was to study, do conditions, and do anything else required of me. I thought all of this was over with by now, but, apparently, I was wrong.

My first session with Mr. Hansen was called the "Truth Rundown." I was required to do this one on the grounds that I had challenged Mr. Rathbun on the morning that I had spoken to my parents. I had only questioned why they had ever been told that I would be leaving with them against my will, but the consequence of that was I now had to do a session of the Truth Rundown, a procedure to uncover the "Black PR"—the bad propaganda—that I had been exposed to during my conversation with my parents. I was going to be directed to the moment when I had believed what my parents had told me, and once I found that, I had to locate the overt I had committed just before that moment, which had led me to believe it. Looking back now, I see it was the ultimate brainwashing technique.

When I tried to insist to Mr. Rodriguez that my mother had most likely been telling me the truth, as indeed Mr. Rathbun and Mr. Rinder *were* planning to send me on my way, she wouldn't hear any of it. Eventually, I made up some moment in time and its earlier overt and withhold, and we finished the session.

Next, I was informed that I would be doing the PTS/SP course, a major Scientology course dealing with SPs and PTSs, Potential Trouble Sources. In this study, you learned LRH's thoughts and techniques on how to identify and handle SPs, and what happened when you were connected to such an evil person. The purpose of this course was to interconnect those times when you were sick or not doing well in life, locating the occasion and properly handling or disconnecting from the root source, the Suppressive Person. The victim of the SP was the PTS, the Potential Trouble Source, because in the presence of an SP, the PTS would undoubtedly mess up, get sick, have problems, lose something, and basically have a hard time in life.

The implied reason I had to take the course was that my parents were SPs; thus, I had to learn the mechanics of suppression so I could confront and no longer be affected by their suppression. Still, they didn't seem like SPs to me. Trusting my own intuition instead of the Church's labels, I refused to see them as the toxic force that Scientology said they were. Of course, I was not in a position to share my point of view.

I spent the next several weeks on the course, during which I had to learn all the characteristics of an SP and the Tone Scale verbatim. Mr. Rodriguez and Mr. H., who were extremely rigorous coaches, didn't know that I still wasn't buying into the concept that my parents were the SPs as outlined in this course. My parents had never "invalidated" me, a Scientology term for making less of me, or making me feel bad about myself. "Suppressive," another term we discussed in the course, was described as something that held you back or confined you, and there was little in my parents' behavior that fit this description. Sure, they had gotten mad at me maybe once or twice, but to say that they were suppressing me was preposterous. I certainly had plenty of problems with my parents, but words like "invalidated" and "suppressive" had nothing to do with them.

Several times during the course, it even crossed my mind that I felt more suppressed by the organization. Even my Aunt Shelly had made me feel more invalidated than my parents. She would tell me that I was unethical, or say preposterous things like I caused the downfall of the Ranch. But, of course, I liked her, and making my observation known would have been a disaster. Anne Rathbun was someone else I seriously considered as being much more invalidating of me personally.

For the next few months, everything about my life was incredibly controlled; concerned about the risks I posed, they were pretty much trying to reprogram me to ensure that I didn't discuss my parents and didn't use their departure to spread suppressive thoughts. I couldn't go anywhere, unless it was the bathroom, and for that, I had to knock on Mr. H's door to get permission and secure an escort. I had to eat every meal with Mr. H and Mr. Rodriguez, only being able to wave to the friends I'd see in the dining room. I had thought I was done being held prisoner when I had come to L.A., but, instead, the reward for my loyalty was more punishment. I had to be under the supervision of one or the other of them at all times. During meals, Mr. Rodriguez would often trash my brother, telling me how off the rails he was. She would also tell me things about my mom and Don and about Justin that were inappropriate and sexual in nature. I felt this was downright vile.

Mr. Rodriguez would also quietly gossip with Mr. H about how she was auditing Lisa Marie Presley. From their behavior, I concluded that nothing was private or protected but, rather, fodder for whispering. RTC was supposed to be the most on-policy, rule-respecting, and enforcing group in all of Scientology, charged with keeping the tech pure to its cause. However, in my experience, they were the worst. I had had many other auditors outside RTC, and not one of them had ever gotten angry at me in the way that RTC Reps had, or treated me with such disrespect, like answering a phone call in the middle of a question in session, which was against the auditor's code. I didn't realize it at the time, but I was really depressed at having been cut off from everyone I cared about. At mealtime I hardly ate. Mr. H once yelled at me so loudly to eat my food that everyone in the dining hall looked over.

Nothing about this situation was unfolding as I'd thought it would. The freedom I'd once enjoyed at Flag prior to my parents' leaving the Sea Org was gone, and it was hard to imagine ever getting it back. I'd thought I was choosing between my parents and returning to Clearwater, when, in reality, I was choosing between leaving my friends to live with my parents and leaving my friends to live in L.A. Neither option was what I'd wanted, but still I couldn't bring myself to regret my decision. In retrospect, I hadn't been given much of a choice, but bad as life was in L.A., it seemed better than living in Mexico with my parents. At least it left open the possibility of seeing my friends again someday.

Perhaps the most frustrating thing about all this was that, regardless of the specific location, I'd chosen the Church over my parents. And, yet, for that loyalty, I was being punished. Rather than recognize my sacrifice by returning me to Clearwater, their response was to strip me of my freedoms and regiment my life.

This new reality cast a shadow over every part of my life. Depressed, I was prone to bouts of crying that I tried to hide in the bathroom or in my room at night. I was often in trouble with Mr. H for refusing to eat and not communicating. However, Mr. H, unlike Mr. Rodriguez, wasn't all bad. She could see I was struggling, and did take pity on me, once even asking me if I was upset about Martino, whose name she'd apparently gotten from my security checking reports. At night, she started taking walks with me, which is what LRH said you should do if you can't sleep, and on those walks we would chat. She had divorced her husband for some reason, and from how she talked about him, I could tell she really missed him. In these moments, there was a humanity to her that was comforting, even if it didn't change anything about my situation. I at least felt like she understood a little.

AFTER ABOUT TWO MONTHS OF THE PTS/SP COURSE, MR. H. allowed me to do minimal work outside the course room, which consisted of bringing select CMO execs coffee or drinks. I was happy to discover I already knew many of them, some of them from Flag and some from Int.

A lucky chance encounter with a friend from Flag, who was now posted at PAC, brought me news about Flag. As Mr. Rodriguez and Mr. H were walking me to my room, the friend passed me in the hall, and just as Mr. Rodriguez yanked me away, I whispered I'd be right back. I gave Mr. Rodriguez and Mr. H sufficient time to get to their own rooms before sneaking back to the elevator door, where he was waiting.

The friend was happy to see me and he told me how my friends had said I had just disappeared, that they had no idea where I was, and that he was super-happy that he could tell them he had seen me. We finished talking with a quick hug, and just as he was promising to tell everyone I said hi, Mr. Rodriguez, not by coincidence, stepped out of the elevator and grabbed me. Apparently, she had been alerted by security, who had seen me on their cameras.

"What was that all about?" she asked me, annoyed and exasperated. She had the nerve to ask me why I felt the need to sneak around.

"Because every time I see someone I know, you yank me away from them," I responded. Thankfully, she half laughed instead of accusing me of backflashing.

Christmas came a few months later, and I was miserable. Christmas had always been a festive time with my friends, but this year, not only had I not received any letters from my friends, but I was also told I couldn't write any. This was a first, as writing letters had always been allowed. I heard nothing from anyone in my family. For Christmas, I got to go out to dinner at a restaurant with Mr. H and Mr. Rodriguez, which wasn't much different than eating with them at the dining hall every day. For the big treat, I was allowed to watch two episodes of *Dharma & Greg*: Jenna Elfman, who played Dharma, was a public Scientologist.

Actually, the best part of Christmas was that Mr. Marty Rathbun sent me a present, my first Harry Potter book. I stayed up late into the night until I finished it. I *loved* it. It was an escape from my actual life.

At some point in January, I finally finished the PTS/SP course. Mr. H said I would be allowed to have some kind of post now but would have to wait a couple of weeks before knowing exactly what it would be. She told me that, no matter what, I would be posted in CMO IXU instead of CMO PAC. I was happy about that, because I had gotten to know many of the people, but her words effectively ended my dream of being allowed to return to Flag.

Two weeks later, I had my post: I was going to be a Word Clearer, which bummed me out. I had wanted to be in Services, but instead I would be stuck helping people who were bogged down or in trouble in their studies or their job to find their misunderstood words. The good part was that I could eat among friends, no longer being obligated to eat with Mr. Rodriguez and Mr. H at the RTC table. The bad part was that the crew food was gruesome. Everyone's pay was usually spent in the canteen.

I now lived in a dorm with five other girls in the Hollywood Inn on Hollywood Boulevard. Our twenty-foot-square room was on the eighth floor of the berthing. There was no AC, the water temperature was either freezing cold or boiling hot, and the elevator didn't work. At night, crowds of people always walked by outside the building making noise, partying, screaming, or fighting—sometimes all three. I was told to count my blessings, because the Hollywood Inn, which was the berthing for CMO and executives, was nice compared to the Anthony Building on Fountain Avenue, where the crew lived. Despite the yucky food and the berthing, I was so happy to have at least some sort of freedom, where I could live with friends, eat with them, and not have to be escorted to the bathroom. If I couldn't have my old life and my old friends, at least I was now allowed to find new ones, which proved easier as the staff at CMO IXU were much more laid back.

I was given an office to use for my word-clearing duties during the day. It was outfitted with a surveillance camera for Mr. H to view in her office, so that she could make sure I wasn't stepping out of line. I still couldn't use the phone, and I was required to check in with Mr. H at least once a day. It was still better than it had been, and I felt things were starting to look up. I had many new friends.

All my mail went straight to her, too. One day, she mentioned something in passing about my friends writing letters to me, which made me ask her if any had come. She shocked me when she said yes. Many friends had been writing for several months now, including Martino. She said that she hadn't passed them along because some letters contained inappropriate comments about seniors, and that the letters had been sent to ethics. I was so upset. All these months, my friends had been writing, and I didn't even know it. They had probably thought I had been ignoring them, or, even worse, that I had reported them to ethics myself.

When I heard about the letters from my old friends, I started to hope I could find a way back to Flag, only to realize quickly that that was never going to happen. Equally disappointing was that more than likely none of my Flag friends would ever be posted here. I started writing to everybody, even though I didn't know who specifically had written to me. Mr. H still read through all of them, so I was very restricted as to what I could say.

Martino wrote me a few times, apparently being more careful

about what he wrote now, after having gotten into trouble for his previous letters, which I never did get to read. He told me he was doing really well at Flag, and that he had actually reconnected with his long-lost father, who he learned was a lot like him, and that it was really cool getting to know him. I could tell Martino was getting more and more into being a Sea Org member and Scientology than he had before; he even told me he had gotten some auditing. He sent pictures and told me he missed me. I missed him, too, but the geography being what it was, it was now more futile than ever to go back to those feelings, so my letters remained casual. More than ever, I knew that we would never be together. It simply wasn't workable.

CHAPTER TWENTY-FOUR

DALLAS

THE FIRST TIME I EVER LAID EYES ON DALLAS HILL, I WAS WALK-ing out of the canteen with a friend. Sparks didn't fly or anything like that. I mostly noticed him because he was good-looking. He wasn't particularly dark or mysterious like Martino; rather, he was attractive in a boyish sort of way. He glanced at me briefly as I passed, and I smiled at him. That was the extent of our exchange.

After that, I would see him in the hallway when he came to the fifth floor to make a delivery to Mr. H's office, but I didn't even know his name.

"Hi, sir," he'd say, the proper way to address me, as I was in CMO.

"Hi," I'd reply and smile back.

Being called sir always made me feel a bit uncomfortable. But telling people not to call me sir was not an option, because the fact that I was a superior had to be acknowledged. I resolved to try to be gracious with everyone who greeted me, by smiling and saying hello back. One day in the future, I might need these people if

I found myself in my inevitable serious trouble, and they might take pity on me because I had always been nice to them.

Less than a month after I first saw Dallas in the canteen, I was checking my in-basket and found a "Goldenrod," announcing a justice action against someone in the Church whose name I didn't recognize. Goldenrods were the kind of announcements that no one wanted his or her name on. They were usually written because a person had messed up on his or her job, or had done something else the Church considered wrong, and the Church wanted to make an example of that person, putting their head on a pike. They only mentioned personal things that were considered unethical, and that could be anything from stealing to being externally influenced, such as taking gifts or getting help from family members without exchange. An example would be allowing someone to buy your groceries or pay your car insurance without paying him back, which was rarely possible because Sea Org members were paid so little money. In addition to calling out people publicly for mistakes, they often also made mention of highly personal things that were unethical, like that person's masturbation habits or some other personal thing that would embarrass him or her. Usually these announcements were gruesome exaggerations of the truth, but what made them worse was that they were always sent out to the entire base of five hundred people, so everyone knew your business.

"Court of Ethics, Dallas T. Hill," this one began.

"Are you kidding me?" someone in the office blurted out. "This guy got them to put the 'T' of his middle name in his Court of Ethics!" Everyone laughed, including me. They rarely used middle initials on these announcements; the fact that he wanted to make sure his full name was on his punishment; who did that? I assumed by the formality of his name, Dallas T. Hill, that he would be a really old man.

When I learned he was actually the cute guy with whom I had

been exchanging smiles in the fifth-floor hallway, I was shocked. He seemed like such a clean-cut guy. I was reluctant to read any further. Much as I knew these were often gross distortions of the truth, I worried that reading it would make me think less of him. In his case, though, it turned out the Goldenrod wasn't about anything personal or sexual. In Dallas's case, he had gotten in trouble for not doing his post properly, because he hadn't answered some telexes, which were communications between management and lower Scientology churches. The crime wasn't so bad, but the punishment, that he would get a Court of Ethics for it, was a little ridiculous, but I guessed he had neglected it to the point of it being problematic.

I didn't have much time to feel bad about Dallas's situation, though. That same week, I had become embroiled in a drama of my own. I was now defending myself against an allegation that I had been flirting with a married Italian guy in CMO. We were friends and enjoyed each other's company. He was someone who had seen me enter the conference room my very first day here, when I was meeting with Mr. Rathbun and Mr. Rinder about my parents. He had seen me again the following day, when I was going into the ethics interview room with Mr. Rathbun. We bonded over the fact that he knew something, although he had nothing specific. Nevertheless, I certainly wasn't flirting with him, and I was a little bit grossed out, to be honest, that I was accused of it.

Of course, I denied it, but once an accusation was reported, it was assumed to be true, and nothing less than a full confession by me would be acceptable. I knew how it worked, no matter how tired of it I was. If it hadn't been for Mr. H's short but sweet apologetic speech, disguised between her best attempts at trying to sound authoritative and formidable. I wouldn't have even done it, but would have just taken one for the team instead. Basically, she told me she knew I was a person who was friendly and outgoing with both sexes, and it was possible that something I had done had been taken the wrong way. However, she was still asking me to please confess and get it over with, for both our sakes or take responsibility for the "effect" I had created. I was always resistant to misrepresenting what had happened, but their procedures always allowed them to have the last word, and I knew that even if I didn't actually confess, they would end up phrasing it in a way that would be the same thing as a confession. In the end, I got it over with, confessed, and never again spoke another word to my Italian friend. Upset as I was about it, having received so many sec-checks during which both the auditor and I *knew* that half of what I was saying wasn't true, ending a session with a false confession was nothing new.

Things got better temporarily with the arrival of my friend Molly, whom I'd known since I was about five years old, when she and I were both living at the Ranch. Later, when the kids from the Ranch were sent to Flag, she wound up in CMO with me. Down-to-earth, very smart, and a bookworm extraordinaire, she had always been my friend, but we were never as close as we were now. Not only did Molly know everything about me, but she had also been at Flag and was on the EPF with Martino, Cece, and all my other friends, and had been friends with them, too.

In no time, I felt comfortable enough to tell her everything that had happened with my parents. It was risky. I knew I wasn't supposed to confide in anyone, but I felt Molly would understand. She had her own issues with her father. She hadn't seen him in three years. She hadn't seen her mother in years, either. Molly knew what it was like to feel alone in the world and to know that friends meant everything. She also knew the importance of keeping a secret. For the first time since coming to L.A. I told someone the story of my parents' departure. I knew that I was forbidden to speak of it, but it was such a relief to share my feelings and finally have someone else who knew.

Molly's arrival was a welcome change and, for the first time in a while, I felt like I was establishing my life again. Then, one day, Mr. H dragged me into her office and began yelling at me. She had found out that I had told Molly about my parents being out of the Sea Org. What made her even angrier was the fact that Molly had lied to protect me, and Mr. H had to trick her by saying that I had already confessed, in order to get her to admit to this. Though the tactic was incredibly underhanded, it was to be expected. I was just upset I'd gotten caught.

Even though Molly and I would both be in trouble for my secret, I was touched by her loyalty. Real friendship wasn't something you came by frequently in the Sea Org. When you got into trouble, people who were your friends previously often shunned you, and rejected any association with you in order to save themselves. Your loyalty was always supposed to be to the group, not to any individual, which was part of the reason why we were all encouraged to be suspicious of each other: so that we would never trust each other and always put the groups' well-being first. On top of that, lying or disrespecting an RTC Rep was probably the worst infraction there was. Being insubordinate to any superior was out ethics, but disrespecting people from the highest governing body of the Church was practically treasonous. They had the power to send you to RPF, no questions asked.

Molly's heroic effort to keep my secret was not lost on me. It was something only a true friend would do, but still it caused a mess. We both had to do amends for weeks on end, then had to ask each member of the group to accept us back. For better or worse, accepting us back was what they did.

In the aftermath, Molly was transferred to the PAC base, which, although it was only a fifteen-minute drive from where I was, might as well have been a thousand miles. Being at PAC meant that, from now on, I would see her only a few times a year. Yet another friend had been taken away from me.

• • •

WITH MY PUNISHMENT BEHIND ME, MY ROUTINE BEGAN TO settle again. I still missed Flag, and I wasn't as happy as I'd been there. In addition to my friends at Flag, the environment there was just different. I'd had more freedom, and it was hard not to look back on that with a bit of longing.

At the same time, I was seeing Dallas more often and I kinda had a thing for him. To my surprise and dismay, my friend Suzy told me she had a crush on him, which was a bummer. I didn't know much about him, just that he was from San Diego, was pretty laid-back, and was good friends with a mildly creepy Italian guy he worked with. He also hadn't grown up in the Sea Org, which was refreshing. The more Suzy talked about him, the more I liked him.

As the girl talk went on, I learned that Dallas had asked out another girl named Katie, although that had been a couple of months earlier. Katie was quite a guy magnet, a tall blond model-actress who had all of the boys chasing after her, even though her reputation was for turning them down. She had recently joined the Sea Org after a brief acting career with small roles in big-screen movies such as *American Pie* and *Never Been Kissed*. Her parents, who had won awards for their valiant efforts to disseminate Scientology, were also big money donors. Needless to say, her glamorous life of perfection represented everything I wasn't. Here I was, a parentless lousy student, a dispensable Sea Org member, and a teenager with a crush on a boy I probably wasn't good enough for. As it turned out, Katie also turned down Dallas.

For the next few months, I tried talking to him whenever I saw him. He noticed me now and even seemed slightly interested, but I could never tell for sure. One late night in September 2001, a friend and I were in the laundry room, waiting for one of the seven washer/dryers for the two hundred staff to free up. We were all supposed to use the machines on the designated laundry day, which meant we had to stay up half the night waiting for our chance. We were there only a few minutes when a huge cockroach made its appearance on the laundry room floor. We ran across the room screaming, only to encounter Dallas just walking in with his dirty clothes. Laughing, he chased it down and saved us. I liked that he was a little shy, but I felt awkward and slightly embarrassed knowing that one of our friends in CMO who was dating Dallas's roomate, had told him about my crush on him.

The excitement of my late-night encounter with Dallas in the laundry room was completely overshadowed the next evening by a strange request from a supervisor to report to Mr. H's office at once. I had barely knocked when her door flew open. "Follow me," Mr. H ordered, already making her way to the stairs. We went to a conference room and, minutes later, in walked Mr. Rathbun and Mr. Rinder.

Mr. Rathbun did the talking. "We've only got a few minutes here," he began. "Here are some letters that have come in for you over the last few months from Ronnie and Bitty. Why don't you go ahead and read them?" He slid a stack of six or seven letters across the conference table. It had been nearly a year since I had told them I would not be joining them in Mexico.

My parents' handwriting was unmistakable. I had assumed that she and Dad would know not to send letters, aware that they wouldn't get through. Seeing them gave me a moment of nostalgia. But then I immediately started worrying that them contacting me might be getting me in trouble again.

"Should I read them now?" I asked, knowing full well that the two men were aware of their content.

"Yes," Mr. Rathbun replied, gesturing to me that he and Mr. Rinder were waiting.

It was somewhat awkward reading the letters in front of them.

I skimmed them quickly, looking for something major that might cause me trouble. Dad wrote about what he and Mom were doing for work, which I didn't really understand, something about selling time-shares something I had never heard of; there was talk about visiting my grandmother in Clearwater. Mom said they got a car that they would eventually give me (I didn't even have a driver's license) and that they were moving to the United States and wanted to see me. I knew at that moment that their wanting to see me was going to be the problem.

"Okay," I said, to let Mr. Rathbun and Mr. Rinder know I had finished reading.

"Do you have any questions?" Mr. Rinder asked as he took the letters from me.

"No, not really."

"Okay, well, they will be arriving at the airport tomorrow, and we would like you to spend the day with them. Is that okay?"

I hadn't expected that. I wondered if Uncle Dave knew they wanted to see me. He never talked to me anymore aside from a Christmas card and a small gift. I hadn't had a conversation with Aunt Shelly in quite a while, either. I could never understand why my uncle didn't talk to me about family business himself. I assumed everything was church business to him; after all, family wasn't real. It was just a distraction to those people who were clearing the planet. Plus, as the head of Scientology, he had to be protected against any kind of suppression at all costs.

I seriously hadn't known if I would ever speak to my parents again, and here I was being asked to spend a full day with them with no Scientology or work responsibilities. I hadn't done that since I was seven years old, and they both had the day off, aside from Christmas and Sea Org Day, which I had last celebrated with them when I was eleven.

I was so conflicted. On the one hand, I would not have to work if I was with them, which was always a great thing, and being off the base might be exciting. On the other hand, I was not really looking forward to the awkwardness that would undoubtedly occur. Not only had I not spent time with them in years, but they had basically been declared SPs, as Mr. Rathbun had made clear to me on my first day in L.A. I was suspicious this was some kind of test. If I went and didn't argue with them about their anti-social, personality-induced decision to leave, I would be a bad Sea Org member. If I went and did argue, I'd be miserable.

"Um, yeah, I guess I'll go," I stammered.

As if reading my mind, Mr. Rinder said, "Look, we don't want any trouble for the Church, so I would like it if you could just play it cool. Just fair roads, fair weather. I don't think they will try to pull anything. Okay?"

"Yes, sir," I said with great relief. All I had to do was spend time with them. I had no idea what was happening or why.

It was extraordinary that my parents, out of the Sea Org, out of the country, and out of my life, wanted to see me, and I was being allowed. Actually, even being subtly encouraged to do it. The "trouble for the church" Mr. Rathbun was referring to was something I was completely unaware of at the time. I didn't learn the details until much later, but my father had let Uncle Dave know that he and my mother were going to be on vacation in the L.A. area, and they wanted to see me. There was some back-and-forth on it, but finally it got to the point where they said either the Church had to present me, or they were going to come and get me, even if it required legal action.

When they got to L.A., they were told by Uncle Dave to meet him and Aunt Shelly at their hotel, which was by the airport. Years later, Mom told me that by the time she and Dad arrived, their frustration was peaking. The first thing Uncle Dave did when they walked through the door was try to calm them down.

"You are going to see Jenna," he assured them. "It was never my intention to keep you from her."

The meeting was all about PR and appeasement. He told them how Marty and Mike were messing up handling them, and that he was going to take charge of the situation himself. They could even have his hotel room for a couple of days. He was basically appeasing them in any way he could, even giving my father some of his back pay. He added that there would no longer be a restriction on their communication with me.

I knew none of this when Mr. Rathbun and Mr. Rinder gave me my final instructions. They told me that Maddie, my escort for the day, would meet me in the reception area of the HGB the next morning. I was to wear civvies, not my uniform. They would meet with me again after the visit to see how it went.

Mr. Rathbun smiled as he and Mr. Rinder walked out of the room. At times like this, I got the sense that he actually felt bad for me. In all my dealings with him, I always had the notion that he had to act a certain way and do certain things because of who he was and his position, but that deep down, he was more human and cared about me a little bit. Unlike his wife, who seemed to enjoy raking me across the coals, he had a hidden compassion. It might have been my imagination, but I figured senior executives were under pressure to do whatever my uncle told them to do.

On the way back to my berthing that night, I looked at the other Sea Org members all jam-packed onto the bus with me. In the few months I had been in L.A., many Sea Org people, complete strangers to me, had approached me randomly, telling me how they had once worked with my mother or father and how much they admired them. I wondered what they would think now if they knew that Ronnie and Bitty Miscavige had left the Sea Org and were currently living in Mexico, where they were selling real estate. It would have shown a crack at the top. A lot of people liked my parents. Learning that they had left the Sea Org might have caused alarm and rumblings and maybe would have started quiet speculation that they had had a falling-out with my uncle. That was why I had to protect the secret at all cost. After what had happened with Molly, I knew there was no one I could confide in about seeing my parents the next day.

Maddie met me in the morning as scheduled and took me to the hotel at LAX. As she pulled the car to the curb, I saw my mom smiling broadly and heading toward us. I was completely oblivious to all that she and Dad had been through to make this reunion happen. Maddie handed me a cell phone. "This is for you to use for the day. Push this button to call me when you are ready to be picked up." I felt so trustworthy at this moment, in authorized possession of the forbidden cell phone.

Stepping from the car, I started to smile. It was hard not to be happy to see someone when they were so overjoyed to see you. Mom gave me a huge hug, and I hugged her back. I felt awkward knowing that Maddie would see me hugging an SP, but when I turned around, she was smiling and waving to my mom as well. My mom waved back before leading me toward the hotel.

The day with my parents went great. They looked older but like they were doing well and taking care of themselves. They seemed to know what topics to avoid and just what to say. We never talked about the Church, for example. We spent the first part of the day shopping at Universal CityWalk. Occasionally, I felt guilty for enjoying myself. It was especially weird because they were SPs, but it was hard to think of them that way.

Mom and Dad never tried to convince me to leave the Sea Org and live with them. In fact, they didn't ask me anything about the Church. If they had questioned me or pushed me to do their agenda, I would have been ready to argue with them. They would have been providing me with the excuse I needed to disconnect from them once and for all, and they knew it. My parents were aware that it was my choice to remain in the Sea Org, but they also knew I was brainwashed. The last thing you want to tell a person who is brainwashed is that they are brainwashed. They realized that the best thing they could do was to be nice and loving toward me, causing me to question the validity of them being SPs. By acting kind and not trying to change my mind, they were laying the groundwork for me to leave on my own.

In the evening, we were getting ready to go our separate ways when Dad pulled out a wooden box with a leather top.

"I want you to have this," he said handing it to me. "This way, you have something to remember us by."

When I opened it, I found photos of them and their new house, and a credit card with my name on it.

"What's this?" I asked in confusion.

I think my dad expected me to refuse it, or at least make some sort of objection.

"It's just for emergencies," he told me, really hoping I'd agree to keep it.

In a certain way, it made sense to me. I didn't have any other money or anyone to contact if anything ever happened, or if I ever needed to leave the Church. I knew that Mr. Rathbun and Mr. Rinder would probably not approve of this, but my dad's simple explanation was convincing. It also made me feel cared for and safe. I decided to keep the card but not tell Mr. Rathbun or Mr. Rinder about it unless they asked.

When Maddie arrived, my parents hugged me one last time. I was surprised at how sad I was when we said goodbye. I also knew my life was back at the base—seeing my parents had not made me waver in that regard. As Maddie drove me away, we waved one last time.

Next thing I knew, I was back in the conference room on the twelfth floor. After a quick debrief of all that had gone down with my parents, I was sent home. I had even come clean about the credit card, and to my surprise, Mr. Rathbun didn't confiscate it.

It was well after midnight by the time I got back to my room. I wasn't particularly tired, so I went down to the basement to do my laundry. Most unusually, the laundry room was empty, and as I was shoving my dirty clothing into the washer, I looked up to see Dallas walking in with a laundry bag.

"Hi," he said, likely not noticing the red glow of embarrassment on my face. Actually, he also looked somewhat embarrassed.

A few awkward moments later, we sat down outside the laundry room door to chat for twenty minutes or so. It was only when we heard people coming down the stairs that I realized how late it had gotten. Dallas smiled and said we should get to know each other more, and I agreed. Before we said good night, he leaned over, put his hand on mine, and we kissed.

What a day it had been.

CHAPTER TWENTY-FIVE

THE CELEBRITY CENTRE

IT WASN'T LONG BEFORE I OFFICIALLY STARTING DATING DALLAS. Not only was he smart and kind; he always had me laughing and I could be myself around him. A total family person, he'd tell me about his parents, his older brother and younger sister, and how he had grown up spending time with his cousins. It was obvious that he loved his family. He'd had a carefree upbringing and was proud of it.

The stories I shared with him about my family were full of holes. Since I couldn't tell him where my parents were, and I didn't even know where my brother was, I tried glazing over the specifics as much as possible.

Mr. H was annoyed that I was dating Dallas, saying that she didn't understand why I couldn't just be single. Technically, romances did not have to be approved. There were broad rules, such as Sea Org must stay within their base, the same for CMO, but individual dating choices were not subject to approval, as long as the policy concerning the rules of dating was respected. She had authority to weigh in on my relationships, as she was the one who had daily contact with me. She would report to her superiors, most likely Aunt Shelly or Mr. Rathbun. I was a Miscavige, and my decisions were taken to be a reflection on the Miscavige name.

I didn't mind that Mr. H made jokes about Dallas. I actually thought they were her way of giving approval. We had gotten closer, now that her crony Mr. Rodriguez had been posted at Flag. At heart, Mr. H was a good person, even though she could be ruthless. She was about Taryn's age, and, in some ways being only a few years older than me made Mr. H like an older sister. She would talk a lot about her own younger sister, who, like me, enjoyed drawing. Her sister was not in the Sea Org, and Mr. H obviously loved her and missed her a lot. Mr. H always bought me Christmas presents, and because I had always had to eat at her table, she would tell me stories about the movies or books she read. Eventually, when I was allowed to eat elsewhere, I think she was sad because it meant that she had to eat by herself; the fact that I was happy to be free of her probably made her a bit sad. She was also an RTC Rep and so had to keep up her front. Mr. H's RTC position gave her a lot of authority, but it allowed her to have no friends. It really was lonely at the top.

Pretty quickly, all of my friends liked Dallas. They got to know him because he ate at my table now. He was just an all-around nice guy who was easy to talk to and extremely polite. He always opened doors for me and offered a hand whenever someone needed assistance. He and I would sit on the fire escape right next to my dorm and talk late at night when we got off duty. He was born in 1980, so he was actually four years older than I. His parents were public Scientologists and not Sea Org members. They had been on staff at the local San Diego mission when he was born. They weren't recruiters per se, but his father was good at getting people into the Church to become regular parishioners. Dallas's parents had gotten into Scientology when they were eighteen. Despite not joining the Sea Org, they were important money donors to the Church and very active in recruiting.

Dallas's childhood seemed so traditional compared to mine. He would tell me the stories of growing up and the family trips with his aunts, uncles, and cousins—few of whom were Scientologists. He lived with his parents, rode dirt bikes, went to public school, and hung out with his friends, both Scientologists and non-Scientologists. He was particularly fond of the ocean and had traveled to Mexico with his cousins to surf. He was also a fan of snowboarding and promised to teach me one day. My childhood had never had that sort of family time or even just the luxury of free time. I would replay Dallas's stories in my head when I got into bed in the evenings, wishing that they could have been mine.

His exposure to Scientology was also drastically different. Dallas was raised with Scientology in the background, not the foreground, and even attended a San Diego public school until sixth grade, when a bad grade and sassing the teacher had gotten him in trouble. His parents sent him to a local Scientology school for seventh grade. It was held in a classroom with only twelve students for sixth grade and above. There was also a section of thirty to fifty younger kids for the earlier grades, which was where his sister went.

Dallas made me laugh when he told me how it had taken him more than a week to grasp the meaning of "beingness," his first Scientology word. He hadn't realized that Scientology had its own language and how confusing a lot of the concepts were. He attended high school at a Scientology boarding school about an hour outside L.A., which was run out of the home of a married couple who had once been in the Sea Org. I was impressed that he had completed the four-year curriculum in just two years. He said recruiters from the Sea Org would visit frequently, trying to sign the kids up, but he wanted to be an actor and had no interest in enlisting.

Only sixteen when he graduated from high school, Dallas was too young to go to college, but he said he hadn't wanted to go. Many Scientologists looked down on college as a waste of time. His parents owned 50 percent of a large, successful jewelry store in San Diego, so he started working there to save enough money to move to L.A. and start his acting career. He was also saving the six thousand dollars he would need to take courses at the Celebrity Centre. That way, he could do Scientology studies and mingle with the celebrities, and maybe even make a helpful contact. His dream was to be an actor, not a Sea Org member. He had a beautiful singing voice, was great at improv, and could even tap dance.

It was at the San Diego org where he witnessed firsthand that Scientology worked. He was taking auditing sessions and decided to skip one, because he had come down with a head cold. The auditor called, freaking out, saying he needed to come in right away, as his sickness was a sign something had gone wrong. The next day, despite still being sick, he went in to the org, as he figured they knew what they were doing. It was the best session he ever had, he told me. Right there in session, his sickness left his body and didn't exist anymore. At that moment, he knew Scientology worked for him.

When he was eighteen, he went to the Celebrity Centre in L.A., where he wrote a check for six thousand dollars to pay for his Key to Life and Life Orientation courses—the courses that I'd taken at Flag all those years earlier. He was assigned to twin with fifteen-year-old Dylan Purcell, son of actress Lee Purcell. Dallas said he was a real jokester, so he was always getting pulled into ethics on account of Dylan's antics. He hung around with a lot of budding actors, some of whom now have established acting careers. In the evening, he took acting lessons with a Scientologist/actor who had trained Juliette Lewis and Giovanni Ribisi, themselves Scientologists.

Dallas often asked me questions about my family. When he'd ask if he could meet my parents, I created excuses, but he wasn't buying them. Mr. H specifically reminded me every day that telling him my parents were out of the Sea Org was forbidden. She would even drill me on how to behave if he got too nosy. She'd pretend to be him asking questions, and I would have to figure out ways to skirt the topic. None of it ever made it any easier to dodge the questions when he brought them up.

One day, I finally decided to ignore all Mr. H's warnings and just tell Dallas everything about my parents. He felt really bad for me, but at least he had understood why I had been so weird every time the subject of my parents was broached. Of course, now I had to lie to Mr. H when she'd ask me if my secret was still safe. But I had to tell Dallas; otherwise I felt like I was deceiving him.

Unlike most Sea Org members, Dallas had a car, which allowed us the opportunity to go off base and have breakfast on Sunday mornings, as long as we finished our work. The morning was supposed to be dedicated to getting our berthings clean enough to pass inspection; we had until noon, so if we completed our cleaning expeditiously, we could use the remaining time to go somewhere.

On one such occasion, despite Mr. H not approving it, we went to the Celebrity Centre to meet his mom at the Renaissance Restaurant for brunch. Not only had Dallas done course work there as a public Scientologist, but he had also worked there as a senior in the Hubbard Communication Office in the late 1990s. Therefore, he knew firsthand how differently celebrities were treated. People like John Travolta, Kirstie Alley, Catherine Bell, Jason Lee, Priscilla and Lisa Marie Presley, and Marisol Nichols were always around on services. At the time, Jason Beghe and Jack Armstrong were the two most revered celebrities at the Centre, because they were both on full-time study and very gung ho about Scientology.

In comparison to other Scientology churches, things for all the celebrities were over-the-top in terms of elegance and privacy, starting with their own separate double-gated entrance on the corner of Franklin and Bronson Avenues, and a special area in the underground parking garage that was monitored by security. Celebrities entered through the President's Office, which had its own lobby, Purif delivery area, and private office space. Upstairs were two auditing rooms and a private course room to be used solely by celebrities and other people of importance, such as big donors to the Church. Scientology defined celebrities as anyone influential, so it could be well-recognized names like Tom Cruise and John Travolta, but it could also be someone like Craig Jensen, CEO of Condusiv Technologies, and Scientology's biggest donor, or Izzy Chait, a prominent Beverly Hills art dealer. The security for the celebrities was very tight but deliberately inconspicuous, so that a big celebrity could literally be on services and most people at the Centre would never know he was there.

The Celebrity Centre also had guest rooms. They weren't special rooms designed just for celebrities. Any of the paying public could reserve any room as long as they were able to afford it; some rooms commanded a hefty overnight rate. It all depended on the size and level of elegance of the room, but the prices were in line with upscale hotels in the city. Back when my mom had been working on the renovations of the Celebrity Centre, I'd even stayed at the hotel a couple of times. The room we stayed in was a duplex, and was super nice. I was told that Kirstie Alley had actually stayed in that particular room. When Dallas was working there, Kirstie was the only celebrity he knew who would stay overnight. The others would just come for the day for their services, then go home.

As Dallas explained, the celebrities who would come to the center were very human there. Some were quite nice and social; others were more reserved and didn't want to be bothered. And, of course, some sucked up to other celebrities and were rude to the staff who worked there. All in all, it was a mixed bag of attitudes—as varied as the celebrities who frequented it. According to Dallas, John Travolta, at least, was very appreciative of Sea Org staff members at the center and their hard work. On one occasion, he met Travolta, who praised him for his service.

Hearing all this, it was hard not to be curious about the most famous celebrity Scientologist of them all, Tom Cruise. Dallas told me how, during the time he worked at the Celebrity Centre, Tom was not coming there. Tom was still a Scientologist; he just wasn't actively involved at that time. Dallas was told by members of the CC staff that because of Tom's marriage to Nicole Kidman, who was not as committed to the Church, Tom had been labeled a "Potential Trouble Source," which had interfered with his progress in Scientology.

Because Nicole's father was in the psychology field, this made perfect sense. We were taught that those in the mental health field were bad and evil. We believed what LRH had written about them was true, that they were the reason behind people like Adolf Hitler and everything else bad that had ever happened on the "whole track," the whole record in our minds of things that had happened to us over trillions of years.

When Dallas told me all this, it reminded me of something Aunt Shelly had once said when I was at Flag. At the time, Tom Cruise had just been getting back into the Church, and it was being mentioned in magazines. I said something to Aunt Shelly about it, and she proceeded to go on about how similar Tom Cruise and Uncle Dave were, in that they were both very intense. Apparently, people called them by the same nickname, which had something to do with the word "laser." I told Aunt Shelly how it seemed to me that Nicole wasn't really into Scientology, and she seemed surprised that I had figured that out, saying I was exactly right and it was a problem they were trying to solve.

No matter what level of star they were, one of the big draws for the celebrities was the Communication Course offered at the center, which claimed to get people comfortable for auditions and helped them to network effectively. Another attraction was the fact that the auditing sessions had a priest-penitent privilege stamp of secrecy, meaning that the contents of each session were guarded, similar to the way that a priest would guard secrets heard during confession. This level of security made celebrities comfortable with relating their problems and the oddities that they wanted fixed.

While the facilities and the hospitality that celebrities received at the Celebrity Centre went far beyond that which regular public Scientologists encountered, the differences weren't just superficial. There were also numerous financial and course-related benefits that celebrities received. Money and the art of selling Scientology were crucial differences that the ordinary public Scientologist experienced compared to celebrities. For one thing, celebrities didn't have to endure the constant "regging," the harassment from the Church to give money for projects or further services. They were still asked to give donations and pay for next services, but they dealt with one designated person, instead of being solicited by various staff members, like the normal public Scientologists were. In addition, celebrities were allowed to do Scientology at their own pace, whereas everyone else would begin that way but soon get pressured and pushed constantly for the next level, which meant they'd also have to pay more money.

For other Scientologists, these requests for money weren't limited to course work. Dallas's parents, for example, were always pressured to give money and sign up for more courses, even if they'd already paid for their next three courses. This sort of thing was never allowed with celebrities. Similarly, when Scientologists would travel to San Diego to fund-raise for the church projects, they would often go to Dallas's parents' house late at night to try to get his parents to donate. Not surprisingly, that kind of house call would never happen to a celebrity.

The end result of all this was that the celebrity experience of Scientology was vastly different from what most Scientologists experienced. It was never entirely clear whether the celebrities knew the full extent of their special treatment, or if they had any idea what life was actually like for the Sea Org members who waited on them hand and foot.

In many ways, the Celebrity Centre was the perfect stage for the act that Scientology put on for the celebrities. The accommodations were gorgeous, and the beautiful grounds made the experience enjoyable. Everything was tightly controlled and orchestrated, and if the celebrities themselves took things at face value, they'd simply see the act and never witness what went on behind the curtain. There was never a risk that they would get exposed to child labor or something similar that the Church didn't want them to see. Sea Org members at the Celebrity Centre appeared happy because it was their job to do that, so celebrities wouldn't know from talking to them or watching them whether they'd been paid their forty-five dollars that week, or if they missed their families.

This act of the Celebrity Centre was crucial to how the Church reached out to celebrities and encouraged them to join. Simply put, it operated almost identically to any other Church where people take courses and get auditing, but it focused on the famous. You didn't have to be famous to go there, but they targeted up-and-coming artists or forgotten artists trying to rebuild their careers. There were numerous policies about celebrities that explained how celebrities are good PR for the Church since their wins will be in the public eye.

In the end, all this amounts to one of the most powerful recruiting tools that the Church has, offering celebrities a chance to mingle with other like-minded Scientologists and enjoy their time in Scientology outside public scrutiny. In that way, it plays to many celebrities' sense of entitlement and selectivity. To that end, even non-Scientologists find themselves there on occasion. When my mom was originally working on the Celebrity Centre, she saw Brad Pitt there because he was dating Juliette Lewis. On other occasions, I heard stories of people like Bono and Colin Farrell attending galas there despite not being Scientologists themselves.

The morning of my Sunday brunch with Dallas and his mom, the restaurant wasn't particularly crowded. The décor was in a very flamboyant Renaissance style. We sat at a table in the garden. Dallas's mother Gail was small, cute, and always smiling. I could tell she and Dallas had great affection for each other. She was very nice to me, despite my being extremely shy and saying very little.

At some point in the conversation, she asked me my last name and discovered I was David Miscavige's niece. "I'll be sure not to do anything bad in front of you," she joked.

IN THE NEXT FEW MONTHS, THINGS WITH DALLAS STARTED GET-ting serious. I met the rest of his family, who were every bit as kind as he and his mother. Dallas soon became my best friend. He was my boyfriend, which meant I could marry him one day. Sometimes, on Sunday mornings, his parents would come to visit the two of us, treating me like I was a member of their family. Whenever I felt down, Dallas made me feel better. I could talk to him about anything and vice versa.

One night on the fire escape, Dallas proposed to me. We had been together only a couple of months, but in the Sea Org, it was not unusual to date for such a short time before a proposal. I hadn't expected anything out of the ordinary that particular night, but I was hoping a proposal would come soon.

That night, in the neon-lit darkness of Los Angeles, on the old iron fire escape bolted onto my building, Dallas got down on one knee and pulled out a ring. He was stuttering and jumpy, as he usually was when he was nervous. He prefaced the proposal by telling me that he hadn't been able to ask my father first, because he had no idea where he was. Then he asked if I would marry him.

Every important line of the conversation was interrupted and punctuated by a honking horn, a siren, someone yelling, or a rattling shopping cart being pushed by a homeless person. We also had to talk over the constant music blasting from the Pig 'n' Whistle restaurant right next door to my building. But I was beyond noticing or caring, and I screamed out "Yes!" in overwhelming happiness. Finally, I was going to be in a family of my own.

Chapter Twenty-Six

A SECRET ENGAGEMENT

When I told Mr. H about Dallas and me getting engaged, she didn't know whether to be excited or worried. The next day, she told me that I was not supposed to tell anyone the news. I wasn't sure who had asked her to relay this information to me, but I assumed it had come from Uncle Dave or Aunt Shelly or Mr. Rathbun. Mr. H didn't say I *couldn't* get married; she only said I shouldn't tell anyone. I had no idea why, but it was too late. We had already told just about everyone, including all my friends at Flag.

I didn't believe that Dallas was my fate or destiny. I didn't believe in that stuff. I just felt like he was the best one in the whole world for me. He was fun, adventuresome, and extremely kind. I was attracted by his nonconfrontational attitude. He always took the time to hear all sides of an argument, and respected everyone's position equally. Despite everything I had been through, I was going to be with the man I loved. I would finally have a happy ending. My ring was gorgeous, too, thanks to Dallas's father owning a jewelry store. It was simple and classic, two smaller diamonds on either side of a bigger one, and it represented every dream of mine coming true.

I was eighteen and Dallas was twenty-two. The majority of the people in the Sea Org married at a young age, for a couple of reasons. For one, you were not allowed to have sex before marriage. Also, married couples were allowed to have their own room, as opposed to sharing with up to seven roommates. I knew lots of people who had married at fifteen. Any younger than eighteen, you had to go to Las Vegas, because in California you were required to meet with a mental health professional if you were under the age of eighteen.

As things stood, Dallas and I weren't going to be able to have children, because of the Flag order. However, Dallas actually believed the current rule in the Sea Org would change again and the ban on children would be lifted. I thought this was unlikely, but being with Dallas and being a part of his family was easily enough for me.

Christmas came and everybody was given a day off. The downside was that Dallas went to San Diego to see his family, and I was forbidden to go with him, so I went out to dinner and a movie with the rest of the crew. I did get some presents in the mail from my parents: a stuffed animal, a watch, and some books which I loved. I was not aware that as a goodwill gesture my uncle had allowed them to communicate with me without restriction. I think he was just trying to keep them calm and happy so that the Church didn't suffer legal ramifications if they decided to sue. However, this was still the only time that I had heard from them since our last meeting.

A WEEK OR TWO AFTER MR. H HAD GIVEN ME ORDERS NOT TO announce my engagement, I was called to meet with Mr. Rathbun in his office on the twelfth floor. He said he had heard I was getting married and was delighted to see me so happy. However, he needed to advise me to hold off a little bit on the wedding and telling people we were engaged, as it seemed that someone in Dallas's family, specifically his uncle Larry, was under suspicion of looking at some anti-Scientology websites. I was told that the last thing the Church needed was Larry, who might be a PTS, meeting my parents, whose status was anything from declared SP to some version of SP. The fear was that Larry, Mom, and Dad might work together to bring down the church.

I didn't think there was anything to fear, but it seemed like it was a real possibility to Mr. Rathbun. As annoying as it was, I figured it would be just a few weeks. Plus, Mr. Rathbun was being so nice, and I was anxious to try to make everything easy for him.

Despite the kink in the plan because of Uncle Larry, I liked daydreaming about what my big day might be like, although I probably would never be able to afford the things I was dreaming about. I didn't have a father who could pay for my wedding, but that didn't stop me from occasionally looking through bridal magazines and picking out dresses I liked, selecting the music for the wedding, and naming my bridesmaids. I even entertained the idea of asking my grandmother to lend me the money, and that I would pay her back, although that would be virtually impossible on my meager pay. I hadn't been in touch with her since I left Florida, although she did send me presents and a card for Christmas, saying how much she missed me. Looking back, she would have never made me pay her back anyway.

Not long after my conversation with Mr. Rathbun, though, Dallas started getting pulled off his job to be given metered ethics interviews. They focused on ensuring that he and I had not gone out 2D. Once, Dallas was given a "Roll Back," an auditing session used to trace the sources for "enemy lines." In Scientology, an enemy line was any criticism of the Church or its units. Dallas was asked questions in an attempt to uncover and expose his motive for marrying me. "Where did you get the idea to marry Jenna?" the auditor asked him.

It was a gross misapplication of the Roll Back, which was certainly not intended to decide if marrying me was an enemy line, or if Dallas's intentions were sincere. But, since the Church was paranoid, the Roll Back was trying to see if Dallas had been told by someone to marry me to get information about my family or something along those lines. He would never have been put through this had my name not been Miscavige.

I had a Roll Back, too. The Church seemed to be looking for a reason to get us into trouble. Any time people were dating there was a suspicion of an out 2D, but this was much worse. I wasn't sure why or who was behind trying to stifle the wedding plans, but who else could it have been but Uncle Dave or Aunt Shelly? The most infuriating part about it was that they were mostly interrogating Dallas, likely because he was the weaker target, not having been as experienced at security checking as I was.

Months went by, and despite my asking when we could get married, we were still given no answer and no hope. Dallas was as frustrated as I was, but it seemed there was little we could do to expedite things. Finally, I received a letter from Aunt Shelly saying that she was happy that I was getting married, and warning me not to be stupid and go out 2D. She said Linda from the Office of Special Affairs, would keep me updated on when Dallas and I should be able to get married. Frustrated, I spoke to Linda myself, who told me handling Dallas's uncle was extremely slow and time-consuming, and there hadn't been any progress and probably wouldn't be for a long time.

I wasn't the least bit sure what "handling Uncle Larry" entailed. There wasn't much they could do about him. I didn't even believe that the wedding was being delayed by somebody as peripheral as Dallas's uncle. Dallas's parents were held in high regard, being both money donors and disseminators of Scientology. That should have trumped the role of a possible wayward uncle. It would have been almost impossible to investigate anybody's extended family and not find somebody in there who was skeptical about Scientology or had once looked at an anti-Scientology website. The whole thing was bizarre. My parents were the ones who were disaffected with Scientology, yet any objections to the wedding always circled back to the concept that there was danger in my parents meeting Larry at a wedding.

Dallas was getting very frustrated, because none of the executives would talk to him, only to me. He wanted me to ask my uncle Dave for help, but I didn't want to, figuring he must already know and didn't care. I worried that it might backfire and get me in more trouble for trying to use influence. Dallas didn't understand, perhaps because the only person who could help us was truly Uncle Dave. If my uncle was really the only one standing in our way, no amount of persuasion on my part would have made a difference.

I tried to rationalize the objections to the wedding at face value, telling Linda many times that my parents didn't need to be at my wedding and neither did Uncle Larry; problem solved. Linda didn't care; she wasn't the one calling the shots.

Finally, after months of nonsensical excuses about Uncle Larry, Dallas and I went out 2D and had sex out of wedlock. If anyone was aware of the consequences of an out 2D it was me, but I did it anyway. Dallas and I wanted to be together beyond any repercussions. If consequences arose, we would address them when the time came. In my mind, having sex with Dallas was not wrong, no matter what policy said. As far as I was concerned, no one was going to find out anyway. Only the two of us knew about the out 2D, and I assumed our secret was safe. We were young, in love, and committed to being married; it was the Church that was not allowing us to move forward with our relationship.

I knew that out 2D was bad if you were engaging in adultery or were promiscuous, but in our case, we were in a committed relationship and we'd been dating for months. We were the ones trying to follow the rules and get married, while they were simply coming up with excuses about why we couldn't move forward. We'd wanted to do the right thing and they'd made that impossible—we were all too aware that following their rules put happiness out of reach, so we did what we wanted and what we felt was right for us—to hell with the consequences.

I didn't feel an ounce of guilt and managed to withhold the incident for weeks. Dallas, however, eventually caved under questioning, as he now thought we *had* done something wrong. One day in early June, after intense pressuring, he confessed it all to Mr. H, who, of course, was shocked by the admission. She had been clever in the questioning, but she hadn't thought it would ever uncover anything. She confronted me next, and she was already calm, to me indicating she had already processed her shock. I told her I didn't feel bad about it, only that we had been caught.

Of course, I was extremely angry at Dallas for talking, but that conversation would be had later. For now, I told Mr. H. that the fault of the out 2D was squarely on whoever wouldn't let us get married. Surprisingly, she didn't disagree. She was just upset and anxious about what would happen next. No Sea Org members got away with an out 2D, and Dallas and I certainly weren't going to be the first, although I might have been the first not to feel bad about it.

I was immediately placed under watch, where someone was supposed to follow me. Mr. H told me that I was going to be in big trouble. I could tell that she was even scared for me.

"Where is Dallas?" I asked Mr. H. I was fully aware that when out 2Ds occur the first thing that happens is that the offenders are separated and often sent to different continents, or at least different bases, to do the RPF and never see each other again.

Mr. H's answer was very disturbing but unsurprising. She told me I didn't need to know, that I shouldn't even be thinking about him, given the amount of trouble I was in. All I could really focus on was that if I didn't find Dallas, I would likely never see him again.

I was terrified and furious all at once. Sea Org rules and policies demanded that I sit there quietly and do whatever I was told at times this grave, but I simply couldn't do it.

"Where the fuck is he?" I demanded of Mr. H.

She was shocked and said she didn't know. "Bullshit!" I yelled, not sparing words. I stormed out of her office and started opening doors up and down the hall, trying to find him. I went downstairs and checked the bus, asking his friends along the way if they had seen him, but they hadn't. I was being tailed by someone who kept calling at me to stop, but I went to every room in the entire HGB looking for him.

Next, I walked two miles to the Hollywood Inn, but he wasn't there, either. I saw my life falling apart all over again. This time, I sure as hell wasn't going to let it happen. Just then, the Hollywood Inn's security guard told me I had a phone call in the office off the lobby, so I ran in, hoping it was Dallas, only to find Mr. Rathbun standing there in person, looking very serious. I was briefly ashamed that the second-most-important person in the Church had to come here to deal with me and my out 2D, but I was over trying to do right by RTC. They fucked up everything in my life. All I wanted was to be allowed to get married, and be assigned a post in the Sea Org for my value, not because of who my uncle was. I was exhausted from always having to be sec-checked because of my family name and the Church's paranoia-driven PR. Other people in my situation would have either been in or out, cut off from their family or not. I was in a constant in-between, which was a complete mind-fuck. Mr. Rathbun tried to sit me down.

"Jenna, I know what's been happening," he said, trying to shame me into submission. "You just need to come clean right now."

It was obvious to me that he was interpreting my behavior as "wild animal reaction," the most well-known symptom of a missed withhold. Clearly, he thought he could calm me down by having me come clean to him. However, I was in no mood to come clean. I just wanted to know where Dallas was.

"He is being dealt with," was all he would give me. I pushed out of the office, unwilling to deal with his mind games.

It was now dark, as I walked the two miles back to the HBG to continue my search for Dallas. While charging down the sidewalk, I heard the sound of a car engine slowing down behind me and the voice of Mr. Rathbun yelling for me to get in, saying we needed to talk. After some convincing I finally got in, thinking he'd tell me where Dallas was.

Mr. Rathbun was rambling on about not knowing how this whole thing had gotten so far out of control. Now, however, he said he had no choice but to report my actions to Aunt Shelly and Uncle Dave. I couldn't believe that he thought I was so naive that I didn't think they already knew everything. I didn't challenge him, though. I just told him that I didn't see what any of it had to do with them. Another Sea Org member wouldn't have had to endure the scrutiny and level of security that I did.

Mr. Rathbun agreed, but he was clearly torn between feeling he was supposed to be yelling at me, and understanding my dilemma and feeling sympathetic, in a way very similar to Mr. H. He drove up to the top of Mulholland Drive, until he finally stopped the car at a scenic overlook so we could get some air. This was the first time I had ever been on this road. With all of Los Angeles lit up in front of us, Mr. Rathbun seemed to think that I would calm down, but when I didn't suddenly melt into submission because of the gorgeous view, he became furious and began yelling at me that I was an SP. We started screaming at each other again, and he got so pissed-off that he got back in his car and drove off.

Now I was stranded in the middle of God knows where,

having gotten no closer to finding Dallas. I didn't even know I was on Mulholland Drive. Luckily, I spied a couple of lovers up the hill from me, who, from their appearance, had seen the entire argument. Trying to look as normal as I could in a Sea Org uniform with my eyes red and swollen, I approached them to see if I could please borrow a phone. The girl in the pair, obviously feeling bad for me, handed me hers. I thanked her, looked at it, then looked back at her, suddenly realizing that I had absolutely nobody to call.

CHAPTER TWENTY-SEVEN

THE EDGE

I STARED OUT AT THE SAN FERNANDO VALLEY, TRYING TO FIGURE out what to do next. I started walking down the road toward Los Angeles; I was about fifteen minutes along when Mr. Rathbun came back for me. This time, I got into the car without argument.

"Look," Mr. Rathbun began, "if you do your program, you will see Dallas again." I had no idea what my program was going to be, but I knew it would consist of countless sec-checks, at the very least.

"I'll do it," I replied, "but only because of how much I love Dallas."

"I understand. I just want what's best for you."

We sat in silence for a bit before finally starting back toward the base.

Before he dropped me off, we stopped at the Celebrity Centre, where he had to drop off a hugely important auditing folder from a session he had with Tom Cruise.

"When I get out of this car, please don't take off," he said. "I will be right back."

Tempting as it was, I was exhausted. Besides, there was no point in bolting. Where would I go?

By the next morning, I had calmed down enough to think rationally and decided I would cooperate, go in session, and try to get through whatever program was required of me. For the next five days, I went in session with Sylvia Pearl, from the Office of Special Affairs, which operated like a kind of secret police known for sec-checking people who were security risks. The video camera in her room was pointed right at me.

In the sec-check, she started with a question she already knew the answer to: Had I had sex with Dallas? She then proceeded to ask me about every single aspect of it—where, when, how, how many times, how long—in excruciating detail. Although the probing questions were expected, as this was a sec-check, I still found them disturbing and invasive. Not only were they intended to be demeaning; they were also designed to make me feel violated. The hallmark of a good security checker was his or her willingness to invade privacy, and Sylvia Pearl did it commendably. It felt wrong to cooperate with something that was clearly intended to be used against me and to control me.

As if having my most intimate moments exposed to Sylvia weren't bad enough, I knew that there were unseen eyes in the room with me. Most likely, there was somebody watching through the camera in the room or someone who would watch the video later. Then, of course, somebody else would read my session worksheet. I felt nauseated just thinking about how many people would learn about my private life before the day was out. The exercise was supposedly for my own good, but this institutional voyeurism was too much for me.

All this interrogation did was to make me doubt the purpose of the whole ordeal. It would be one thing if I simply had to confess what I'd done and repent, but the additional details could not have served any purpose. According to Scientology, the more details you gave, the more relief you were supposed to get, but after everything I'd revealed, I didn't feel relieved, I felt used.

They seemed committed to making me repent for my out 2D and for my behavior, and to admit that I was wrong. It would have been easier for me if I thought I was wrong. However, for reasons that I couldn't describe, that were out of my control and beyond my understanding, I couldn't submit in the way in which they asked of me, and in which I had in the past.

When I wasn't in session, I would ask where Dallas was, assuming that he was going through the same process somewhere else. After five days, I was given permission to write him a letter, but Mr. H. still had me change a few things after she read through it. Two days later, I got a letter back, which was just a few lines long and didn't sound like Dallas. In short, he was getting through his program, I should do mine, and he loved me. The brevity of the letter worried me more than the content did.

After a few more days of questions from Sylvia, I found my attitude changing. Whereas earlier I had resented the questions yet answered them, suddenly, cooperating in any way became a struggle. Sitting in the auditing room, waiting to begin the questioning, I wasn't sure I could handle another round of confessing in front of an audience.

"Could you please turn off the camera?" I asked Sylvia. All I wanted was a bit of privacy. I was going to do the session, but I just needed some help or comfort—at the very least, a one-on-one conversation.

"No," she said, leaving it at that.

When she began to ask questions, I just shut down, refusing to talk to her. I had nothing to say. I couldn't find any words to say that she would listen to anyway. As she became increasingly impatient, all I could think about was leaving the room, and how much I needed to get out of there. The only problem was, I wasn't allowed to go anywhere.

I got up to leave the room. Sylvia wouldn't allow me. She was strong and clearly prepared, even though she was at least fifty. I tried to escape her grasp for at least fifteen minutes, until I promised not to run if she just let me go to the back stairwell. It was the least confrontational way in which I could handle the situation. She eased up, and that's when I made my move.

I got by the first security guard, but he radioed someone to get to the bottom of the stairs, four flights down. Practically jumping down a flight at a time, I beat the next guard to the exit.

Once I was on Hollywood Boulevard and out in public, I was untouchable. No one would dare make a scene. I started walking down the street, then I noticed that Sylvia had found me and was following me.

"Jenna—Jenna, wait! Stop!" she shouted over the sounds of passing cars.

"Get away from me!" I yelled back. "I'm not going back. I'm going to find Dallas."

Beginning with the Hollywood Inn, I checked every floor, asking anyone I saw if they'd seen him. Back at the HGB, I charged up to Mr. H's office.

"Where is he?" I demanded. She didn't even open her mouth to respond, just simply looked at me. We studied each other for a minute, waiting to see what the other would do next, until I made it clear that the rapport we'd built over the last several months was gone. "I'm going to find him—and you know what else? I'm never going to sit down for another session so somebody can get off on my sex stories. I'm through with that."

She shut the door in my face, and I tried knocking. She wouldn't answer, so I knocked louder and louder, raising my voice until, with nothing to lose, I got a running start and crashed my body into her door, which burst open on my second try, despite the dead bolt. Her fed-up expression was replaced with shock. She just stood and watched as I began grabbing at the papers scattered around her office, looking for clues as to where he might be. In one of the piles, I discovered a report from someone who had been security checking him. It included all the explicit details of our intimate encounter, which didn't surprise me, but it was unnerving just the same.

Glancing at one of the pages, I saw the name of his auditor, Tessa, in the Office of Special Affairs. With Mr. H still standing there, I ran downstairs to the OSA auditing rooms looking for Tessa. Nobody in OSA would tell me where she was, so I waited for her outside the building.

A few minutes later, Tessa and another woman emerged from the front door of the HGB and started walking to a car. I followed them, demanding that they tell me where Dallas was, but they refused to talk to me. They drove off, advising me that I should stop worrying about Dallas and take care of myself.

FOR THE NEXT TWO WEEKS, I CONTINUED MY SEARCH FOR DALLAS, enduring exhausting days of combing through Sea Org buildings in L.A. and hoping to find where they'd stashed him. Wearing my regular Sea Org uniform, I'd wander the halls, quietly doing my own detective work to see what I could discover. While I wasn't smashing down doors or sprinting down the street, with each passing day I became more agitated and my resolve grew.

Though my approach had little to show for it, my investigation gave me time to look back at the last several weeks and consider their treatment of me, treatment that, in many ways, had been unusual. Once upon a time, an outburst like the one I'd had with Sylvia in the auditing room would have easily landed me a severe punishment, most likely RPF. Instead, they made constant threats of putting me on RPF, but it appeared to be all talk and little follow-through. If there had been a time to crack down on me, it would have been after that session with Sylvia. Instead, here I was, walking through the corridors of PAC Base. Although someone was following me, she was not trying to stop me.

The disconnect in their actions was hard to understand and made me wonder what was going on behind the scenes. Clearly there was conflict on their side; they seemed to want to punish me but something seemed to be preventing them from actually doing so. It didn't take much to see that most likely my parents factored into all this. After all, if the Church put me on RPF, they'd have to explain that to my parents, who likely would not be thrilled, not to mention anyone else who would wonder why a Miscavige was disobedient enough to get the Church's most severe punishment.

While my family was surely part of it, it didn't seem like the whole story. After all, I'd refused to accept my punishment for the out 2D; anyone aware of that knew I was in a major violation of the mores of the group, and, instead of contrition, I gave them spite. Yet their actions seemed to show a larger ambivalence on their part, almost as though they could not make up their minds about how to deal with the situation.

Perhaps, in the end, the powers that be knew the reality as well as I did: I would not accept being sent to the RPF. They already had Dallas, and I didn't feel I had much else to lose. I would have sooner called the police and filed a missing-person report on Dallas than submit to another punishment that I didn't deserve. Though I doubted that they had any remorse about preventing Dallas and me from getting married, it seemed like at the very least they didn't know what to do about it now. To allow us to wed now would essentially condone our actions; they couldn't punish us for an out 2D and let us stay together. Instead, they seemed to think they could just keep us apart until I decided to give up; as my persistence was making clear, that was not going to happen.

Finally, I grew so desperate and depressed that I went back to Mr. H for help. It didn't take long for our conversation to escalate into a screaming argument that ended with her slamming the door in my face again. Undeterred, I broke it down a second time, even though it had just been fixed. Within minutes, three security guys grabbed me by the arms and legs, pulled me into a small room, and held me down. Even then, I tried breaking free as best I could. I kicked one of them in the balls and almost got away.

My bad behavior must have been reported up the chain of command, because two days later I got a phone call from Greg Wilhere, a top executive in RTC who said he was already en route from Int to see me. He made a deal with me: if I stopped going nuts, he'd let me talk to Dallas. A few minutes later, he kept his end of the bargain. I was on the phone with Dallas.

I quickly broke down in tears, the emotion of the moment and my exhaustion being too much to control. Dallas was on the verge of tears himself, but something sounded wrong in his voice. He was being very weird and deliberate in what he said; there were exceptionally long, extremely noticeable pauses in his speech. I knew that someone was standing over him and telling him what to say, a very common practice for people in trouble. It only made me angrier. I wanted to see him face-to-face. I was furious that they felt like they owned us

"Tell me where you are," I demanded.

"Jenna, I can't," he said before another long pause. "I'm going through the program. I'm getting there bit by bit. If I finish this, the word is that we can be together again."

"Do you believe that?" I asked him.

"I think there is a chance, and that is all I have right now," he said rather hopelessly.

"Just tell me where you are," I begged. I'd been through too much to simply leave it to chance, but he was adamant.

"I can't tell you where I am."

I felt a flush of anger. I had risked so much trying to find him, yet his loyalty seemed to be more with the Church than with me. Despite my best efforts, the Church, it seemed, had already won. He was their puppet, and they seemed to be enjoying throwing this in my face.

Hysterical and desperate, I took the phone with me and climbed halfway out the window.

"Listen, Dallas, and whoever else is also listening to this—if someone doesn't tell me where you are, I'm going to jump out the fifth-floor window. I'm serious."

"Jenna, I can't tell you!" he said.

Standing on a ledge five stories up and looking down on the cars speeding by, I couldn't believe it had come to this. It was starting to get dark and the wind tugged at the hairs of my sweater, the streetlights below merging into a blur. I had no control over anything, but the prospect of taking my own life was a way to change that. I knew that the Church had great fear about what happened when someone died or committed suicide on their watch. They didn't need another PR flap; they would likely do anything to prevent it, especially after Lisa McPherson. This was my last-ditch effort to regain what they'd taken from me, to use the only leverage I felt that I had left—their fear of bad PR and my own life.

Still, Dallas refused to reveal his whereabouts. I was just hanging up when Mr. Wilhere called someone else in the office asking for an update. He had someone tell me Dallas was coming over now, and I would see him, so I came inside. Finally, someone had taken me seriously enough to let me see Dallas.

About an hour later, Dallas got off the elevator, looking miserable and worried. I wanted to hug him, but, all at once, my feelings of fury came raging back.

"Where have you been?" I demanded through tears. "Why haven't you been looking for me?"

"I'm sorry, Jenna, I just can't tell you."

With those words the relief that I'd felt upon seeing him evaporated, and all that was left was the painful reality of the choices he'd made. He could say he wanted to be with me, but when he'd been forced to choose between me and the Church, between my safety and obeying orders, we both knew that he'd chosen the Church. I had finally found him, but somehow he was already lost. It was more than I could take. I started throwing punches at him. He was bigger and stronger, so my actions were futile, which angered me even more.

And so, for the second time that night, I stepped out onto the ledge.

I know now that people who have been abandoned feel the need to test people in their lives by seeing what they will do, seeing if they will abandon them like everyone else if pushed hard enough. Thinking back to that night, it's difficult to say whether I was testing him, them, or myself. I still don't know if I really was going to jump each time I took up my five-story perch, but what I do know was that, in that moment, as I stood outside the window, I experienced the pain of every loss I'd faced at the hands of the Church over and over again: my parents, my brother, my friends. If the Church was going to take Dallas, too, then maybe jumping out the window wasn't such a bad idea.

The sky was darkening, but I tried to look down not up as I contemplated my next step. I wondered how much it would hurt, or whether I would die instantly. I pushed aside thoughts of pain, and thought about the Thetan that was me, which, somehow, I still believed in. And yet, instead of giving me strength to continue in this life, the idea of that Thetan pushed me in the other direction, as I realized that, if I died, I would simply come back in another body. There was comfort in that, comfort in ending it all to start again, maybe with a new family. After all, I was in this for a billion years. What was so bad about throwing one life away, when apparently I had thousands to lose?

Dallas finally realized how serious I was when I asked him if I would die. His eyes filled with tears, and taking my hand, he promised to tell me where he had been and what had been happening. With his promise, I let him pull me in through the window and we embraced. Maybe my life did matter to him after all.

He told me he was being kept at PAC, in the basement under full-time watch, doing manual labor such as demolition and laying tiles, and had been getting security checked all the while. He said that in the letters he had written me, he was instructed what to say and to make it sound like his own words. Just as I had suspected, he said that our brief phone call had been monitored by Linda, who had told him what he could and couldn't say. The threat they were holding over his head was that, if he didn't cooperate, he would be declared a Suppressive Person and would never see his family or me again. He said he was just trying to do right by everyone.

I wanted to feel relief, knowing that Dallas did think my life was important enough to break at least one rule. I could see that he was really hurt, that he had been in a horrible bind and didn't know what to do, and for that, I felt as though I was the worst person in the world, which I had always been told that I was. Still, I struggled to get past my own ordeal. I had risked everything out of love for him and fear of being separated, but, as far as I could tell, he hadn't felt the same way. He had a lot more to lose than just me.

We weren't together long when Mr. Wilhere arrived to speak to me privately. He asked Dallas to wait in the other room.

"Jenna, if you get through your program, you'll be fine," he began. "Most people would go to the RPF for what you've done, but you're lucky. It looks like you're going to be spared."

"What about Dallas?" I asked.

"I don't really care about Dallas. He'll probably be thrown to the sharks."

So, Dallas had chosen the Church and this was his reward: he was dispensable to them. He was just a tool to get me to do what they wanted, which was to not cause PR issues for the Church by acting out. They didn't know what else to do with me.

Soon after, Linda came to take Dallas. Emotionally and physically worn down, I was ashamed by the way I had treated him. I agreed to go home and think about the best way to approach things. No sooner had I got to my room than I realized what a mistake it had been to let Dallas go, especially after Mr. Wilhere talked about him being thrown to the sharks. Now that I knew where he was, I had to go find him before they moved him somewhere else.

Eager not to repeat past mistakes, I hurriedly walked over to PAC and found him in a room, with a security guard posted outside the door.

That night, I slept in a room with him. It was the first time we had slept in the same berthing, and I took comfort knowing I was finally close to him.

CHAPTER TWENTY-EIGHT

A NEW NAME

THE FOLLOWING MORNING, MR. WILHERE MADE AN ANNOUNCE-
ment: the Church was going to send Dallas and me somewhere to
calm down and "destimulate," an LRH method of dealing with
someone who had gone insane. I didn't care what he said. The
only words I heard were "get away." I knew I couldn't continue as
I had been. My body couldn't handle it. I only weighed ninety-
four pounds, and there wasn't much more I could take.

That day, Mr. Wilhere drove Dallas, our two security guards,
and me up to Big Bear, where we were taken to a two-bedroom
cabin, one with bunk beds and one with a queen-sized bed. My
guard and I stayed in the one with the queen and Dallas and his
stayed in the room with the bunk beds. Looking around at the
comfortable cabin and the two guards, I couldn't understand why
the Church was seemingly spending so much money on us. I'd
experienced many different forms of punishment in my life, but
never anything quite like this. Two days earlier, they'd seemed determined to torment me; now I was at a retreat. The arrangement
struck me as strange, but given what life had been like, I wasn't
about to complain.

For the next few weeks, the four of us just hung out, cooked, hiked, swam in the lake, and read books aloud to each other. Once a week, someone would come by to visit and bring us mail, any clothes that we needed, and food. I felt guilty about all the money and resources being spent on me. We'd been there about a week when Sylvia Pearl arrived to continue my sec-checking and stay in a cabin near ours. However, her presence didn't work out. I still couldn't handle the security checking, and again, I just walked out of the sessions. At the same time, Dallas was being sec-checked, too, except his questions were about me, as they tried to get him to report on me, which only made me angrier. In time, Sylvia was replaced with an RTC auditor, and eventually, with some difficulty, we finished my sec-check.

Mr. Wilhere came up once a week to check on me, bringing with him any news that he cared to share. It was during one of these visits that he told me there had been a significant development in the Lisa McPherson case. Bob Minton, the key financier in the civil case brought by her family, had changed sides. He was no longer supporting the cause of Lisa McPherson, but instead was supporting the Church. I remembered that Bob Minton had been the leader of the Lisa McPherson Trust at the base. OSA often referred to him when talking about our enemies who were picketing and trying to bring down the Church. Minton and his wife had been the most vocal opponents at the Flag Land Base. He had testified at a court hearing that the lawyer representing the McPherson estate had made him lie, change court documents, and pump up anti-Scientology sentiment. The McPherson family lawyer responded by saying that Minton had been extorted by the Church. Already, the criminal charges against the Church had been dismissed in 2000 after the medical examiner changed the cause of death from "unknown" to "accident."

Aside from periodic stories from outside, our stay at Big Bear was incredibly secluded and peaceful. I never learned exactly why

I was sent there. It could have been to make my parents happy. It could have been because I had threatened suicide, which meant that I was insane and a Potential Trouble Source. It could have been that I was a Miscavige, and the only alternative at that point would have been having me leave, thus creating bad PR. I'm sure they assumed that isolating me at Big Bear would settle me, make me happy, and allow enough time for the whole incident to blow over without other people seeing that my punishment wasn't so harsh.

Whatever the Church's intentions were, staying there did help me to calm down. Before Big Bear, I was an accident waiting to happen, but after weeks without fear of losing Dallas or having him taken away, and eating and sleeping properly; I'd finally regained my footing.

However, it didn't put an end to my doubt of the Church; in fact, in some ways, I left Big Bear more determined than ever not to give in to their demands. I knew there were things about Scientology that I disagreed with—the invasive questions, the pointless auditing, the endless security checks—and I understood that, while these things had helped some people, all I'd ever gotten from them was aggravation. Furthermore, I found it completely unfair and unreasonable that I had to be punished over and over again for things that weren't my fault. As I looked back on what I'd been through, one thing was clear to me: the only way that people in the Church would stop taking advantage of me was for me to say *no* to them, even if it pushed them to the edge.

At times, this attitude put me at odds with Dallas. While he too had issues with the Church and found a lot to suspect in how they'd treated us, he struggled to understand why I refused to cooperate and do the various punishments they gave me. In his eyes, we should tolerate these things, get them over with, and move on; to me that would only result in them pushing us around more. The more power we gave them over us, the more they would take.

As long as we weren't married, nothing had really changed. Everything that had happened before could still happen again, and, until we were married, we would always be at risk. Sure enough, when we returned home after six weeks, that risk was made perfectly clear.

Before we all went back to L.A., Mr. Wilhere came to talk to me and let me know what our fate would be. Dallas and I were going to be removed from out posts at the Flag Liaison Office, demoted, and posted at the PAC Base doing manual labor in the mill, where the carpentry jobs were carried out. Their final warning was that we were on the verge of being RPF'd.

The idea of doing manual labor at the PAC Base wasn't that bad. It would have been nice to have less responsibility. We would be doing carpentry. What I objected to was the fact that we were right back where we'd been six weeks earlier, still being punished for the same supposed crimes: our out 2D, my suicide attempt, insubordinations, the list just went on. They had paid for us to go to Big Bear, only to return us to our lives in exactly the same place: receiving an unjust punishment that we were simply expected to take. We were guilty in their eyes and had to pay the price.

Dallas agreed to work at the mill. I refused. After several weeks in limbo, things were finally settled. I was going to remain at CMO IXU and be posted at the Landlord Office at FLO, as a "renderer," meaning I would render designs and help put design boards together. Dallas was transferred back to PAC, which was considered a lower org. Even though the two were just a few miles apart, they were separate bases, so we couldn't eat together or see each other at night.

Though being married doesn't guarantee husbands and wives staying together, this separation was exactly what I'd feared. Worse, when I did see Dallas, he told me he was still being security-checked by Jessica Feshbach, who would soon be famous for being Katie Holmes's auditor. As had been the case with Sylvia at Big Bear, he told me that his sessions were being used to find out about me, not him. This enraged me all over again. Dallas was upset, too, and together we wrote letters to Mr. Rathbun and Mr. Wilhere, requesting that we be together at FLO. Mr. Rathbun never wrote back, and Mr. Wilhere told me that I cared only about my first and second dynamics, myself and Dallas, and I didn't care for anything else, like the group or our mission to save mankind. When his response arrived, I shredded it and sent it back to him, which only got me in more trouble.

Despite how rebellious I was being, I still wasn't sent to the RPF. Instead, I was honing my ability to say no. The realization I'd had at Big Bear meant that they could only control me if I were willing to accept their treatment. For whatever reason, they wanted me to stay, which meant that the Church was in a compromised position: simultaneously trying to punish me for things I'd done, while attempting to keep me calm. So I pushed back on everything I disagreed with, which, by that point, was quite a lot.

Even though I was unhappy, I couldn't bring myself to take the next step and leave the Church. All the ingredients were there, but as long as Dallas remained committed to the Church, I couldn't truly contemplate leaving, if we wouldn't be together. They'd almost succeeded in splitting us up when we were both in the Church, so I could only imagine what would happen if I left and he stayed. My involvement in Scientology became mostly about Dallas. Frustrated as I was, I tolerated it because it enabled us to stay together. It was a relationship worth saving. As a result, I limited my behavior to criticism and insubordination, rather than all-out mutiny.

We still held out hope that our marriage would become a reality. Despite the fact that Dallas and I didn't always agree as to how we would get out of the mess we were in, we still wanted the same thing: to be together. We were best friends and loved each other. Everything we had been through, had only brought us closer, and, one way or another, we were determined to emerge from all of this as husband and wife.

SEVERAL WEEKS AFTER OUR RETURN FROM BIG BEAR, I WAS TOLD that I needed to get onto the daily van run to Int, which was odd, since I hadn't been there in years. I spent two hours on the van wondering who I would be meeting and why. My meeting was with Mr. Wilhere, and it was about marrying Dallas. He wanted us to hold on a little bit longer, saying things weren't resolved with Dallas's uncle yet. Unsurprisingly, handling Uncle Larry was never-ending.

I told him that I would be willing to cooperate and hold on a little bit longer if he was willing to have Dallas posted at FLO so that we could at least be together. He agreed so quickly that it surprised me.

With that out of the way, I figured that, since the only reason they cared about Uncle Larry was based on the premise of my parents coming to the wedding and the possible ensuing conspiracy, I told him I was sure they would be willing to not come, if that was the problem. I could just write them a letter saying as much. To my surprise, after thinking about it, he had me write one, watching while I untruthfully described how happy I was and how well I was doing. I told them I had found someone whom I loved, and that I thought they would love him, too. I had my own life now, I told them, and I hoped they understood. I didn't ask them not to come to the wedding, but I hoped that they would get the gist without me having to spell it out.

Mr. Wilhere kept his word. The next day, Dallas was posted as a typesetter in the Dissemination Division at FLO. This division was responsible for creating promotional pieces for Scientology materials, magazines, and other publications. We were now able to spend mealtimes together, see each other occasionally throughout the day, and even take the same bus back to the berthing at night.

A few weeks later, Mr. Wilhere unexpectedly arrived in the office, saying that he needed to speak to me. He handed me a letter from my parents, already opened. They said they were no longer in Mexico and were now living in Virginia. They said how happy they were for me, and that they understood about not attending my wedding.

I was pleased with their words, but a bit baffled by how it had all unfolded. What I didn't know was that my uncle Dave had actually traveled to the East Coast on Church business, and had hand-delivered my letter to them, proving just how aware Uncle Dave was of what had been going on with me. According to what my parents told me, my uncle, along with his entourage, met them at a fancy hotel in Washington, D.C., where Uncle Dave was staying. Not only did he give my parents my letter; he hooked my father up with a local real-estate guy for employment guidance and found my mother a job at a law office. He also told my parents they were no longer SPs; they had lived in Mexico as the Church had asked of them, and had basically done their A–E steps required for someone to become "undeclared," or no longer an SP.

At the meeting, Uncle Dave said my father could now talk to their mother, something my dad had wanted to do. With regard to my wedding, my mother said that she had expected to hear that I was getting married, being in the Sea Org, so the news wasn't surprising. Uncle Dave had told them he had heard that Dallas was a nice guy, but that he didn't know him.

Of course, I knew nothing about this at the time. I was simply relieved that they weren't coming to my wedding; it was only after I left the Church that I heard the story from my mother.

"So," Mr. Wilhere asked sardonically, "are you going to get married tomorrow?" I could tell how annoyed he was that I was about to get everything I wanted and had even gotten Dallas to be posted at the base.

"Pretty much," I answered unapologetically.

"Well, good luck," he said, mumbling some obligatory advice on how to have a good marriage. I barely heard what he said. I was going to be married.

Early the next morning, Dallas and I drove to the courthouse to get our marriage license. We were too nervous and excited to notice that the car was almost out of gas, and had to coast down a hill to get to the gas station. Dallas's gas cap had to be opened with a key; he was shaking so much that it broke off in the key-hole when he tried to open it. He borrowed pliers from the gas station attendant and fished out the broken part, which took almost an hour. We prayed that it would work when we put it into the ignition, cheering ecstatically when it did. We paid with the five dollars' worth of change we had saved from our pay. I could only imagine what the attendant thought when we handed her the pile of mostly dimes and nickels. We still had to coast a lot of the way to the courthouse, because the gas wasn't necessarily going to get us as far as we needed to go. When we finally arrived, we had to leave the car unlocked because the key was still stuck in the ignition, but we got our marriage license.

Dallas's dad was a Scientology minister as well as a jeweler, and had agreed to come to Los Angeles to perform a quick ceremony. The plan was to meet him at the Celebrity Centre at midnight, as that was when we got off work.

To my surprise, Dallas's mother; his sister and her boyfriend; and his brother, wife, and baby girl were all there, too. The only one who was not a public Scientologist was his sister's boyfriend. Two of my friends, Phil and Clare, were my chosen witnesses. There was no Bitty and Ronnie Miscavige, no Uncle Dave or Aunt Shelly, and no Uncle Larry. I got pretty emotional that Dallas's family was there to make it special. Even though I didn't know them well, they had obviously cared enough about us to make the two-hour drive from San Diego.

It wasn't exactly the wedding of my dreams. Dallas and I were both in our uniforms. I hadn't even touched up my makeup, and my shoes were caked with spray glue from that day's design boards. The ceremony was five minutes long, no flowers, no fancy food, no champagne or music, but none of that mattered. We were married now.

I still cherish the moment that Dallas placed the ring on my finger. I promised myself that, no matter what it took, I would protect him and take care of him, and I would never be separated from him again. I knew that it was wrong to make him more important to me than the Church, but I didn't care. We had finally done it. On September 20, 2002, I became Jenna Hill.

Chapter Twenty-Nine

AUSTRALIA

Dallas and I were given no time to enjoy our special moment. I had to return to work immediately, where I stayed up all night finishing design boards. In the morning, we had breakfast on the down low at Denny's with Dallas's parents. We weren't supposed to eat out like this when it wasn't a Sunday morning, but we did it anyway. That day, I proudly told anyone who would listen that Dallas and I were married, and that I was now Jenna Hill. I was delighted to distance myself from the Miscavige name, but even though my name was different, it didn't change the fact that sooner or later Dallas would have to meet my family.

In December 2002, Dallas and I were given permission to celebrate our first Christmas together, with a trip to San Diego to spend the holiday with Dallas's family, followed by a trip to Clearwater to see Grandma Loretta and Aunt Denise, then to see my parents in Virginia. Everyone in Dallas's family was incredibly nice, possibly the nicest people I had ever met. His parents' house was a log home, as cozy as they come, with a stone fireplace. The flannel sheets on all the beds and the soft lighting made everything warm and inviting. The feeling of home hung in the air;

the familial setting was so contrary to the communal upbringing I had experienced.

After San Diego, Dallas and I flew to Clearwater, followed by Virginia, where we arrived on a gorgeous snowy day. It was really odd to see my parents in their little house, with a fire crackling in the fireplace, just like at Dallas's parents' house. My mother had even cooked a meal for us, which really surprised me. It was foreign yet familiar at the same time; being there made me feel as though I perhaps did have a place to come home to, at least for the holidays.

Over the next couple of days, Mom and Dad showed us around their community and told us about their lives. They seemed to be doing really well. I had anticipated that being with them would be really strained, but it wasn't. My mom loved decorating her new house, and made it sound like a lot of fun. Strangely, my father's Christmas present to us was a television and a VCR/DVD player, which was awesome, but against Church rules. We would just have to keep it well hidden. By the time we left, I felt almost like I had a family with parents who were truly there for me, that maybe it wasn't just Dallas and me after all. For the first time since I was little, I felt as though I really did have a mother and father whom I could turn to in time of need.

When we got back to California, our little room on the base looked drearier than ever, but at least it was our own place. One of the perks of being married was that Dallas and I got our own room, small as it was. With our own space, I now felt like I had a family of my own, even if it was just the two of us. Together, we had a place to go that was ours. We could also eat together, and, in the unlikely event we ever had time off, we could spend it together. We received a couple of Christmas presents that made it look homier, which helped. Aunt Denise had given us some curtains, and my grandma had given us a quilt. I was given permission to talk to my parents on the phone, which was huge, having been forbidden to speak to them for more than two years.

Being married felt like a huge sigh of relief, and while it didn't make any of my issues with the Church disappear, it encouraged them to stay dormant for longer periods of time, long enough to settle into a routine as best we could. I couldn't forget the past, but I didn't have to confront it every day.

Dallas and I had been married a little over a year when my senior at the Landlord Office told me I had been selected to go on a mission to Canberra, Australia. There was a small, failing Scientology Church there, and I was to go on a mission to find a new building for it and raise the funds to buy the building.

When I heard that this mission was going to be at least six months long, I freaked out a little. I didn't want to be away from Dallas for so long. From my own experience, I knew how common it was for husbands and wives to be split up by their jobs in the church. In addition to my parents and other people I'd known over the years who'd been in a similar situation, there was a woman in the Landlord Office who had been separated from her husband for nine years. I had two friends who had been posted away from their spouses for two years and were now both divorced.

Dallas and I were going to do whatever we could to make sure this didn't happen to us. So I proposed that Dallas go on this mission with me. I sent a telex to the Int Landlord with Dallas's qualifications, and the next thing I heard was that he had been approved for the mission as well. It was odd that they had agreed so easily, but I wasn't going to complain.

Neither Dallas nor I had ever been on a mission before, which made the whole thing even more odd. In addition, our pre-mission clearance process was strange. People going on these long-term assignments were supposed to get opportunity checks, when they were questioned as to their motives to go on a particular mission.

Dallas and I did not get one. We were also supposed to be issued full Mission Orders with comprehensive targets, approved by RTC; read by us; star-rate checked out for our full understanding of them; and, finally, each target demonstrated by us in clay. None of this happened. We were given mission orders that appeared to have been written two minutes before we departed for the airport. Even these were hastily constructed, copied, and pasted on top of somebody else's earlier orders. Our mission orders still read, "Find a Building in Kentucky."

The whole thing was extremely peculiar. Why this mission, and why us? It seemed as though it was some sort of plan to take us "offlines," or out of sight. Neither of us had any idea what was behind this, but we didn't ask too many questions. We were just grateful to be going to Australia together.

In January 2004, we boarded our plane for the eighteen-hour flight to Sydney, Australia, and from the moment we stepped off the airplane, it was clear that Australia was going to be quite an experience.

From the start, we had a lot more freedom in Canberra. We could walk to wherever we were going. We even bought ourselves bikes to get around, as renting a car was too expensive. This was the first time I really had to navigate the real world on my own in any way. Clearwater had had far more Scientologists; in Canberra, there were only a handful of them. Everywhere around us there were Wogs. At first I was a little worried, but as I met more of them, I became more comfortable.

The Church covered our living expenses, paying for our apartment and our food, although it was often a struggle to get this money on time. I had to learn how to cook, as my whole life I had been fed by a galley; not having a mess hall was a strange adjustment. It made me feel like we were constantly dealing with food throughout the day, whether it was grocery shopping or actually cooking. At first I was afraid of the stove, so Dallas did most of the cooking. We'd also eat out once in a while. Eventually I tried following recipes and had fun with it, but the meals almost always turned out disastrously. Everything I made was disgusting.

Learning how to cook was just the tip of the iceberg. Probably our biggest challenge was the job itself. We were supposed to find a new Scientology Church building in Canberra, raise the funds to buy it, purchase the building, and have it renovated. Because Scientology was in the process of trying to standardize the layouts for all their new churches, the building itself had to be a minimum of 25,000 square feet or it wouldn't be approved. In addition, it had to be on a busy street, not too industrial, preferably something more traditional and decorative so it had the look of a church. As we did our research, it quickly became clear that a building fitting all those specifics would have cost several million Australian dollars.

And there was the problem. In all of Canberra, there were only about fifteen to twenty practicing Scientologists. The whole operation in Canberra was quite different from what our mission orders had described. In fact, the whole organization in Canberra was composed of ten people who only delivered Intro courses. There was not even auditing, the primary service of any Scientology organization. Not only that, but they were being kicked out of their premises, as they had not paid the rent for six months.

The Church's lists for potential donors included anyone who had ever given their name to the Church for a course, stress test, or any other purpose, the majority of whom had never come back. Complicating things was that Dallas and I had never raised a dime in our lives. The third person on our three-person team had some fund-raising experience and had been on many other missions, but she was quickly recalled home, leaving us there on our own. Still, we were given an impossible task. The idea of raising several million dollars from a group of approximately fifteen public Scientologists, none of whom earned more than $80,000, was ridiculous. Additionally, many of those Scientologists had already paid for services that the Canberra church wasn't able to deliver, so asking them for money seemed wrong. We brought up these observations in our daily reports, but we were nonetheless pushed to get them to donate. In addition, we were not allowed to raise funds from other Australian orgs, as they were doing their own fund-raising. We ended up raising $75,000, the result of a lot of promotion and small fund-raising events like raffles, games, and shows.

Looking back, this was pretty good for people who had never raised a dime in their lives. It was largely possible because of a few friends we made there who knew a lot of people and helped us make connections and raise the money. Still, we were told this amount was not acceptable, and eventually Dallas and I started running out of ways to raise more. Unless they changed the mission plans or the specs of the building we were supposed to purchase, we had done everything we could. We had asked to come home several times, but it wasn't allowed.

Still, Dallas and I struggled to keep asking the same people for money. I could see these people's lives and I knew that they really couldn't afford to donate. This was not something that either of us had ever encountered, and we were in disagreement with the Church about what we were being asked to do. The focus was not on building a Church to deliver Scientology by which to make money; it seemed more about making money and having a nice-looking building. They wanted the new buildings to be filled with gimmicks and high-tech video displays, but all this seemed to trump the delivery of Scientology itself. It felt as though the focus was on the material aspects, instead of Scientology, which was why we were there. Asking for money from these people in return for nothing, especially when they had already given so much, seemed greedy.

The more we pushed to make money, the more we ran into the general public, not always with good results. In one fund-raising effort, we made promotional pieces and sent them to the public Scientologists on our list. Sometimes we would get them back with rude things written on them. I remember one person said that L. Ron Hubbard was a fraud and that we were all idiots. I was surprised, especially when we received ten or so others with similar sentiments. Based on everything that we heard from Uncle Dave and the senior members of the Church my whole life, I had been under the impression that everyone loved L. Ron Hubbard, and that Scientology was flourishing and expanding all over the world. However, it seemed like most people in Australia did not even know what it was, and those who did often were skeptical.

In part because of the freedom that we had, we began to encounter ideas that ran in the face of Scientology's teachings. Even though it was against the rules, we started watching TV for an hour or two a day. I especially liked watching *Queer Eye for the Straight Guy*, a makeover show featuring five gay experts in home décor, food, culture, fashion, and more. I liked the characters and enjoyed the show, and found myself a bit surprised that what I saw didn't match what I'd learned in Scientology. We were taught that homosexuals were sexual perverts and covertly hostile, qualities that made them close to SPs. However, when I watched these guys on television, they didn't strike me as any of those things. It didn't make sense to me, and I just didn't see how it could be true.

We also had Internet access, although I didn't know how to use it very well. One time, Dallas called my attention to a website called "Operation Clambake," which was highly critical of the Church. When we saw what it was, Dallas and I looked at each other in disbelief, knowing we had stumbled on something we weren't supposed to, but neither of us could deny it was interesting. We had to exercise self-restraint, but what we did see was pretty revealing. One story in particular on the site said that

Uncle Dave had usurped power when he took over the Church. That was the first negative implication about his leadership that I had heard. I was a bit curious about the site but didn't fully understand how websites worked. I also knew that people got in trouble for looking at stuff like this. I saw that Operation Clambake mentioned OT III materials on its site; I had been warned about what would happen if you accessed information from levels that you had not yet attained; I figured I would stay away, because I didn't want to go crazy.

Still, I couldn't fully shake the allegations from the website about my uncle. I knew Scientology had detractors because of the protesters at the Flag Land Base, but I hadn't known there were whole websites devoted to opposing Scientology, or how much a part of everyday life the Internet was. The fact that Dallas had come across this site so easily surprised me, but it was also somehow satisfying, although I didn't really know why. It was almost like the moment at the Ranch all those years ago when I'd seen the outside contractors and secretly wished that they would advocate for us. It felt like there was an awareness of what our experiences were in Scientology that was reassuring, even if that awareness wouldn't necessarily change anything.

When I called my parents that night, I asked them if the story about Uncle Dave could be true. They said they didn't know much about it, but they were not sure that the Internet was a reliable source of information. Because my parents brushed it off, it sort of left my mind for a bit.

It wasn't just things that we read and saw that deepened our thinking about the Church; it was the people we met and the vastly different lifestyle we were living. Gone was our incessant regimentation and constant security checks; instead we were actually getting to live our lives, more than before, at least. In Canberra, we became friends with most of the public Scientologists there, especially since they were our only source for our fund-raising. Spending time with them gave me a chance to experience what life would be like if Dallas and I were public Scientologists, living on our own. I had never been around Scientology staff that worked at the Church and moonlighted with normal jobs.

It wasn't just the lifestyle; it was also the presence of the Church that started to change us. I started to see that places like Flag and Int were the exception, not the rule. I had always heard that there were five hundred Scientology Churches around the world, and I thought they were all on a similar scale to Flag, or at least close to it. Clearly, I hadn't really thought it through. To see this small, struggling church in Canberra, and then be around this small handful of casual Scientologists, was to become aware that Scientology wasn't taking over the world in the way we'd always been told.

Of all these experiences, perhaps the most eye-opening wasn't anything subversive or illicit—it was my friendship with a lady named Janette. When we met her, she had two little girls, and a baby boy on the way. We spent a lot of time with her, coming over for her kids' birthday parties and just hanging out. Her two-year-old, Eden, was so precious. She was full of quirks and mischief and I spent a lot of time around her. When I went to the Org, I would sometimes carry her with me and play with her there, even though I was supposed to be a Sea Org member on a mission. I was aware of the effect Eden had on me, but it just seemed natural—I couldn't really help myself. Still, the way I was acting was considered unbecoming of a Sea Org member on a mission.

Janette was pregnant, which was also something that I hadn't really been around before. She would tell me about it, and it just seemed like such an amazing thing for a so-called meat body to be capable of. I felt as though I could ask Janette about anything. We saw her in the days after her son was born, and it seemed like such an incredible thing.

All this time with Janette and Eden got me thinking, in a way in which I never had before, about what it would be like to have a family. Dallas was also great with her. He loved to pick her up and twirl her around until she burst out giggling. He adored children, and always remarked about how cute and special they were. But knowing kids were not allowed for Sea Org members, the thought of being a mother hadn't really occurred to me. Yet, for the first time ever, I found myself wondering if I was missing out.

A YEAR WENT BY, AND THERE WAS STILL NO END IN SIGHT TO OUR mission. While we enjoyed our time there, we tried hard to follow the rules and not go too far off the rails. Even though we tried some new things, we still were very beholden to the Church and our responsibilities. Looking back, I wish we hadn't been so afraid and had gone to the beach and other places; however, we weren't at a place where we were comfortable dismissing the Church's rules so blatantly.

Overall, though, the year was refreshing. I no longer felt on edge because of my frustrations with the Church. Because the level of monitoring we faced was so much less than what it had been, it made it much easier to put aside the issues with which I'd been struggling. Even though I still disagreed with aspects of the Church, I was more relaxed than I'd been in years, not to mention well fed, well rested, and having a lot of fun.

Christmas 2003 rolled around, and although we got permission to come home for the holidays, Dallas's parents had to pay for our round-trip flights. My dad then flew us to Virginia, where my grandma Loretta was going to meet us, but at the last minute she canceled her trip, saying she wasn't feeling well. I was sorry that I hadn't been able to see her, as she was the person I was most looking forward to spending time with.

On our way back to Australia, Dallas and I stopped by the

Landlord Office in L.A. to receive what were supposed to be our revised mission orders. The new Landlord told us, completely unexpectedly, that we were going to be posted at the Sea Org base in Sydney. We were shocked. When we asked when we were supposed to return to California, he said never, that Sydney was to be our new Sea Org post.

It was so out of the ordinary for anything like this to happen. More important, it was against Church policy. We hadn't even properly terminated our Canberra mission. No one had even worked out posts for us or done transfers for the Sydney job. We expressed complete outrage at this development, but, in the end, we went to Sydney on the promise that we weren't being posted there, that we were only on a mission and would receive our mission orders shortly. They never came.

We were in Sydney for two weeks, demanding to receive our mission orders. When that failed, we demanded to come home. It was at this time that I learned that my grandmother had passed away. She was found in her car, not breathing, in a mall parking lot. She was in a coma and never woke up. I was told that her death was a result of her emphysema.

I cried uncontrollably that day. It was horrible to think that I would never be able to see, hug, or speak to her again. It made me wish that I had spent more time with her during the time I had had with her. But I tried to reason that at least she was getting another, younger body somewhere without pain, and that she was happier.

We tried to get the Church to book us a flight back to the States for her funeral, but they wouldn't get us home in time. My parents, however, were permitted to go to Florida to be at her service. I was devastated that I never got to say goodbye to my grandmother. I sometimes talked to her when nobody was around, just to say goodbye. But I don't think she heard me.

CHAPTER THIRTY

LOWER CONDITIONS

ONE WEEK AFTER MY GRANDMOTHER'S FUNERAL, DALLAS AND I were told that we could terminate our assignment in Australia. We boarded a flight home, only to find our room at the FLO Base had been given to someone else. We had painted, carpeted, and tiled that room, on our own dime, but it been given away. Our new room on the seventh floor had really old, peeling linoleum floors and smelled like mold. There were little piles of sawdust everywhere, and a tiny dresser to serve both of us. The bathtub had clogged and overflowed, and hadn't been fixed. The bed must have been at least twenty-five years old, because it creaked when you walked by. In spite of all this, we were happy to be home. As strange and unexpected as our year in Australia had been, it felt good to return to our lives. We knew that it would be difficult to give up some of the freedom that we'd had, but we assumed the adjustment would pass quickly. It didn't. The adjustment was much harder than we'd expected, not just because of what we'd been through abroad, but also because the base itself was worse than it had been.

The next day, we had to be at the base by eleven in the morning and, from the moment we stepped out there, it was clear that things were tighter than they ever had been. We quickly learned that the base's schedule had changed. There was no longer time for personal exercising; meal breaks had been reduced to fifteen minutes; Clean Ship Project—the only time during the week when we got to do our laundry and clean our rooms—had been reduced by two hours; and canteen privileges had been canceled, meaning we were not allowed to buy anything from the canteen, including food. The entire base was being punished with lower conditions and had been for three months.

This time, it wasn't just me who had a problem with all this: Dallas was quite troubled by it as well. More than was the case before Australia, he and I were on the same page about the Church. When we finally got our standard post-mission sec-checks, I was a little surprised when Dallas confessed that we had been watching movies and other programs, which was unfortunate. I had decided to offer as little as I could in confessionals, especially in matters the Church could not possibly know about, but Dallas's obedience made it futile. During my own sec-check, I was asked to estimate how much org money we had wasted by being unproductive and squandering our funds, so I calculated three months of rent, plus bus fare and the cost of food. That was just how confessionals worked. If I were to say the org wasted its own money and that we had actually made them $75,000, I would have been asked for more withholds.

Bad as things seemed to have gotten on the base, the March 13 annual celebration for L. Ron Hubbard's birthday offered us a clear look at just how bad things really were. For events like this, we were expected to sell new or updated releases of LRH books or congress lectures to the public using the sales patter, "cash or credit?" During these sales pushes, we *had* to make our sales quota, which was always impossible, and this year, the whole crew of five hundred people stayed up all night at the Shrine calling around the world to get people to buy the lectures. If we weren't on the phone, we were told to get busy. No food or water was available, and we weren't allowed to get any. Security guarded the door, making sure we didn't leave until seven-thirty in the morning.

Some people did manage to leave early, like a seventy-year-old woman with emphysema, who left at three in the morning. However, such people were dealt with harshly at the next day's muster. They were called to the front of the group and reprimanded, told that they were despicable and that their behavior was disgusting. They were put onto a punishment of scrubbing a Dumpster, inside and out, for an hour. For the next week, we were warned that if any of us walked one step out of line, the whole group would be put on boot camp, cleaning Dumpsters.

After the release of the new congress lecture, each night at eleven, the whole base would assemble in the dining area and listen to audio tapes. Each tape was at least an hour long, and was preceded by a lecture on how unethical we all were and how we had better listen to these lectures, so we could learn what Scientology was all about.

During the lectures, the supervising staff would walk around, noting who was falling asleep. The next day, their names would be published for all to see; they then would be assigned to Dumpster cleaning. It was a constant struggle to keep all my friends and Dallas awake at these tape plays in order to keep out of trouble.

Seeing all these people sleep deprived and exhausted, I found myself thinking of our fund-raising experiences in Australia, and the fact that here—just like there—the emphasis seemed to be much more on making money than caring for people or sharing Scientology. In fact, the welfare of the Sea Org members appeared to be the least important thing. To some extent, I'd noticed this before, but Australia helped me to see just how crucial this search for money had become to our duties in the Sea Org.

Looking around, I saw that the small realizations we'd had

in Australia had a big impact. Suddenly, everywhere around us, we could see not the rules we had to obey, but the freedoms they made us give up. Shortly after we arrived, they began asking via written questionnaire if anyone had a cell phone or had spoken to ex–Sea Org people, or had an Internet connection that was able to view anti-Scientology websites. At the base, computers were kept in a locked room and key holders required special clearance from OSA. The computers had been loaded with software that blocked known anti-Scientology websites. We were told very clearly that, if you failed to report anything, penalties would be high.

I revealed that I had a cell phone, given to us by Dallas's parents, which we used once per week to call our parents. Before I'd first gotten the phone, I had it approved, but now they told me that the approval was incorrect and I needed to surrender it. Meanwhile, they were also enforcing a slew of new rules: no food or snacks allowed in our desk drawers, even though we were up all hours of the night and had only fifteen minutes for meals; no music at our desks; no more civvies one day per week; nobody allowed to go home before midnight. Staff meetings were a long stream of insults and public humiliation for anyone who stepped out of line.

Still, I refused to turn over my cell phone. Five people confided in me that they were not going to give up theirs, either, so I figured we could make some sort of stand together. I wound up being the last person on the base who had one. I was told that the newly issued policy banning all cell phones and laptops was because people trying to infiltrate the Church could pick up on cellular waves and listen to our conversations; thus, it was for our own safety. I argued that this was ridiculous and paranoid. Then the next reason given was that some people looked at pornography on their phones. I told them that was equally ridiculous, and besides, it would be none of their business. Then, they gave the reason that they didn't want family members calling with upsetting news. None of it convinced me to give up my phone.

All of their excuses were perfect examples of punishment and deprivation for their own sake. They didn't care about the phone itself, and truthfully, by that point, neither did I. I wasn't fighting about a phone; I was fighting about the principle of it. They were trying to take something that belonged to Dallas and me. It was our property, yet they felt entitled to take it. They had already taken away our room, confiscated our television, and removed food from our drawers. What made it even more hypocritical was that, by definition, one of the main characteristics of a Suppressive Person was that they had no regard for personal property.

It was the kind of object and the kind of argument that made both Dallas and me stop, think about our experience in Australia, and consider just how much we were giving up by living in the Sea Org. If they could take away something as meaningless as a cell phone and treat our belongings like their own, what would happen with the more important things? What about our relationship? They'd already tried to break us apart. Dallas still held out hope that one day they would lift the ban on us having children; what then? We'd learned for ourselves that there was a whole world of people out there who saw flaws with Scientology, and, increasingly, we were becoming like them. Maybe the real purpose for taking away our phone was to cut us off from the outside world, to control what information we were exposed to.

NOT LONG AFTER WE RETURNED FROM AUSTRALIA, I WAS TOLD I couldn't stay in the Landlord Office. The entire Landlord Office was moving to the Int base, but, since my parents had left the Sea Org, I was not authorized to work there. When I was asked what post I wanted instead, I chose auditor.

In retrospect, it was something of an odd decision, but, at the time, it made a lot of sense. For the last several years, I'd found myself constantly at odds with the Sea Org, their rules, and their actions taken toward me. I felt that Scientology was moving away from its mission to help people and becoming more about getting money from the public. Staff members were treated in demeaning ways, despite the fact that they were the ones who had dedicated their lives to the Church. A few months earlier, my Uncle Dave had named Tom Cruise the "world's most dedicated Scientologist," despite all the staff and Sea Org members who had sacrificed everything for Church. This was exacerbated by having to watch clips of Tom Cruise interviews during our fifteen-minute meal breaks, where he touted the amazingness of Scientology. Everything was upside down and backward. Nothing was for the greatest good for the greatest number of dynamics anymore. The base was so dreary that I had heard of several people who had seriously considered suicide, and been routed out of the Sea Org because of it.

However, in spite of all these concerns with how the Church was being run, I still, somewhere in the back of my mind, held on to positive feelings about the practice of Scientology itself. In my more frustrated moments, times when I found myself questioning, I was always uplifted when I thought back to all the wins I'd heard over the years, and all the ways that Scientology had supposedly helped people. Those memories were the only positive things that I had left in Scientology. And they were all possible because of auditing. Auditing was the embodiment of the only thing in which I still believed.

As a result, I decided that if I were an auditor, I could finally be in a position to help people in the most direct way possible. Unlike security checks, during auditing sessions, the auditor was supposed to be nice to people, never becoming angry at the pre-Clear. The objective in auditing was to listen and guide, whereas sec-checks were much more investigative and uncomfortable. With auditing, not only would I be helping to clear the planet, one person at a time; I'd also be helping people to help themselves.

I was excited when my auditor post was approved. I had to

do some training before I started, and rose through my levels in a couple of months. For the first time in a long time, I enjoyed my studies, because they had a purpose. I was taken into auditing sessions for my own advancement. However, I started to notice that the sessions in which I was audited made me feel very anxious. They were too introspective and started to make me feel like I was going crazy. If a session didn't go well, the auditor would assess list after list of what was wrong with me on the session, and it just started making me spin. This was not how auditing was supposed to make me feel.

Things only got worse from there. We'd start a session with her asking me if I was upset about anything, and I would burst into tears and start telling her how much the rules and restrictions on the base were just too much. My auditor would then ask me if a withhold had been missed because of my nattering. Her response never failed to frustrate me, and, usually, I just made up withholds, but after several sessions, I decided I was done accommodating. I was tired of being intimidated. I sat there for an hour saying "no," while she grew more and more demanding.

"We are going to get to the bottom of this," she warned. I wasn't interested.

I stood up to leave, but she blocked me. I tried to push her out of the way, but she kept trying to force me back to the chair. After two hours, I threw the cans on the floor and squashed them with my foot. She still wouldn't let me out. She tried to give me two more cans, but I smashed them, too. I threw my pc folder over the table, causing the papers in it to fly everywhere. She wouldn't let go of my arm or let me out of the room. I pushed her, kicked her, tried to do anything to make her let me go. I was screaming at her, begging her, but she just kept saying, "We are going to get to the bottom of this. What have you done that you can't tell me about?" She wouldn't let me use the restroom. I was sure people outside in the hallway could hear the commotion, but nobody came to see what was going on. After several hours, she told me that we were going to go on a walk. We spent the rest of the day walking and decompressing.

The next day, I woke up bruised, exhausted, and very on edge. I was told that as a result of my behavior, I would not be allowed to audit. I was assigned lower conditions. I was told that I had disturbed the sessions of other people in neighboring auditing rooms while trying to get out of my room; this was a suppressive act. I insisted that denying my right to audit was not per policy, but they didn't seem to care.

Meanwhile, because I had never given up my phone, people were going to see Dallas several times a day, telling him that he had to give them the phone. He would tell them that it was not up to him and that he wasn't going to battle me for it. But they would harass him nonetheless.

Eventually, someone came to me for my phone. When I told him I was not giving it up, he said that he would physically make me. I threatened to call the police. Threatening to call an outside authority for internal issues was so taboo that I would hear about it again. After days of hashing it out with the Ethics Department, they finally got me to grudgingly agree to amends by paying for the cans, fixing the room, apologizing to my auditor, and apologizing to other auditors. Even then, I was told that I still could not audit.

At that moment, I decided I was done with the Sea Org. I had finally gotten to be an auditor, only to realize that the rules were not any better for that than they were anywhere else. All at once, everything that had been building for several years—it all just snapped. I wanted to be gone.

The first thing I did was run to Dallas's office and tell him how I felt. As I suspected, he was okay with it; and he almost seemed relieved that I was the one who was saying it. But while I was ready to be gone, Dallas wanted to route out properly and cooperate with the Church. His method was the only way we could remain in contact with our Scientology family members still in the Church and continue to be Public Scientologists, paying to take services if and when we wanted. I agreed that I would do this for his sake and he told me that, as long as we did, he would leave with me.

In the weeks that followed, several people spoke to me. I was taken into session a few times, and people were trying to work things out so that I would stay. They even decided to move Dallas and me to the PAC Base, because we would be allowed to take libs there and have more time off, as things there were slightly more lenient. It didn't work. I just knew that I needed to be out of there.

In my secret calls to my parents, they were extremely supportive. They told me that their disillusionment with the Sea Org had progressed in a way similar to mine. They didn't want to go into details, instead choosing to stay vague and cautious, as they knew if they outright attacked the Church, it might turn me off to them and the idea of leaving, but told me that I could call them at anytime.

Over the next week or two, I started speaking with them more regularly; they would tell me about people who had been declared SPs, including my old friend Claire Headley and her husband, Marc, both of whom were out of the Sea Org and now SPs. Teddy Blackman, my brother's friend, was also out. I knew that Marc, Claire, and Teddy were not Suppressive People. The "declare" was ridiculous. With my aunt Sarah having been recently declared, too, I felt that perhaps they were declaring people who they felt they could no longer control, regardless of whether or not they were actually suppressive people.

My parents also began to open up more about their experience leaving the Church. In the years since they'd left, I'd wondered about their reasons for doing so. Given how committed they once were, I'd assumed that things must have been bad, but I never knew that Uncle Dave had been a part of it. After Marc Headley left, he told my parents that my uncle physically beat staff. Mom said she knew it was true, because she too had witnessed him beating someone, and that had been one of the major turning points that led to her leaving the Sea Org.

This was the first time I'd heard something of this nature about Uncle Dave from someone whom I actually trusted. It wasn't so much shocking as it was disturbing. Those in my circles never spoke badly about Uncle Dave, but people were afraid of him. I knew that my uncle had a bad temper, but, sometimes, in Scientology, a temper meant that you cared. Still, as much as I'd known that people feared him and that he possessed a domineering personality, I hadn't thought him capable of physically harming people. According to my parents, he wasn't afraid to use money to acheive his purposes. My father said that, when they left the Sea Org, Uncle Dave offered to pay my mother one hundred thousand dollars, as long as she left and my father stayed. He didn't even make the offer to my mother; he made it to my father, who he must have figured was the more malleable of the two. Of course, my father declined, but they were both put off by the gall of my uncle in thinking he could buy people.

In the coming weeks and months, I'd learn even more about why my parents left. My mother told me about a girl, Stacy Moxon, who had died a few years earlier. The death was deemed an accident, but the circumstances suggested suicide. Her sister had been inconsolable; I wonder if she knew how depressed and desperate Stacy was. It was so hard hearing stories like this, because the environment of the Sea Org, with all its rules and restrictions, made it impossible not to get depressed and feel hopeless. At the same time, any kind of psychological ills were discounted and ignored, so those in psychological trouble had zero resources.

She told other stories, about long-married couples, parents of kids I knew at the Ranch, being forced to divorce because they were married to someone in a lower org. She finished by referencing several people who had been told to make a choice between an abortion or the Sea Org. It was during the course of these phone calls with my parents, that my father told me that Uncle Dave had told him that he had personally supervised the Lisa McPherson auditing, instructing that she be attested to the state of Clear shortly before her death. All this news served to reaffirm my suspicions. I believed my parents because I felt they had no reason to lie, and that these stories would be hard to make up.

The more they told me, the more it confirmed what I already knew or suspected. This type of coercive behavior was widespread. I had been at the Int Ranch, Australia, PAC, and Flag, and I knew how conditions were and how people were treated. I was glad that I had made my decision. Even Justin, who I hadn't spoken to in a long time, started calling me as well, offering me support if I needed help getting out of there.

The pressure to stay came daily. Linda, who was a high-ranking member of OSA, was trying to convince me that I was a valuable asset to the Sea Org, and that I had just hit a few bumps. When I told her about some of the things I'd heard from my parents, her response was simple: "People make up lies to suit their own ends."

The church also sent friends to convince me to cooperate, but I warned them to stay out of it; I didn't want to ruin these friendships when my beef was with the Church, not them. After a few days of one person or another visiting me, I knew I could no longer cooperate. I just wanted out and Dallas was coming with me. And, so, I holed myself up in our room until they decided to give me my leaving security check.

CHAPTER THIRTY-ONE

GONE

I SPENT SEVERAL DAYS IN ISOLATION IN MY ROOM, WAITING FOR someone in the Office of Special Affairs to give me the necessary materials and sessions to route out properly. Policy dictated that, before I could leave, I had to undergo the leaving staff security check. In order to do this, I had to first complete the auditing I'd been in the middle of when this whole mess started, but I physically and emotionally could not do any more auditing, and told Dallas as much. He hadn't told Linda that he was leaving with me yet, as he was waiting for me to start my security check, and hoping to avoid the manual labor that was usually part of the leaving process. That way, he could stay in his post until the very end.

Dallas and I argued about my finishing my auditing for several days. He was frustrated that I was being so difficult. He couldn't accept how done I was, no matter how hard I tried to explain it. He wanted more than anything for me to route out properly; otherwise, he would have to make the choice between me or the Church and his family. His family meant everything to him. The only way for him to be with me and still have them was if I weren't

an SP. The only way for me to avoid this was to complete my auditing, do my sec-check, and sign a few documents.

I could sense Dallas was growing more withdrawn, so I tried
to give him space. It was a stressful time. He was coming home
from work later and later, and was not as excited to see me as he
had been.

"What's wrong?" I'd ask.

"Nothing, just working," he'd say, without much elaboration.

I knew something was going on; Dallas always wanted to talk
to me, but he wasn't responding to even the simplest questions. I
called my parents who were certain that somebody in the church
was talking to him. This had been my first thought as well. However, when I had asked him, he said no. Based on their own experience, when they had left the Church, their words felt right to
me. The next time I saw Dallas, I asked point-blank who he had
been talking to. He said nobody, and we left it at that, with unspoken questions. We both were being paranoid and suspicious,
unsure of how to move forward. Never in our three-year marriage
had we encountered a crossroads like this.

One morning, as he was leaving for work, Dallas told me he
would be back at lunchtime to visit, but never showed up. Concerned, I pulled out my forbidden cell phone and called reception.
No one there knew where he was, either. I began to panic, that
they had him somewhere, all over again. I almost couldn't stand
the anxiety. Not knowing what else I could do to find him, I lay
down and drifted off to sleep.

A few hours later, I was awakened by a knock on the door. I
opened it to find Linda. I asked her where Dallas was. She said
she didn't know, but I could tell she was hiding something by
her forced tone. She opened her briefcase and pulled out a small
packet of legal-sized papers that were stapled together.

"Okay, so this is the checklist for leaving staff," she said.

I squirmed at the sound of the words "leaving staff." I knew

I was at the end of my rope, but hearing the words out loud was another thing. Never in a million years did I think that *I* would ever be the one doing the "leaving staff" checklist. I tried to take comfort in the fact that I had attempted everything I could to make it work.

Linda showed me the various steps on the routing form. The first one, as I well knew, was that I was required to receive a staff security check. This gave me the chills all over again. According to LRH, the only reason people left staff was because they had done bad things that they were hiding from others. He believed that taking a confessional and admitting to their actions before they left would actually help them live with themselves, possibly even convince them to stay. This was why the confessional was a requirement to route out properly. If you refused the confessional, you would be declared a Suppressive Person.

Next, Linda explained that the next step on the checklist called for me to sign a bond. She explained that it was a document I would be required to sign, swearing that I would never speak out against the Church. If I ever violated this bond, I would have to pay $10,000 for each violation. She said if I didn't sign it, I would be declared an SP. This pissed me off. LRH had never written a policy like this, and I told her as much. One of my main objections to the current management of the Sea Org was just this kind of thing, making up policy that did not originate from the gospel of LRH. Linda got aggravated and told me I was going to sign it.

I didn't like her tone or her attitude. I told her I would do my confessional, which I had been waiting to receive for several weeks now, but I would not sign anything. She burst out yelling that I was unethical and being a Suppressive Person for refusing to sign the bond. She dropped the checklist and bond on the bed and directed me to read it myself.

"You mean this?" I said mockingly as I picked it up, shredded it into a hundred pieces, and told her to get out of my room. She was not used to people being insubordinate and shot me a look of disgust before she stormed out, all the while screaming that I was not going to get away with this. I slammed the door, flushed with anger and fear over what I had done, and what might happen as a result. I still hadn't heard from Dallas, and I was getting worried.

Finally, at one-thirty in the morning he walked through the door, looking tired and not particularly happy to see me, which, at this hour, was a concern. To me, this could only mean he'd been in protracted meetings with Church people. I wasn't in the mood to argue, but I did ask him if he was still going to leave with me.

"I don't know," he said.

If it weren't for all of the awkward silences and mysterious disappearances, I would have been shocked. Still, I couldn't believe that he was about to turn his back on me, let me go through all this by myself, and not even bother to tell me how he really felt until I pulled it out of him.

"I just don't know," he continued. "You aren't really cooperating and getting through your confessional like you promised."

When he said that, I knew for sure somebody had been feeding him lies. He knew I had been waiting obediently for them to come to me.

"You know just as well as I do that I have been sitting here for two weeks waiting for them to give me the confessional, and they haven't."

"Yes, but that's only because you won't agree to finish your auditing first," he said.

"I don't want any more auditing. I just want to get my confessional and get out of here!"

"Well, if you would just cooperate, then you could," he said stubbornly.

"So, does this mean that you won't leave with me unless I do the auditing?" I asked. I wasn't prepared for what Dallas said next.

"Well, I don't want to leave."

"So, you are saying that you won't leave with me no matter what?" I asked in total disbelief, trying to get to the heart of the matter.

Dallas looked ashamed. My worst fears were confirmed.

"Who have you been talking to?"

He looked like he had expected this question. "Nobody. I just don't want to leave."

"You are lying. Who have you been talking to?"

"Nobody, I swear."

Looking at him now, I could tell that he was finished with me. He saw me just as Linda did: an uncooperative, rebellious SP.

We spent the next few hours arguing, with neither of us giving any ground. All I wanted was to leave and be done with it, and Dallas, for the life of him, couldn't accept why I refused to cooperate. He kept saying that he "didn't understand," no matter how many times I explained. He was convinced that I cared less about him and his relationship with his family than I did about my own welfare. He said if I really cared about him, I would do what was being asked of me. I just couldn't bear another auditing session and Church policy was to never audit someone who didn't want to be audited. From my point of view, if he didn't leave with me, then I had endured all this hell for nothing.

Finally, at four in the morning, our discussion came to an end. The decision had been made: I was going to leave, and he was going to stay. There was no other solution. We were both devastated and crying, but I knew that I would not be able to keep my sanity if I stayed in the Sea Org any longer. And I couldn't argue anymore.

I spent the rest of the night packing my bags with his help. As we packed, we both were trying to figure out how we could possibly make this work. We'd said the words that I would leave without him, but neither of our hearts was in it. I wrote a letter to his parents, telling them I loved them and to take good care of Dallas. Dallas gave me a couple of his sweaters to remind me of him.

In the morning, I called my father, told him what we had decided, and asked if I could live with him and Mom in Virginia. He said he was sorry that things didn't work out, but I could certainly live with them.

Dallas had to leave for work but promised he would be back to drive me to the airport. I felt sick, but determined to carry forward with my plan. I just couldn't continue to live in a place that had to control my every thought and move. Around eight o'clock that night, Dallas returned home from work. He looked tired and out of it. When we hugged, I saw Linda standing in the door behind him.

"What the hell is she doing here?" I demanded.

Dallas made her wait by the door while he talked to me. He sat down on the bed and took my hands in his. "Okay, so they are going to let you leave without a confessional," he said. I didn't get why he had said they were "letting me," since I was planning on leaving anyway, regardless of whether they were going to "allow" it.

He told me the Church had booked me a flight to Virginia for that very night. "Are you coming?" I asked hopefully, even though I knew the answer.

"No," he said, looking down to avoid my gaze.

There was nothing else I could do. I had tried everything to convince him, but I simply couldn't. It was my biggest failure of all. I burst into tears.

I reached for my luggage and asked him if he would at least take me to the airport. He promised me that he would.

"Are you ready?" Linda asked from the doorway. Words couldn't express how much I hated her.

"Was Dallas with you today?" I asked. When Linda said no, and Dallas rolled his eyes, I was sure they had been together. I was furious and started shouting at her. I totally lost it when she tried to convince Dallas to stick me in a cab and not take me to the airport himself. I was his wife, for God's sake. This was going to be the last time we would ever see each other. Yet she was so vindictive, she couldn't even let us have that.

Dallas finally announced that he was taking me, despite Linda's objections. She was forced to make a few phone calls, but finally permission was granted, on the condition that she accompanied us. I knew the Church didn't want Dallas and me to be alone, lest I use my power of persuasion on him. The car ride was tense, with Dallas and I trying to savor our last hours together, and Linda invading our space by parking herself in the middle of the backseat and leaning forward to keep us from getting too close or saying too much. We arrived at LAX two hours before my departure. I checked my bags, and still had lots of time to be with Dallas to say goodbye. However, Linda was lurking not far away and crowding us, so I told her to back off. I warned her that if she didn't, I would make a scene. Knowing that would be bad PR for the Church, she reluctantly walked away.

Dallas and I had been sitting together in the lounge for only twenty minutes when Linda walked up and told Dallas she needed to get back to work and to leave me there to wait for my flight. I felt Dallas's body tense up. He was visibly frustrated with how little respect this woman was showing for the obvious emotional anguish we were both feeling. Yet somehow he managed to show restraint, a quality I had always admired in him. "Okay," he told her, "just give us a few more minutes." I just snapped and started screaming at her. Linda hurried off, probably to phone somebody else, but I didn't care.

I stood there looking at Dallas, struggling to believe that I would never see him again. I'd wanted out for so long, and yet standing here listening to Linda disrespect us and our relationship, I knew, all at once, that there was no way I could get on that plane without him. I knew his heart wasn't in this decision, just as mine wasn't. I couldn't leave Dallas with a group of people like this. The Church had an endless supply of Lindas and, when all the dust settled, their wrath toward him would likely be harsh and unforgiving. I refused to let that happen. I was leaving the Church and I was leaving with my husband.

I didn't open my mouth about any of this—at least not yet. I told him I'd be right back and went to phone my father to tell him I wouldn't be coming home just yet. Dad understood and said he would be there for me if I needed him.

When I got back to the bench, I told Dallas about my change of heart. "I can't leave you," I said. "I don't want to be without you. I will stay and try to fix things." I really had no intention of surrendering to the Church, but I wasn't going to tell Dallas that. I just needed the time it would take to convince him to leave with me.

Dallas's face lit up and he pulled me into an enormous hug. As he held me close, I could feel the tension in his body release. "I will do anything you need to help you get through this," he said with pure enthusiasm. I smiled at him, relieved to see how quickly things had changed, even though I still didn't exactly know what I was going to do.

As we headed toward the airline office to get my bags, Dallas's cell started to ring. It was Linda, demanding to know where we were. Dallas excitedly told her how he'd convinced me to stay, and we were just going to retrieve my bags.

"She can't stay!" I heard Linda shout.

Dallas was completely blown away. "I thought that we wanted her to say!" he said.

"She can't stay!" Linda repeated.

Dallas was in disbelief. The contradictions of the Church were on full display; perhaps more clearly than ever before, he was able to see how the Church said one thing and meant another.

The fact that I'd agreed to stay should have been a good thing; it meant that I had seen the error of my thinking and was back on board. Wasn't that the goal? Yet Linda was adamant that I was not allowed back.

The next thing I knew, Dallas was whisking me outside. He pulled me around a corner to where Linda couldn't hear us.

"I need to tell you something," he said. "I have been meeting with Linda and Mr. Rinder the last couple of days. They have been telling me all kinds of horrible things about you and your family. They even told me that if I left with you, I would never see my family again. The only reason they didn't separate us earlier was because I promised not to tell you I was talking to them."

My mouth dropped. I knew it. My father had warned me, and I knew myself what the Church was capable of, but somehow, I didn't understand how they thought they could get away with it. I guess I was just naive. I tried to contain my fury when Dallas told me that they had made him submit to a sec-check and prevented him from coming to see me during lunch, and had made him come home late almost every night. They had also locked him up in a boardroom, where Mike Rinder had told him I hadn't been cooperating, I was no good, my parents were evil, and that he should leave me.

Dallas looked back at me, waiting for me to say something. It was a scary moment. I was shocked, angry, and relieved all at once, shocked that the Church would go to such lengths to break up a marriage, angry that Dallas had not told me, but ultimately relieved that he was back on my side. He had taken a big risk by even telling me, and I understood and appreciated that. I hoped that I had made the right choice to stay. Linda kept calling us on the cell phone, constantly, demanding to know where we were. I was so sick of her harassing us and was so angry at what she had tried to do that I stupidly broke the cell phone when I flipped it all the way back to pick it up. At last, Scientology had finally claimed the cell phone that they'd so desperately wanted.

She found us a few minutes later, when we were gathering my bags. I was already on edge because of everything I had heard, and now even more so because I had agreed to stay. I suspected that Dallas knew I just wanted time to get him to leave, the hard part was going to be convincing everybody else I wanted to stay and serve the greater good. I wasn't sure how I was going to tolerate being back there, but I'd figure something out. Hopefully this wouldn't take too long.

LINDA WAS RELENTLESS IN TRYING TO SEPARATE US AS WE EXITED the airport on the way to Dallas's car. She wanted Dallas alone with her so that she could talk to him. I told her to leave us alone or that we were going to call the police. This really freaked her out. She walked away, saying that I was creating another scene.

Finally, we made it to the parking lot, and drove back to the base in Dallas's car. Dallas and I were exhausted and just wanted to go back to our room, but Linda said that was forbidden. "It's not a God-given right to be a Sea Org member," she told us. Instead, she said, we had to go to the Blue Building. There, a security officer, took us to a room and gave us a list of conditions that would allow me to remain in the Sea Org. Linda stood watch over the whole discussion, frustrated that I had won. As usual, we were told that we each had to do a manual labor program and that we would be separated. By now, Dallas and I were fully cognizant that, by separating us, the Church was in a much better position to control us.

"You've tried separating us," Dallas told the officer. "It just doesn't work! We will do the labor, but we are not separating. You guys are just crazy. We are doing everything you are asking of us, but we are not doing this."

I was really happy to have Dallas back on my side. For the first time ever, he was standing up to them, and, in his voice, I could hear someone who was approaching his breaking point. The room was getting tense. Someone said that Dallas needed to go into the next room to talk to someone, but that he had to go alone. Dallas refused, until he realized it was easier to hear what they had to say. He told me he'd be right back, and this time I believed him. It was a complete turnaround from just an hour before.

When he returned a few minutes later, he told me that they had tried to get him into a car. They wanted to take him to meet with Linda and Mr. Rinder, but he'd resisted. From his tone and the look on his face, I could tell that Dallas's desire to stay was slowly dissolving.

As it became clear to them that we were not going to accept their terms and were a united front, they gave an ultimatum: either separate or leave the Sea Org. Dallas told them it was because of them that we were going to be leaving. With that, we said we were going back to our room to get our stuff, but they told us we were no longer allowed on the base.

"Well, if you leave, you're blowing," the security officer said. "You'd be leaving without authorization."

With this, Dallas flipped a lid. "How can we be blowing?" he said in disbelief. "If you're telling us we can't stay here, how can we be blowing!"

I had to try to calm him down, which was kind of weird, since he was always the one trying to calm me down. I told him not to waste his energy on these people. We tried to head to the room, but the security guards blocked us.

Frustrated, we went back to Dallas's car. Neither one of us had any money, so we used my dad's credit card, taking him up on his offer to use it if I ever needed to get out. We spent the night at a Travelodge not far from the base, trying to figure out our next move; the following day we went back to the base, only to accomplish nothing. We were both scared and traumatized, and not sure if we were doing the right thing. When I made this decision for myself, in a certain way it was easier. Now that I was responsible for Dallas's leaving, too, it was much riskier. I could tell that Dallas was frightened. I hoped to God he wouldn't switch sides again.

The next morning, there was a knock on our door. I couldn't imagine who it was, since nobody knew we were staying there. It was the security officer, dressed in a business suit, not his uniform. He handed us an envelope and pointed to a U-Haul in the parking lot. Inside the envelope were pictures of all of our belongings, with corresponding numbers to indicate which box they were in. All the boxes had been methodically packed in the U-Haul. There was a corresponding list of everything we owned, down to the number of pennies and Q-tips we had.

The officer walked us to the parking lot, while another security guard circled us on a bicycle. "Just so you know where you stand, you guys are blowing and that is suppressive," he told us. Pointing his finger in Dallas's face, he warned, "I am going to do everything in my power to make sure you never talk to your family again."

I didn't know what the Church planned to do to make good on its threat, but hearing this made me very uneasy and infuriated Dallas.

That morning, we set off for Dallas's parents' house in San Diego. He had called them already, and they were expecting us. Each mile that we put between us and the base made us feel safer, as though we could feel the ropes that had bound us there breaking one by one. No longer would we have to wear uniforms. We could determine our own wake-up times, or decide to go see a movie. We could earn our own way in the world, and make our own rules. It would truly be the greatest good for the greatest number of dynamics, only now, for the first time in our lives, the math worked in our favor.

CHAPTER THIRTY-TWO

THE REAL WORLD

DALLAS'S PARENTS GREETED US WARMLY WHEN WE ARRIVED. They were glad to have Dallas home with them, but had mixed feelings about his leaving the Sea Org. They were worried about what it would mean for their future in Scientology, as well as the ramifications for his siblings and their families. I was grateful that they took us in, but it was going to be a minefield negotiating it all. Everybody had his own vested interest in how they wanted us to behave when it came to the Church. While I wanted to keep them happy, my main concern was being in a marriage with Dallas in which only the two of us made the decisions.

Dallas's parents said we could stay with them, and that they would give us jobs at the jewelry store, which was Scientology-friendly. All new employees were required to do an introductory course in Scientology, whether they were Scientologists or not. Despite hiring many Public Scientologists, Dallas's dad had told himself that he'd never hire ex–Sea Org members again, because it usually meant trouble, but that he'd make an exception for us.

When we reported for work our first day, I was terrified. I was given a job in the human resources department. Even though I was shy, I found the people to be extremely welcoming. They were friendly, honest, caring, and supportive, more so than anyone I had ever encountered in the Church. The one uncomfortable thing about the job was applying Scientology to problems that came up. I was trying to distance myself from Scientology; I still believed in it, but I needed a break from it and didn't like subjecting non-Scientologists to the techniques.

Adjusting to life outside the Church was a lot more of a process for me than it was for Dallas. I didn't have a driver's license, and was not used to talking to Wogs. I also had nightmares every night. I was either being chased by people in the Church trying to get me to come back, or they were trying to convince Dallas to return and that I had to save him.

We'd been in San Diego only a few days when Linda began calling Dallas's father, asking him to find out where we stood with the Church and what our plans were. This created a lot of tension between Dallas's parents and us. They were trying to get us to sort things out with the Church, and since we lived and worked with them, we couldn't catch a break or have any privacy. At one point, they even traveled to Los Angeles to meet with Linda, and she showed them our negative reports. I didn't like the underhanded way the Church was using Dallas's parents. First, they wanted to be sure that we weren't going to make trouble for them now that we were out of the Sea Org. Second, which was even worse, they were using an audience with his parents as a way to point out what a bad influence I had been on their son. They were sharing records about when his behavior had started to turn and highlighted how it coincided with his befriending me.

In spite of all this, Dallas and I enjoyed our freedom outside the Church. Once we started making some money, we were able to get our own place, a condo in central San Diego. We even got two dogs. We were able to visit my parents in Virginia, where we also saw Justin and Sterling, who was now also out of the Sea Org.

At my job, I often talked to people who were curious about the Church. They would ask me questions about growing up there and would be utterly horrified by my responses. They would tell me that these things weren't normal, and even offered their support. Through their eyes, I slowly learned how weird my upbringing had been.

We'd been out of the Church less than a year when Dallas and I received a summons for a Committee of Evidence to establish our standing in the Church. In a CommEv your actions are put on trial, and four people sit in judgment, deciding if you are guilty of the crimes against the Church that are listed. I wanted to return the summons to them with my dogs' poop in the envelope, but Dallas's dad convinced Dallas to go sort things out. His parents wanted the security of knowing that he was in good standing with the Church, and that neither he nor I would be declared SPs.

It took a lot of convincing, but in the end I agreed to do the committee of evidence to appease them, knowing it was going to be excruciatingly hard and humiliating.

The Church was charging me with five Crimes and four High Crimes, citing various incidents that had occurred in August, 2005, and some as far back as October, 2003. My High Crimes included failing to apply the Scientology technologies I had been taught to difficulties I encountered in my life; threatening to call police in the weeks prior to my leaving the Sea Org: refusing to follow standard procedure for routing out of the Sea Org; and telling Dallas that I intended to leave, which was considered a "suppressive act." I had also damaged the auditing room and cans when I tried to leave my auditing session, engaged in an altercation with Linda at the airport, and disagreed with and yelled at my superiors at various times while on post, all considered Crimes against the Church.

Dallas was also facing a number of Crimes and High Crimes, but the majority of them had to do with his failure to "handle" me, when I violated the standards for Leaving Staff by refusing to do my auditing, and when I threatened to call police. He was also being cited for his failure to handle me when I "blew up at others" upon our return to the base from the airport after I had changed my mind about leaving the Sea Org.

After finally being out, the last thing I wanted to do was hear a bunch of nonsensical evidence against me, or worse, for the Church to feel like it had the power to summon me at will. It was an extremely hard pill for me to swallow, but I decided to do it for Dallas, because it could clear up our standing in the Church. He was still holding out hope that he could have a relationship with the Church, which would make life a lot easier for his entire family.

We all drove up to the PAC Base in L.A. one morning. I knew the entire proceeding was going to be recorded, so I told them that I was also going to be recording it as well, and put my tape player on the table.

Dallas and I were going to have our committees of evidence individually and I was going first. In the proceeding, I was told the various charges against me and was asked if I pleaded guilty or not guilty. I said not guilty to all of them. I told them that I didn't agree with anything that happened and that it was their doing. When they asked me if I was going to take responsibility for anything, I said no. They asked me if I would be willing to route out of the Sea Org in the standard fashion, if it meant being able to continue to speak to Dallas's family. I told them that I would think about it.

Dallas went next. He also pleaded not guilty to most of the charges, but not all of them. On the one he did plead guilty for, however, he told them it was their own doing. For the next few weeks, we waited for our "Findings and Recommendations."

Four months passed before they finally arrived. In the findings, I was found guilty of Mayhem, Mutiny, and telling Dallas that I wanted to leave staff. The committee had recommended that we be declared SPs; however, the International Justice Chief intervened, saying if we wanted to return to good standing with the Church, we just needed to do 250 hours of amends each, get through a security check, pay our freeloader bill, and do lower conditions.

The findings were severe, and didn't even attempt to acknowledge an injustice. They were more severe than Dallas and his parents had expected, but for my part, it was what I expected. Not surprisingly, I had no intention of following through with any of their measures. The whole decision felt like it played out too conveniently in the Church's favor, but, at least for now, Dallas's parents would not be made to disconnect from us.

BEING OUT ALLOWED US TO GAIN MORE OF AN OUTSIDER'S PERspective on the Church. It didn't come to us all at once in the form of one big piece of information from one source. More frequently, we learned little things here and there, but, over time, they added up.

My father sent Dallas and me some online posts written by someone using the screen name "Blown for Good." They illustrated just how bad things had gotten on the Int Base, and told stories of physical abuse, sleep deprivation, separating people from their spouses, all of which had supposedly been orchestrated by my uncle. In many ways, these stories paralleled other things I'd heard from my family members who'd left.

"Blown for Good" was also posting on the Operation Clambake website, so I'd been reading his entries. There was a link to a *South Park* episode that satirized Scientology, which I had heard a lot of talk about. It spoofed the highest levels in the Church, the OT Levels that existed beyond the state of Clear. Specifically its target was OT Level III, "Wall of Fire," which disclosed LRH's theory of evolution.

This was many levels higher on the Bridge than anything Dallas and I had encountered, and we debated back and forth about whether we should watch it. We had always been told that acquiring this information prematurely could result in serious personal and mental injury. I knew it was ridiculous, but honestly, I was a little scared. I might have been out of the Sea Org, but this was something I had been told my entire life.

Even though I was out of the Church, I still had that built-in hesitation. I knew it was irrational. Obviously, tons of people watched the *South Park* episode, and they were still alive, so Dallas and I decided to take our chances. The episode was amusing and a little ridiculous. It was like science fiction. We already believed that we were Thetans, so I had expected that LRH's theory of evolution would involve other planets. However, the details of a galactic overlord and a planet named Xenu were new to us.

We learned that OT III claimed that, 75 million years ago, a galactic overlord named Xenu banished Thetans to Earth to solve an overpopulation problem on his alien planet. The banishment of the Thetans and a series of incidents surrounding it were said to be the source of all human misery. This was not known to many Scientologists, as they would only have known about it if they had made it that far up the Bridge. Because of its far-fetched conceit, OT Level III is often cited by Scientology skeptics looking to demonstrate the absurdity of the religion.

Learning about OT III was eye-opening, both in terms of the fact that Scientologists actually believed that, but also because of what it told me about my own skepticism about the Church. While it was hard to fathom that the highest levels of the Church were focused on what felt a lot like a science-fiction story, what struck me the most was not the story itself, but the fact that, if I had heard this at the peak of my faith, I probably would have believed it.

As an outsider now, I could plainly see that it raised serious questions; however, it was only because I'd left that I was able to see it for what it was—a web of stories that seemed to have little basis in reality. Once we learned about OT Level III, more than ever before Dallas and I began to feel that this whole thing had been made up, and that LRH had just kept going and going with his stories, making it up as he went along. OT Level III didn't feel like belief—it felt like fiction.

In the aftermath of learning about the OT levels, I found myself thinking of all the Public Scientologists I'd encountered while we were fund-raising in Australia, and how much time and money they would have had to invest to get to OT Level III. I found myself thinking about what it would feel like for them to finally have that truth revealed, and how natural their skepticism would be, but how hard it would be to embrace that skepticism knowing that you'd devoted such a big part of your life to it. A person who was a Public Scientologist would have already invested thousands of hours and paid in the range of $100,000 to be at OT Level III; by then, she would be pretty deeply invested both financially and socially. She would have already turned all of her friends and family to Scientology, and would have garnered a lot of respect for accomplishing so much; thus, it would be hard to not embrace the reveal.

This is to say nothing of how Sea Org members like my parents and grandparents, who would have invested not just money but years and decades of their lives, would react to the revelations in this level.

In part, because of all this, but also because of our own curiosity, Dallas and I were both becoming more interested in seeing what people outside the Church thought of it. Dallas started reading the *Bare-Faced Messiah: The True Story of L. Ron Hubbard,* by Russell Miller, a British journalist. The book was an eye-opener for Dallas. I read parts of it, too, and began to see what a fraud LRH had been. Even if only half of what I was reading was true, it meant that he had lied about nearly every one of his accomplishments. I had often wondered how he could have done all the things that he had purported to have done, and now I was seeing that he likely never actually had. For both Dallas and me, this book exposed the founder of Scientology as a power-hungry, egomaniacal, crazy, and charismatic liar. It forced me to examine my thoughts and feelings about Scientology. Did I really agree with its policies and its teachings? Had I ever experienced any of its powers?

Bit by bit, I started questioning everything I had ever been taught. I had always believed that I was a Thetan, and that one day I would be able to come out of my body. I had no real evidence of that, as it had never happened to me. I also wasn't convinced about millions of years of past lives, or the recollections of them, and wondered if they were nothing more than my subconscious, not true experiences from the past. I also questioned whether Scientology's organizational methods, such as whether Knowledge Reports, really worked. We used them at the jewelry store, and I had started to doubt their effectiveness. In my opinion, the Big Brother concept of internal policing made people more paranoid than productive, and alienated people from each other.

My biggest question with Scientology came from the overts. Growing up in the Church, I had never realized outright the importance of my own individuality and how valuable it was. Anytime you had an individual thought or opinion that was contrary to Scientology teaching, you were told you had an overt or a misunderstood word. I was now realizing this was just to stop you from challenging them on any level. It was nothing but complete suppression of free thought.

Now that I was no longer in the Church, I bristled when I felt they still had influence over even my minor personal choices. On Myspace, I was being pressured to unfriend SPs like Marc and

Claire Headley and Teddy Blackman. Claire had been a good friend in the Church, and I wanted to stay in touch with her. Not only did I refuse to block them; I also put up a post stating that I wouldn't do it. These people were my friends, and if anybody had a problem with it, then, too bad. Slowly, all of my friends in Scientology began unfriending me, including many of those who had said they didn't care that I was no longer a Scientologist. Many of them contacted me, and told me that they had been told by people in the Office of Special Affairs that they must delete me as their friend, or they would no longer be able to speak to their families.

After that, Dallas and I joined the online communities for ex-Scientologists, using different names. We got a chance to read people's stories and tell our own. They were eerily similar; we had all gone through hell. I was particularly surprised to hear that many of them had experienced recurring nightmares, just as I did. The sense of community I felt with other former members was growing. In January 2008, *Tom Cruise: An Unauthorized Biography,* by Andrew Morton, was published. The pre-publicity was huge, and sure enough, the book was number one on *The New York Times* bestseller list within three days of its release. Dallas and I didn't know much about Tom Cruise's life, but we did know he was the most famous celebrity associated with Scientology. We both read the book with great curiosity, and found that it contained many factual accounts of the RPF, family disconnection, and other Scientology practices.

The release of this book and the publicity surrounding it highlighted many of Scientology's abuses. Dallas and I thought that it was great that this information was getting out to hundreds of thousands of people. Of course, the Church was all over it, and immediately went into damage control mode, denouncing just about everything that had been written. In a fifteen-page rebuttal, it called the book "a bigoted, defamatory assault replete with lies," and went on to list each and every allegation and provided a response. Their outright denial of a family disconnection policy elicited outrage in me. "Does Scientology encourage their members not to speak to their family if they don't know the religion?" the release asked. "This is not only false, it is the opposite of what the Church believes and practices."

Suddenly, I felt an overwhelming need to do something. Their outright lies felt like a spit in the face of everyone who had gone through hell on their behalf. It also showed that they wouldn't be changing anytime soon. With a nudge from Dallas who, like me, was frustrated by the Church's continued pressure on our relationship with his parents, I wrote a letter to Karin Pouw, the spokesperson for the Church and author of the rebuttal. I cited dozens of examples of forced disconnection in my family and in others. I ended the letter with a personal challenge: "If I am in fact wrong, and you want to prove me as such, then allow me and my family to be in contact with our family members who are still part of the Church such as my Grandpa, Ron Miscavige, and his wife, Becky. Allow the same for my friends."

I told her there were too many destroyed families for the Church to be able to get away with denying it any longer. I suggested that she spend less time writing rebuttals and more time repairing the families destroyed by the Church, "starting with the family of David Miscavige himself."

"If Scientology can't keep *his* family together," I wrote, "then why on earth should anyone believe the Church helps bring families together?"

Looking back at my letter now, I wish I had been a bit clearer and a a little less angry. Nonetheless, I had taken a stand and shared my letter with a few friends, who forwarded it to the media, who made it public. Immediately, I received an outpouring of support from all kinds of people: ex-Scientologists, people who had had encounters with Scientology, ex-members of other cults, and regular people. It was amazing as well as eye-opening to hear from so many people with similar stories.

This wasn't about a few isolated incidents, as the Church liked to make it seem; this was systemic and it was widespread and the world needed to be told.

Chapter Thirty-Three

SHARING THE TRUTH

With the publication of my letter to Karin Pouw, my desire to advocate for victims of the Church was sparked. In the months to come, I found myself speaking out in the media and participating in my first organized protest against the Church. It all started with a video of Tom Cruise that went viral on the Internet. In it, he was discussing LRH's famous Keep Scientology Working discourse, in all Scientology-speak. He was saying absurd things, such as Scientologists driving by an auto accident were the only ones who could help the injured people. He made all sorts of egotistical comments interspersed with his maniacal laughter, ending with his awkward salute to my uncle. I heard people talking about it everywhere I went.

Right away, the Church went into damage control mode and tried to keep the video off the Internet by sending threatening cease-and-desist letters to the owner of the website hosting the video. This was a common tactic used by the Church, to use copyright law to sue people. But, this time, it didn't work.

On January 21, shortly after the video aired, a group of hackers/activists who called themselves Anonymous posted a video to the Church on YouTube, telling them that in response to their censorship, they were going "to expel them from the Internet," and they did. They managed to bring down their servers for three days. Almost immediately, Anonymous's message became not just about Internet censorship, but also about standing up to the Church and bringing awareness to its violations of human rights.

I simply cannot express how much this meant to me. Up until then, it felt as though I and a few others had been fighting the Church with our backs to the wall; people were telling me I was crazy, wrong, and suppressive. To see a group of people rise up like this in defense of the many who had been wronged by the Church was a huge testament to the kindness of the human race. Most of these people had no previous involvement with the Church. Unlike the media, this group wasn't afraid of what the Church said, or about getting sued. Now it felt like there was a whole army in our corner.

Anonymous organized a worldwide protest on February 10, 2008; it was the first of many. Members of the group wore Guy Fawkes masks to protect their identities, knowing the Church harassed detractors as they rallied outside Scientology sites all over the world. They bought a huge amount of attention to the subject and made the Church squirm.

In the meantime, many ex-Scientologists who had previously been anonymous were now coming out, including Marc and Claire Headley. As it turned out, Marc was the anonymous blogger with the screen name "Blown for Good."

Inspired by all the activism we'd been witnessing, Dallas and I started putting together ideas for our own website, with some sort of information center and even a nonprofit group for people who had left the Church and needed help. Around this time, an ex-Scientologist, Kendra Wiseman, contacted me. Her father was president of Scientology's Citizens Commission on Human

Rights, a watchdog group with an antipsychiatry agenda. Kendra had her own bad experiences with the Church and wanted to start a website, to be called exscientologykids.com. She told me that she had already spoken to Astra Woodcraft, another prominent Church critic, about the project. Astra had been in the Church since she was a kid, and left the Sea Org because she refused to have an abortion.

The two women asked me to come on board, and I was instantly in. When Kendra showed me the site and what she had put together, I found it both perfect and amazing. It gave great information on the Church that could be understood by anyone. It offered help to those who had left, as well as a community for people to share their views. The site was launched on March 1, 2008. It was immediately the subject of many news and magazine articles and radio interviews. Many ex-Scientologists were active in the online forums, sharing their stories, offering support, and talking about their experiences.

Meanwhile, in the aftermath of my letter, Astra, Kendra, and I were being recruited by the media to tell our stories. I started getting calls from *Glamour,* the *Los Angeles Times,* and ABC's *Nightline.* Shortly after our site was launched, I did an interview with *Nightline's* Lisa Fletcher. By the end of the interview, she was in tears. It was the first time I had publicly told my entire story. Right before *Nightline* was getting ready to air the piece, its producers called the Church for comment. Several days later, they heard back. The Church was extremely threatening, causing ABC to hold off airing the story. That same night, Dallas received a phone call from his father at eleven o'clock. He said he was twenty minutes from our house and was arriving with two very high-ranking Church execs from the Office of Special Affairs, who wanted to speak with us. I didn't know this until later, but they had actually chartered a helicopter from L.A. to make the trip; their business was so urgent. They wanted to stop the *Nightline* interview from airing.

I told Dallas's father that they weren't welcome, unless they were there to apologize. A couple of minutes later, the phone rang a second time. It was one of the OSA execs traveling with Dallas's father.

After a while, Dallas and I agreed to meet Dallas's parents and the two OSA reps at a Denny's restaurant nearby, because it was the only place open that late at night. The meeting started off with abusive comments from the two OSA reps about our behavior, our families, and our attitudes. One falsely called my mother a whore. The other said I was using my uncle's name to get my fifteen minutes of fame. They were clearly living in their own world, and Dallas and I saw no point in arguing with people who were so detached from reality. But Dallas's parents insisted that we stay and try to come to some sort of resolution, so we tried to oblige them. Finally, we got down to the real reason for the visit. The execs pleaded with me to pull the ABC *Nightline* deal, and refuse to do additional interviews. They tried to bargain with me. If I did, they said, they would lift the "declare" on my aunt Sarah and several of my friends, allowing them to speak to their families.

Dallas's parents were also pleading with us to cooperate. Otherwise, they would have to choose between Scientology and us. Everybody was trying to force us to make a decision right then and there, but we said we'd think about it. Before departing, we were asked not to talk to anybody about this meeting and not to post about it on the Internet.

There was no way I was going to pull the *Nightline* deal, but Dallas and I were torn about refusing additional interviews. Even before the Church's plea, we'd been on the fence about whether or not we would continue doing interviews. Through the website, we would continue to bring a good amount of attention to the stories coming out of the Church.

But both of us knew what that decision would mean. It would mean that once again, the Church would have power over our lives. There was something about giving the Church the satisfaction of that, which made us feel like we'd be enabling them to do more to us and others. In the end, we decided against it.

The next morning, we went out for breakfast and to do a few errands. As we got onto the freeway, Dallas took note of a white Ford sedan also getting onto the freeway, although he said nothing to me. As we switched freeways and went another ten miles, he noticed the same car still behind us. We got into downtown San Diego, with its many stoplights and one-way streets. The same car stayed behind us, although maneuvering so as not to be directly in Dallas's rear-view mirror. I stopped by my office to pick up some items and came out fifteen minutes later. The same car was down the street on a side road. After I closed my door, Dallas jerked the car into motion and took off into traffic.

"Jeez, slow down!" I told him, backseat-driving as usual.

"Jenna, I think we are being followed. Do you see that white Ford three lanes right of us? I am going to make the next left, and he will swerve across and follow us."

Just as Dallas had predicted, the car made the exact same moves as we did. We were being followed.

Dallas kept driving around the same few blocks to see how many times this guy was going to keep it up before realizing we were on to him. We managed to get a picture of his license plate when he pulled out in front of us. When we turned into a parking lot, he followed us, but took off when we got out and started walking toward his car.

As if the mysterious car weren't enough, the Church was still trying to get to us through Dallas's parents. In April 2008, Dallas and I decided to participate in a protest organized by Anonymous, to be staged at all the Scientology sites in L.A., as well as at various Scientology sites around the world. Again, the focus was on families and disconnection. The night before the protest, the Church's new PR person, Tommy Davis, called Dallas's father and told him we were going to a rally with terrorists. Upset, Dallas's parents wanted to meet with Dallas alone. Dallas refused, and he and I went out to dinner. As usual, we were followed, this time by a guy driving a car with no license plates.

The driver sped away when he realized we were taking pictures of his vehicle. I called Tommy Davis myself, to no avail. Even though I left several messages, I never got a call back. The guy was obviously a coward, just like so many others in the Office of Special Affairs who would go to great lengths to disparage us to our families, but would never go head-to-head with you.

I'd stopped being surprised by this behavior, but at the same time it was hard not to be startled by the apparent lengths that they were willing to go to in order to disrupt our lives. They seemed to operate in their own small world where they could do what they wanted to whomever they wanted. And yet they had so little sense of what was going on beyond the borders of their own little world. They would take shots from over the walls and then hide behind them just as quickly, so they never came to realize just how removed from reality they were.

Upset as I was about the suspicious cars and their attempts to squeeze us through Dallas's parents, I was more disturbed by what those actions demonstrated about the Church. The distance between their world and the real world was on full display. This wasn't just about controlling the people in the Church, it was about controlling any and everyone around them—no matter what the cost.

On the morning of the protest, Dallas and I drove to L.A., where we met Astra and several other friends. Dallas and I had the jitters, as we had never demonstrated before. However, when we got there and saw how many people had turned out, it turned out to be very uplifting, and made us feel supported. It was a blazing hot day, and there were at least two hundred protesters. Everybody was wearing masks, and we were all picketing outside the Blue Building on Fountain Avenue. There were tons of ex-Scientologists, many of whom had already done so much to raise awareness.

The Headleys also turned out at the protest that day. We started at PAC, where the Church had security guards blocking their road, L. Ron Hubbard Way. We protested on Sunset Boulevard instead. People honked in support of us. Some of the protesters used megaphones to voice their anti-Scientology message. Various media outlets were there to cover the story, and we all readily gave them sound bites.

I was startled to recognize two other protesters in particular, Mark Bunker and Tory Christman, whom I remembered from protests at the Flag base in Clearwater. They had been part of the Lisa McPherson Trust, and had frequently picketed the base. I remembered the briefings we used to get about handling these guys. It was disturbing to think about it now. Yet, here they were, still protesting against the Church.

It was an empowering day and a big success. I felt extremely thankful to Anonymous for organizing it. Many of them have not personally experienced the evils of the Church, so it said a lot that they were there standing up for people they didn't even know. For so many years, I had felt that I was alone in my feeling that something was wrong with the way people were treated in the Sea Org. Now, I felt as though there was an army of us.

As we drove home that night, Dallas and I noticed that we were again being followed, this time by two cars. I called OSA the next day to speak to Tommy Davis, but, of course, he was not available and never returned my call.

Later in the day, Dallas's parents called to say they wanted to speak with Dallas alone. He agreed to meet them at their house, where he learned they had just come from a meeting with several execs from the Church. They had been shown photos of us holding signs at the protest, and told that we had been hanging with people from Anonymous, which they described as a criminal organization. As it turned out, Dallas's parents had been having meetings with Church execs, who had been trying to convince them that Dallas and I were bad people. They even went so far as to say that the only reason Dallas had married me was that he wanted to take over my uncle's position in the Church. These secret meetings often resulted in tension and heated arguments between Dallas and me and his parents, but we knew what we were doing was right. This wasn't just about Dallas's family, it was about the dozens of others we would be helping.

About a week passed, before Dallas's mother called him again. She told him the Church had contacted her to say that ABC was going to air the *Nightline* interview, and they had asked her to write a letter to the producers requesting that they not broadcast it. They wanted her to tell them that Dallas and I were liars, and had asked her husband and son to do the same. She said she told them that she didn't want to get involved. To this day, I don't know if any of them wrote letters against us on behalf of the Church.

Ultimately, despite all the Church's efforts, the *Nightline* interview aired, and even with all of the drama that had surrounded it, I felt a huge sense of relief. The tumultuous few weeks of dealing with the Church had made me more convinced than ever that the only way to bring attention to those human rights violations was to do it from the outside. Theirs was such an all-consuming world that the only way true change would ever come about would be if people out here in the real world came to see the risks that Scientology posed. It was up to all of us who had left to reveal the truth about our experiences, because only then would the world see this organization for what it really was.

In the aftermath of the interview, visits to our website soared. We had so many hits that we moved to the first entry on the Google search page for the keyword "Scientology." We got tons of email from people asking us to help them find their children or other family members in the Church and in many cases, we were able to help. More than anything, these kinds of pleas showed me that we were doing the right thing. The sheer volume of emails was unbelievable.

The site continues to average more than 200,000 hits a month. Even more rewarding is the number of thank-yous we receive from people all over the world. I am proud that the website has become a valuable tool to warn people about the dangers of Scientology, help them find loved ones they have lost to the Church, provide support to those in need, and bring awareness through school programs and the media.

CHAPTER THIRTY-FOUR

ONE LIFE

THE LONGER I WAS OUT, THE MORE I CAME TO UNDERSTAND THAT my life had been owned by the Church. For years, I had sensed that something was wrong; learning the truth about what had gone on behind the scenes shed new light on my suspicions. I was astonished to hear how high up in the Church concern and control over my time as a Sea Org member had gone. In late fall 2007, my parents called to tell me that Mike Rinder was in their living room. I immediately assumed he must be there to either handle them, or gather information about me. To my surprise, neither was true: He'd had a falling-out with my uncle over a BBC television segment about Scientology, and, in the aftermath, Mike had walked out of the Church.

I was shocked. I had just seen Mike on television a few weeks earlier. Defending the Church. Mike Rinder leaving was huge. I wondered what had become of Cathy, B. J., and Taryn. My parents told me that the rest of Mike's family had disowned him. Months later, when Mike had a chance to cool off after his departure from the Church, we heard his firsthand accounts of the so-called handlings of my parents and me. He told me that he and

Marty Rathbun had been assigned to handle my parents when they'd first announced they were leaving the Sea Org, in 2000. They'd made their decision to leave known, then locked themselves in their room at the Int Base and refused to open the door. Mike and Marty were in Clearwater at the time, but Uncle Dave considered this a big enough problem that he ordered them back to Int immediately to deal with it. Mike described my uncle as micromanaging in their dealing with my parents. He demanded reports on anything that transpired and dictated endless orders as to what was to be done. This is what Mike told me:

At the outset, my father was refusing to talk to anyone, especially his brother, so Uncle Dave instructed Mike and Marty to split my parents up, even if it meant physically taking my father out of the room. He then instructed them to security-check both my parents. Everything they said was to be reported to Uncle Dave in detail. Several days later, when my parents still hadn't changed their minds about leaving, Uncle Dave unleashed his fury, calling Mike and Marty incompetent and incapable, before telling them that he would speak to his brother himself. The two met on the *Star of California,* the ship replica at the Int base, where Uncle Dave offered my father $100,000 to have only my mom leave; the move failed to convince my father to stay.

As it became clear that my parents were leaving, my uncle wanted them out of the country, so my father randomly selected Cabo San Lucas, Mexico, as the place they would settle. This worked out well for the Church, as a private investigator for the Church ran a local ATV (all-terrain vehicle) rental shop there, so he could keep an eye on them. Uncle Dave was concerned that they would be subpoenaed for deposition in the Lisa McPherson case if they were in the United States. It was only later that Mike learned why Uncle Dave had been so afraid, which was that Uncle Dave had told my parents that he had supervised her auditing during the period before her death. My parents had no intention of creating problems for the Church, but they had to go anyway. They finally agreed when they were told that I would be joining them there. Uncle Dave had assured them that he would be the one handling me.

Anne Rathbun of course handled me, although it turns out she had been supervised directly by Uncle Dave. I had always wondered how much Uncle Dave knew about what was going on with me when my parents were leaving. Mike said that after I had been sent back to Los Angeles from Flag, Uncle Dave's plan had been to resettle me in Mexico with my parents, regardless of what I wanted. Apparently, my uncle told Mike many times that I was a spoiled brat who contributed nothing to the Sea Org, so it would be no loss to get me out, and would keep my parents happy. When I refused to go, the whole plan had to be rethought. It was telling that Uncle Dave was always pulling the strings, but never showing his face.

All those hours that Marty and Mike had left me alone in the conference room claiming to have forgotten me, they were in Uncle Dave's eleventh-floor office being subjected to his rage. He was furious about their incompetence in failing to deal with a young girl who, in his estimation, was not only lazy and incapable of doing anything useful, but also too stupid to think for herself. I wasn't surprised that my uncle had said these things about me. Doing it behind my back was a way to keep himself unaccountable. From everything I learned about him, he thought he was the only one capable of doing anything right.

Mike said that it was the first time that he had been ordered to persuade someone to *leave* the Sea Org, and didn't feel right about it. My uncle had not banked on how indoctrinated I was. When they told him that I wanted to stay, Uncle Dave was frustrated. He still wanted me to go, but, in the end, he said than I was a better Sea Org member than either Mike or Marty, which was his way of signaling that it was okay for me to stay.

When I was asked to make the phone call to my parents to tell them it had been my decision to stay, I didn't realize how much discussion had already gone on. Apparently, my father demanded to speak to me, but Uncle Dave would not allow it; he wasn't willing to get on the phone himself so he listened via speakerphone and had Mike and Marty speak for him. Only after my mother became threatening did Dave decide my parents could talk to me.

After hearing how involved my uncle had been in my parents' leaving, I wasn't surprised to learn that Uncle Dave had also been responsible for the handling Dallas's and my departure. Not only was he aware of what was going on, he was directing all the action. He'd been responsible for all the sneaking around and trying to convince Dallas to stay. He'd been encouraging people to keep Dallas in, and push me out. It was unlikely that this had anything to do with Dallas himself. Though Dallas and I had been married for three years, Uncle Dave had never met him. It seemed more about making my life miserable and creating as many barriers as possible for us. Family meant nothing to him.

Uncle Dave had kept track of me far beyond that which I had imagined. I knew that I was being controlled and that there was a system in place, but I never knew that it came down to a single person. What struck me once again was how he always had his decisions carried out by others. He insulated himself from his actions and the human toll that that they took. He didn't have to confront the uncomfortable questions that his decisions raised about just how disconnecting people from their families served the greater good, and what any of this had to do with Scientology.

Perhaps the most surprising thing about hearing all this was that I wasn't surprised. By the time I spoke to Mike Rinder, I'd heard so many bad things about my uncle's behavior from former Scientologists that there was little left that could shock me. Everyone who left the Church had a story about him and what he'd done. My story wasn't very different from theirs. In the end, not even my last name could spare me from my uncle's watchful eye.

I AM NO LONGER A BELIEVER. I AM NOT RELIGIOUS. I BELIEVE IN what I can see. Dallas believes in the possibility of God, past lives, reincarnation, and karma. I believe in the *possibility* of these things, but I do not count on them or incorporate them into my thinking.

It was a huge adjustment of perspective to realize that the life I am living may be my one and only. All the people I know who are still in the Church may be wasting the only life they have. However, having one life also allows me to see the beauty of it, what a miracle it is that we can live, and how important it is to be an individual. Nobody in this world was born to be the same as anyone else. Turning people into robots, especially children, is a crime against nature itself.

There is so much beauty in humanity and I've only been able to appreciate it in the last few years. I am touched by actions like those of families concerned enough to try to protect their kids from Scientology; people who have let me cry on their shoulder, and supported me in speaking out against Scientology; Dallas's whole non-Scientology family, who are as genuine and truly caring as they come; and authority figures that I have in my new life, who are caring and compassionate despite the power they hold.

My mother recently moved to California to be closer to her grandchildren. She is a doting grandparent, eager to make up for what she missed out on with me. My father still lives in Virginia. Justin and his girlfriend live there, too. Sterling is living abroad. Uncle Dave is still the head of the Church. As far as I know, my parents never spoke to him after my departure. I have never talked to him. I tried calling Aunt Shelly years ago, but I never heard anything. She hasn't been seen in public since 2007, but, recently, a lawyer spoke out on her behalf, saying she that was fine. He was putting it out there in response to an article in a newspaper or blog saying that she was missing.

In 2012, Grandpa Ron—my dad's father who'd brought the whole Miscavige family into the religion in the first place—caused a stir when word got out that he too had left the Church. Given his long commitment, it was a nice surprise. To hear him tell it, in the end, he simply got fed up with everything and had to leave. In his own words he, "escaped." He and his wife Becky are now living with my dad in Virginia. Grandpa Ron was just one of several high-profile people who'd left in recent years, a rapidly growing list that in addition to Mike Rinder also included Marty Rathbun whose wife Ann remained in the church.

The day I signed my book contract, Dallas's parents were declared SPs for refusing to disconnect from us. Dallas's siblings still talk to us, and we love them and see them all the time. Dallas's parents still believe in Scientology itself but see the corruption within the Church and don't agree with how it is being run. As far as the Church is concerned, we are obviously SPs, although we still have not been declared so, as far as we are aware. We haven't heard from the Church in years, and they seem to have stopped following us.

While I've moved on in my life, some things in the past are hard to forgive. To me, the Church is a dangerous organization whose beliefs allow it to commit crimes against humanity and violate basic human rights. It remains a mystery to me how, in our current society, this can go on unchecked. It is particularly insidious because of its celebrity advocates and affiliated groups, such as Narconon, Applied Scholastics, and the Citizens Commission on Human Rights. I feel that people should be warned about what the Church truly is, who its founder really was, what really goes on there, the lengths it is willing to go to, and what they are willing to sacrifice in the name of achieving their ends. The ends themselves are shrouded in secrecy and conflicting information. Scientology always has been a game of power and control. L. Ron Hubbard was the ultimate con man, and it's hard to figure out how much of Scientology was an experiment in brainwashing and controlling people, and how much of it was truly intended to help people.

While I have plenty of reasons to loathe my uncle, I also try to see him for what he once was: A kid, who, like so many others was duped by the system and was too young and irresponsible to make the right choices. By the time he was sixteen, and joined the Sea Org, he was already in too deep. He made his choice. I don't know who he would be if he had never encountered Scientology, or how much of his personality is shaped by Scientology.

Still, it's hard to reconcile the idea of him as a child with the adult he is now. Many former Sea Org members and Scientologists are quick to blame Dave, and Dave alone, for their experiences. The truth, I feel, is a bit murkier. There's little doubt that my uncle has played a leading role in defining much of how modern Scientology works; but to place blame squarely on him is to miss the larger point. The problem with Scientology is bigger than one man, not just Uncle Dave or LRH. The problem is Scientology itself. The problem is that Scientology is a system that makes it nearly impossible for you to think for yourself. People like my uncle are enablers who create an environment of fear that discourages independent thought. Get rid of them and you would continue to have a system that, almost by definition, restricts individual freedoms.

Today, when we are in Los Angeles to visit friends, we drive by the base there. We see the Sea Org drones coming and going from the buildings and walking along the sidewalks. They are recognizable by their uniforms and their blank stares. They are in a different world. Looking at them, I find myself taken back to a time, not that long ago, when I too wandered mindlessly from building to building. I remember how those walks from one building to another were some of our only encounters with the outside world, and how, even during those brief moments outside, people in passing cars would yell at us that we were brainwashed, as their cars sped away.

At the time, our reaction to the word "brainwashed" was disbelief. We'd look at each other, shocked that we who were seeking the ultimate truths of the universe could be brainwashed. We'd recite Scientology slogans, such as "Think for yourself," to each other, and take comfort that we alone could make the world go right. After all, if we were the greater good, then who were they?

Seeing the followers walk around now, I have been tempted to yell too, especially when seeing some of my old friends. Tempted to help them realize what's going on and bridge the distance between their world and mine. I open my lips to speak, but each time, the words catch in my throat. What stops me isn't fear; it's the knowledge that I can't force them to believe anything that they are not ready to believe.

Ultimately, Scientologists make a choice about what they believe, and make a choice as to whether they're willing to ignore the small but persistent voice inside them saying that something isn't right. The brainwashing by the Church teaches people to go against their instincts, and it is too strong, too deeply ingrained for the outside world alone to set things right. The desire to change must come from within. They have to have the realization themselves to believe it.

I made a choice that I didn't want to be controlled, and in walking away from everything, I learned the value of listening to the voice in my head telling me what was wrong and standing up for what was right. Being the lone voice of dissent is hard and almost always inconvenient and there isn't usually instant gratification. However if you don't speak up, you will most likely regret it and will have to live with the results. In my experience, often, the only reason that the church was allowed to get away with its abusive behavior is that people failed to say no. Saying no is difficult, even brutal at times. But, in the long run, many others will appreciate your courage, even if silently, and someday it may lead to them mustering up the courage to stand up for themselves.

Of all the gifts that my freedom has given me, perhaps the greatest was the ability to start a family. From the moment I began spending time in Australia with Janette and her daughter Eden, I knew that I wanted to be a mother. However, if I'd stayed in the Sea Org I would have never been allowed to. Leaving gave me the opportunity to discover for myself what it means to have a child, and, today, Dallas and I are thankful that we got out young enough to have kids and start a family. Our two beautiful children are a blessing that we never would otherwise have known.

For me, the ultimate beauty of humanity was shown to me when I had my first child. Our bodies are capable of creating miracles, regardless of whether we are spirits. In the end, I learned that just being my body was good enough for me. My body allowed me to be me a mom, which is by far the best thing about me.

Glossary

Auditing—Scientologists will tell you this is similar to counseling. An E-Meter is often, but not always, used. On the lower levels, an auditor guides the PC (pre-clear) through various questions supposedly designed to elicit a certain result.

Blow—"To leave without permission" or "to leave before something is completed." One can "blow staff," "blow course," "blow session," or "blow the org." It is a very, very serious offense in Scientology to blow. People who leave without permission in this way are usually declared. Depending on context, "blow" can also have a positive meaning. It can mean "to go away," e.g., "My pain just blew!"

Bridge, The—Shortened from "The Bridge to Total Freedom." All Scientology doctrines put together are referred to as "the Bridge." If one is progressing through their Scientology studies and sessions, they are "going up the Bridge."

Cadet Org—The Sea Org for children, and for the children of Sea Org members.

Checksheet—A list of steps required to complete a Scientology Course. The steps must be done in sequence; they lay out which policies are to be read, which lectures are to be listened to, which policies require checkouts, what essays are to be written, which practicals or drills are to be done, etc. At the end of the checksheet, the student and his or her course supervisor must attest to the completion of all of its steps and their understanding of the material. There is always a test at the end of each checksheet.

CMO—The Commodore's Messenger Organization. L. Ron Hubbard called himself the "Commodore." Originally created as an elite unit comprised mostly of young kids who ran messages for L. Ron Hubbard himself, enforced his orders, and took care of his personal matters and household. Anything being said to a messenger was considered as being said to the Commodore himself. CMO was the most senior management body in the Church. Only RTC was senior to CMO, but they were not technically considered management.

Comm Ev—Committee of Evidence. This is the Scientology version of a trial. During a Comm Ev, the accused is required to sit before a panel of Sea Org members who evaluate their "crimes." If you are accused of misdeeds and ordered to stand before such a panel, you are said to be "Comm Ev'd."

Conditions, to do conditions—A set of formulas to be applied to one's life depending on the state of one's life. For instance, if you are doing exceptionally well, you would apply the steps outlined in the condition of "affluence." If you have done something bad, the org may require you to do a "treason" condition. The various conditions, from worst to best, are: Confusion, Treason, Enemy, Doubt, Liability, Non-Existence, Danger, Emergency, Normal, Affluence, Power Change and Power. There are specific formulas for each of these conditions. Lower conditions (those below "normal") are frequently used as punishment.

Course—One of many set study programs in Scientology in which the Scientologist studies L. Ron Hubbard's texts and practices using various aspects of the texts. If one is regularly going to church to study Scientology doctrine, they can be said to be "on course."

Declared, to be declared—To be labeled a Suppressive Person (evil) and thrown out of Scientology. People who are declared may not have *any contact* with Scientologists, and Scientologists can be declared just for talking to a declared person.

E/O (or EO)—Ethics Officer. Responsible for the "crime and punishment" division of any given church.

Enturbulate—To upset or cause disruption.

EPF—Estates Project Force. When one first joins the Sea Org, one must do a sort of "orientation boot camp" for several weeks or months. This boot camp is called the EPF.

Flap—A major problem or serious incident. "There was a huge flap at the org."

MEST—Matter, Energy, Space, and Time. The physical universe.

MEST Work—Manual labor.

OSA—Office of Special Affairs. Often referred to by critics as Scientology's Secret Service.

OT—Operating Thetan. This is someone who, according to Scientology, has attained a high spiritual level. There are currently 8 OT levels. One begins the OT levels after attaining the state of Clear. An OT is supposed to be able to control Matter, Energy, Space, and Time.

(Out) 2D—The second dynamic. In Scientology, the second dynamic refers to family, children, personal relationships and sex. It can be used in a variety of ways, including: "She was my 2D" means "I was dating her." "Going out-2D" means cheating on your partner if you are married, or engaging in more than kissing if you are single. "I need to handle my 2D" can, depending on context, mean "I need to fix my relationship with my partner/spouse" or "I need to find a boy/girlfriend."

Overt—A sin or crime.

O/Ws—Overts and withholds, which essentially means sins and secrets.

Potential Trouble Source (or PTS)—Someone who is connected to a Suppressive Person (SP). According to Scientology, a PTS will often be sick (in fact, they believe that PTSness is the only reason anyone gets sick), have emotional ups and downs, and not be able to get very far in life.

PTS/SP (course)—A major Scientology course in which one learns Hubbard's thoughts on evil people and how to deal with them, and what happens when one is connected to a suppressive person. See also: Potential Trouble Source, Suppressive Person.

RPF—Rehabilitation Project Force. When a Sea Org member has done something considered particularly bad, they are isolated from the rest of the Sea Org members in the RPF program. People on the RPF are not allowed to walk (they run everywhere), are not allowed to speak to another Sea Org member unless spoken to, and spend most of their time doing manual labor. This is a very controversial program. Scientologists call it "rehabilitation"; critics call it forced labor.

RTC—Religious Technology Center. This organization is run by the top echelon of the Sea Org. They own all the copyrights to L. Ron Hubbard's material.

Sea Org (or SO)—The inner core of the Scientology parish. Sea Org members run and operate the churches, raise money, give auditing, and perform any number of other tasks. They sign a one-billion-year contract, promising to return and serve in their next life.

Sec Check—Security check. A confessional given while on the E-Meter. Sec-checks can take anywhere from three weeks to a year or longer.

Suppressive Person (or SP)—A person who does not support Scientology. If someone is found to be an SP by the Church, they are "Declared," meaning they cannot have any contact with any Scientologist whatsoever.

TRs—Training Routines. Basic drills meant to improve your communication skills. These include TR0, wherein two students sit across from each other with their eyes closed with the purpose of learning to "be there comfortably," and TR0 Bullbait, wherein one student must sit perfectly still while another yells, screams, tells jokes, or in any other way tries to get him/her to react. See also: Out-TRs.

Twin—A course partner. Twins study everything on any particular course together, and help each other through the course. You can also say you are "twinning" with someone.

Withhold—A secret, something bad that you haven't told anyone about.

Wog—Derogatory term meaning "non-Scientologist."

Acknowledgments

SPECIAL THANKS TO LISA PULITZER, WHO BELIEVED IN MY STORY FROM the very beginning and without whom this book would not have been possible. Thank you so much for all of your care, support, and hard work, and for being so darn nice along the way.

My gratitude to Lisa Sharkey for believing in my story and making it possible for me to get it out there.

Thank you Madeleine Morel for being the firecracker that you are and for being there for me all the while.

Super-special thanks to my editor for working so hard on this book and caring enough to understand my story and for making sure it is communicated as it should be.

I feel like the four of you are such special people and I am very lucky to know you and have you in my life.

I'd like to thank everyone at William Morrow and HarperCollins whose hard work on my book made it the best it can be.

I'd also like to acknowledge Martha Smith for her long hours and attention to detail.

Thanks to my family, firstly my husband, Dallas, for standing up for me, for teaching me about the world, how to drive, and how to cook, and for being such a nice person and for supporting my dreams, being there for me, putting up with me throughout the years and during the book-writing process. My two angels, who are the center of my life and bring me so much pure joy and who make this world so much more special for your being in it. I love you so, so much.

My heartfelt thanks to the all of the Pavlicks for your love and support and for taking me in and being the kind, loving, and caring people that you are. I couldn't have asked for a better family. Love you all.

A special thank-you to my parents and my brother Justin for helping me when I was getting out of the Church and fighting for me and for being supportive and helping me to see the light.

My love and thanks to the Hill family for respecting our choices, staying strong under intense pressure, and choosing our family over religion.

Thank you to Astra and Kendra, my fellow ESK girls and friends for being amazing, strong, beautiful, smart, and well-spoken, and for doing everything you have done and do on a daily basis. You guys have been strong at times when I have been weak and I am just honored to be talked about in the same breath as both of you.

I want to acknowledge all of the ex-Scientologists and even independent Scientologists who have spoken out over the years on Scientology's abuses, negligence, and human rights violations, taking on personal risk and attack to bring forward the truth and still persevering despite everything. Tory Christman, Mark Bunker, Marc and Claire Headley, Mike and Christie, Marty Rathbun, Tom Devocht, Jeff Hawkins, Amy Scobee, Matt Pesch, Lawrence Woodcraft, Chuck Beatty, Paul Haggis, and the many others I have not mentioned. Thank you.

Thanks to Anonymous, especially those I have met, for your continued support and care about this important issue.

Many thanks to my Aussie friends who have spoken out against the Church—the Andersons, Janette, Anna, and Dean.

I'd like to thank all of my friends who have believed in me along the way and have supported me or who have just been so nice and really helped show me what a kind place the world is. Ana, Jane, Lucy, Aimee, Liz, Laurette, and Gus, to name a few who really stood out, as well as my many other friends I met at HK and LHC.

And finally I can't forget the many journalists who have worked over the years to get important stories out there and bring attention to an important matter with integrity, such as Jonny Jacobsen, Lawrence Wright, Tony Ortega, John Sweeney, Tobin and Childs, Anderson Cooper, and many others.